John McCririck's

WORLD OF BETTING

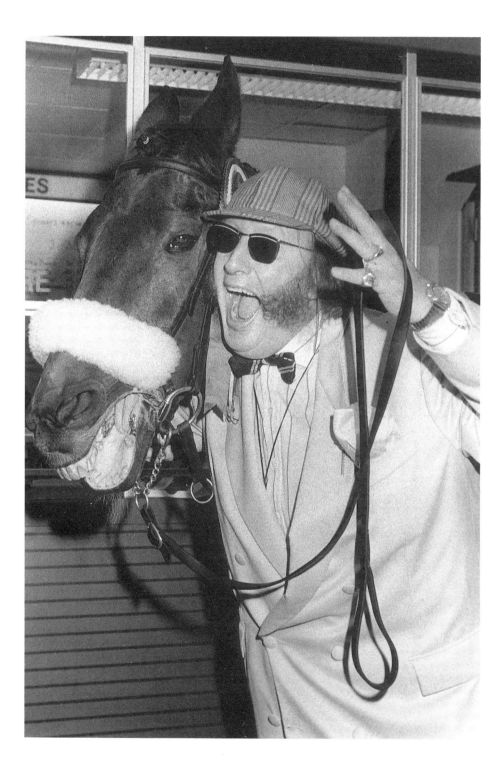

John McCririck's

WORLD OF BETTING

Double carpet and all that!

CARTOONS BY McCORMICK

STANLEY PAUL

LONDON

Stanley Paul & Co. Ltd
An imprint of Random House UK Ltd

20 Vauxhall Bridge Road, London SW1V 2SA
Random House Australia [Pty] Ltd
20 Alfred Street, Milsons Point, Sydney 2061

Random House New Zealand Limited
18 Poland Road, Glenfield, Auckland

Random House South Africa (Pty) Ltd
PO Box 337, Bergvlei 2012, South Africa

First published 1991
Reprinted 1991 (four times)
Revised paperback edition 1992
Reprinted 1993

Set in 9½/11pt Berkeley Book and Futura and Bodoni
by SX Composing Ltd, Rayleigh, Essex

Printed and bound in Great Britain by Clays Ltd, St. Ives PLC.

A catalogue record for this book is available from the British Library

ISBN 0 09 177165 X

Opposite title page: **John McCririck (right)
with Red Rum**

*T*o *the* B*ooby*
So lucky to have hooked her wonderful
boy out of the great fishtank of life

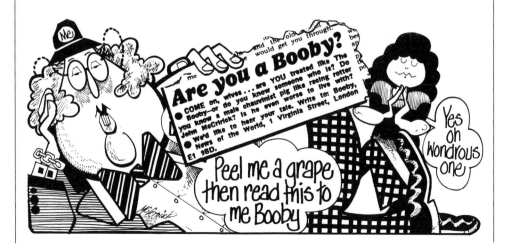

Eat your heart out, Tom Cruise! Britain's latest hunky screen god needs feeding on the set of his epic Oscar-contending video *World of Betting*

ACKNOWLEDGEMENTS

The author and publishers would particularly like to thank George Selwyn for providing all specially commissioned as well as library photographs; also Gerry Cranham, The Hulton-Deutsch Collection, AllSport, Sport & General, Sygma, Camera Press, Sporting Pictures, *Racing Post, Daily Star* and *Daily Mirror*.

They also wish to acknowledge the *Racing Post*, where versions of the 'At Large' pieces were originally published, and *The Sporting Life* for allowing them to use extracts, and Hodder & Stoughton for the extracts from Ron Pollard's *Odds and Sods*.

Contents

Under Starter's Orders

To see you dressed like you are as a tipster is a bloody disgrace especially speaking on TV about the snooker. Why do you have to look like a poof with that style of hair, you look a right jessy, your [sic] an insult to women, & those elaborate jewels all over your fingers and wrists. Your [sic] an insult to a true Englishman. What you lazy sods need is a dose of the ARMY, teach you a bit of discipline. Your generation today is a total disgrace & an insult to hard workers. Trouble is you get too much big money. GROW UP TWERP.

I get many fan letters like that. Some people go on the record with abuse. Television critic Nina Myskow (pronounced 'Miss Cow') in the *News of the World* called me a 'sexist paddock pillock with all the charm of an armpit'. And the BBC's 'youf' supremo Janet Street-Porter labelled me 'repulsive' in *Today*.

Fans write to the racing press:

The recent spate of criticism regarding the behaviour of John McCririck on Channel Four Racing proves that a lot of people are sick and tired of the man and it is high time he was removed. (Sporting Life)

We have seen a bewhiskered clown desecrate Tatts almost daily on Channel Four's racing coverage. (Racing Post)

Linda Halfhide told Channel Four's Video Box: 'I find his rude and abusive manner to the racing public disgraceful.' Comedienne Ellie Lane said – on air – that 'the only interesting thing in your trousers is the label'.

Even the BBC's racing correspondent, and my fag at Harrow (or was I his?), Julian Wilson, wrote: 'John McCririck is a disgrace. A disgrace to his school, his wife ("The Booby") and his profession. He is undisciplined, unkempt and unabashed.' But Jules so kindly, though with uncharacteristic inaccuracy, added: 'He also appears to be by far the most popular individual on racing TV.'

The late and so lamented ex-Levy Board Chairman and Director General of the BBC Sir Ian Trethowan wrote of 'the hairy, loud-voiced, bizarrely-dressed John McCririck' that 'some racing regulars may find him irritating, but viewers in general like him, particularly – and importantly for the ratings – those not necessarily hooked on racing'.

And Ossie Fletcher, former editor of the *Sporting Life* and the man to whom I owe most in my erratic journalistic career, offered this:

A fearless reporter, he dug out some wonderful stories and won two national Press awards in the process. Curiously – or perhaps understandably – he was never popular with less talented colleagues. But for me it was a matter of immense regret when we came to the parting of the ways.

For me, too.

I can't leave out an anonymous missive, penned on a William Hill betting slip: 'You are a typical right-wing twit. You ought to be buried in an anthill up to your big fat neck. At least Labour politicians think about the needy and poor of this world, while you lot just think of more and more money. Get stuffed you fat oaf.'

And the *Mail on Sunday*'s *You* magazine captioned an unflattering picture in which admittedly the usual suede shoes, traditional Old Harrovian bow tie (careworn, never new) and cigar made me resemble a spiv: 'It's reassuring that, even in the normal '90s, there's still a place for real eccentrics like John McCririck: it's right beside the on switch.' Thanks a bundle for that switch off!

But enough of the puffs. If Nina, Jules,

the 'Disgusted Viewer' who sent me those kind words at the top and all the rest can bear to be led by my ring-laden hand – all grotty second-hand cast-offs from Ratners – I'll take them on a safari through the fascinating betting jungle, encountering that rich variety of characters who people such a strange but vibrant habitat.

We'll meet punters – large and small – to whom bookies are 'the old enemy'. We'll examine the ploys and intrigues both sides utilise in their eternal struggle to outwit the other. We'll consider how people bet, and *why* they bet. And we'll see the lengths to which some go to effect the 'right' result – schemes and systems, coups and frauds.

The World of Betting is a universe of plots and hopes, frustration, inner torment and sublime moments of exhilaration. For me, the thrill of gambling – on horses and on a thousand other weird and wonderful possibilities – is the most riveting human activity of all, excluding sex of course. And you can imagine how often I do *that*!

In this book I intend to share with you the magic along with the many faces, facets and moods of the steamy betting environment.

Come prowl with me.

Best of luck,

John McCririck

1

A Day in the Life of Big Mac

FRIDAY 7 JUNE 1991

11.30 P.M.

Half an hour to go to Oaks Day and the Booby is dispatched to King's Cross to buy the first editions of the next day's newspapers for review on the *Morning Line*. While she's away on this vital errand, her gorgeous hunk relaxes, glass of gently chilled white wine in hand, downstairs in The Trap – the tiny mews residence near Regent's Park which Loyd Grossman, David Frost and the highly skilled Yorkshire TV *Through the Keyhole* team made appear reasonably habitable in May 1991.

11.45 P.M.

Back comes the Booby weighed down with newsprint, and the next couple of hours are spent perched up in bed, hoping my own two-page wander and observations round the wonderful, bizarre world of Fleet Street and Malky's way-out cartoons in the *Racing Post* contain the right mix of comment and humour, before scouring the dozen other papers in search of suitable *Morning Line* extracts. And you should also know that, unlike other sporting types, there are no restraints to physical activity on the eve of a big day. How lucky the grateful Booby is. . . .

SATURDAY 8 JUNE

6.15 A.M.

Eyelids ease open to the sight of the devoted Booby in her shimmering nightie hovering with the breakfast tray – tea (no sugar but Candarel sweeteners) and a couple of almond croissants lightly dusted with icing, Marylebone High Street's homemade pride. And a saucer of cream for our neutered tabby, the miaowing Found – pronounced 'Fee-ow-nd', because she was just that.

6.25 A.M.

Time for a tosh (a bath to those not fortunate enough to be Old Harrovians), run by the Booby, who gauges perfectly, after twenty-one years, the correct temperature. Did anyone out there say the fatso smells and never washes?

6.35 A.M.

Thoroughly cleansed, glistening muscles rippling, it's back up the spiral staircase with nothing on – to admiring peeks from the Booby, who has laid out on the bed that day's apparel. She reckons it's time for pink, the colour my house, Headmaster's of course, sported without distinction on the rugger and Harrow football fields.

6.45 A.M.

Epsom being outside the stamina range of my ever harshly handicapped tricycles Hermione and Hermeseta, the car door is opened reverentially by the Booby (she drives, I can't). Along with our yellow Labradors Grub (she's become totally schizophrenic because the Booby keeps calling her Gooby) and Smelly, we're soon at the course, though even at that time of day roadworks cause delays. Is there ever a race meeting anywhere without some bright spark deciding that's just the time to dig a hole in an approach road?

7.35 A.M.

First duty at the course is to sit in the car listening to Radio Five's excellent racing round-up. BBC Radio Sport, from *Test Match Special* to *Sports Report* and that haunting signature tune, is a class apart.

Then it's off to the Channel Four vans huddled together in the car park between the main stand and paddock. In charge from the scanner van are executive producer Andrew Franklin and director Bob 'Heart' Gardam. Even at this early hour they're bright-eyed and buzzing – not so the rest of us.

With the day's other *Morning Line* presenters John 'Greatest Jockey' Francome and John 'The Noble Lord' Oaksey (too many Johns on Channel Four Racing – which one should be sacked?), the running order is gone through. Although the *Morning Line* follows an established format, each programme has to be planned, timings detailed and presenters made aware of the sequence. Segments of the paper review, for instance, have to be discussed with Franklin: it is accepted that for all Channel Four Racing coverage the contents known before going out on air must have his approval.

Just like a newspaper needs editing, so does live television and radio, though obviously this can be done only in outline. If he doesn't want something to go out, it doesn't – which is just as it should be. So a couple of juicy items are given the 'No, John, I don't think so, do you?' rebuff.

Presenters reckoning they ought to run programmes – and during my thirteen-year-stint as a sub-editor on BBC TV's *Grandstand* that did happen on occasions – should count themselves fortunate to have in control an editor they can trust. Without grovelling, it is a fact that Andrew Franklin *is* Channel Four Racing. Without the former editor of ITV's flagship sports programme *World of Sport*, there would be no racing on Independent Television. Apart from Franklin, the late Tony Preston and now John Fairley, both bigwigs in Yorkshire TV, and Channel Four Sport supremo Mike Miller must also share responsibility. If you enjoy our coverage, these are the executives to applaud. If not . . .

End of crawl. Back to Oaks day.

Next on the agenda is delivering to Teresa Wadeson in the CapGen van (where programme captions are compiled and transmitted) quotes for the paper review which are to be shown on screen.

Then comes more important business – a bacon and sausage roll (no fat on the bacon, though!) to keep those almond croissants company.

8.15 A.M.

After being 'wired up' – with microphone and earpiece, linked to the 'scanner' (control van), and having adjusted my pert tea-cosy Channel Four hat, knitted by dear Auntie Mary in Bangor, North Wales, there's a brief rehearsal, checking timings, and so on. Unlike studio-based news programmes we have no autocue to read our scripts off. So allowances for stumbles and stutters would be appreciated! I won't reveal which member of the team said when reviewing a sprint: 'And we pick them up two furlongs out – the winner is nineteenth from the left!'

Immediately after the paper review – while the programme continues – is the time to phone round major bookmakers, and a couple of independents, to check early market moves for a possible 'steamer' (that is, if two or three firms separately report strong early support for a horse).

The *Morning Line* has often been used as a platform for exhorting bookmakers to play fair. The practice now of many companies guaranteeing early prices on advertised races to a certain stake up to a specified time followed a campaign waged by Channel Four, along with other hacks. On Oaks day the call is for course bookmakers to offer the same quarter odds, not a fifth, a place (1, 2, 3) in the nine-runner Classic as in betting shops. For racegoers not to get the same terms as punters off course is totally unacceptable. In their own self-interest course bookies must fall into line. But will they today? We'll find out in a few hours. (As it happened many played fair, but some grasping, thoughtless firms held out and just ripped off their clients.)

It's a typical *Morning Line*, full of joshing good humour – well, we find it amusing, anyway – and anticipation of the cracking good sport to come, with the Noble Lord (the peer who claims to be so old he can't accept 'yes' for an answer) ruminatively magisterial, though the Greatest Jockey (known also as Gypsy John Francome) referring to Big Mac as a 'gypsy' smacks of his own *déjà vu*, and he couldn't even work out the easy Picture Puzzle, the 50-1 Oaks no-hoper, Jet Ski Lady.

9.30 A.M.

Once off air, there's a break with another bite including fried bread and a bacon and sausage roll (two sausages in this one to quench the gnawing pangs of hunger) before the conference which precedes every Channel Four Racing programme. Today it's in a small Portakabin which has been laid on for the use of the team, and would be memorably described by Brough Scott in the following week's *Racing Post* as 'so shakily secured that it all but capsized every time the "Pink Whale" floundered off to the loo'. I wonder who he was referring to. . . .

In attendance are all presenters, plus 'Heart', Franklin, associate producer Mark 'Jacko' Jackson, Bob's PA (production assistant), the indispensable Jane 'Blondie' Garrod, and CapGen wizard Sue 'Neck of the Swan' Nicolle. We go through the running order, worked out overnight by Andrew, with everyone chipping in points – who's to be interviewed, possible past races to be shown and so on. A running order is the skeleton, and the conference fleshes it out. There is plenty of flesh in this Portakabin!

10.45 A.M.

Work begins on two racecards – one for use before each race, the other (yes, you've guessed) for afterwards. All fillies and mares are underlined in red ink. Getting the sex wrong grates with viewers and years of red-inking subconsciously helps eradicate errors.

In all races where there's been morning betting the best odds, culled from 'Pricewise' in the *Racing Post*, are put against each horse to be used as a benchmark for the day's fluctuations. Jockeys are checked to ensure they match those in the papers but, unlike the other presenters, I don't bother with colours. Having once humiliatingly let down the whole BBC *Grandstand* team with a wrong studio-based call when Peter O'Sullevan's mike went down at Ascot – in a four-horse race! – the likelihood of my being summoned suddenly to deputise for our commentator 'GG' (Graham 'The Owl' Goode) is non-existent.

Almost as embarrassing as when live at Longchamp being unable to interpret from the course tannoy whether Carroll House had kept the 1989 Arc after a prolonged stewards' enquiry. *Sacré bleu!*

Then come the stats, updated year by year with new facts being added all the time. So the stat relevant to hot favourite Shadayid, about forty-six One Thousand Guineas winners to have won the Oaks, is in the 'pre' racecard, and in the 'post' racecard the stat, for use should Shadayid succeed, that she was the forty-seventh filly to win both Classics, and the fourteenth since the War. Should she lose she would be the tenth One Thousand Guineas winner beaten in the Oaks since the War, compared though with twenty-four out of thirty Two Thousand Guineas victors to have failed in the Derby in that time.

The Gold Seal Oaks

[handwritten annotations: 33 FAVS this Century — GENEROUS / ONLY ONCE SINCE 1946 Same Owner–trainer / DERBY + OAKS — MARCEL BOUSSAC – CHARLES SEMBLAT / RAE JOHNSTONE – GALCADOR + ASMENA / Since 1960 23 Longheeled Cts tried for Oaks / 3 won – DISQ ALIYSA (4)]

FORM NOTES & BETTING GUIDE

3/4 AUSHERRA: Has produced her two best performances at courses with similar peculiarities to Epsom – finishing a neck 2nd to Jaffa Line in the Group 3 Prestige Stakes at Goodwood (7f, good to firm) on the second of two juvenile starts, and when beating Gai Bulga a length in the Listed Oaks Trial Stakes at Lingfield (1m 3f 106yds, good) last time – and thus looks unlikely to be inconvenienced by the track. Looked well suited by the trip on that latter start and has place claims at the very least today.

5/7 DARTREY: An impressive winner of her sole juvenile start, when showing a good turn of foot to beat Diamond City in a Newmarket (7f, good to firm) stakes race, her racing inexperience betrayed her when unable to settle the principals' pace in the General Accident 1,000 Guineas at Newmarket (1m, good) on her seasonal bow, finishing a never-nearer 6th to Shadayid. She subsequently stayed on really strongly when a head/second to Gussy Marlowe in the Group 3 Musidora Stakes at York (1m 2f 110yds, good to firm) and looks sure to relish the extra 1½ furlongs she encounters for the first time today. Trainer Michael Stoute has already saddled the first-past-the-post three times, and Dartrey has definite claims of making it four.

6/20 FRAGRANT HILL: Won a minor event at Newbury (7f, good to firm) last season, beating Exclusive Native and Silver Braid by ¾ of a length and the same, but subsequently ran well below that form when last of six to Crystal Gazing in the Group 3 Rockfel Stakes at Newmarket (7f, good). No excuses were given for that poor performance, but she reappeared better than ever, beating subsequently disqualified Sipsi Fach a neck in the Listed Lupe Stakes at Goodwood (1m 2f, good). Although that form is someway removed from Gold Seal Oaks victory. She had been held up with a ricked back 10 days previously and is open to improvement.

7/20 JAFFA LINE: Bidden out to beat Ausherra a neck in the Group 3 Prestige Stakes at Goodwood (7f, good to firm) for the latter of two victories there last season, she stayed on well to finish a head 2nd to Horsham in the Group 3 Thresher Classic Trial at Sandown (1m 2f, good) on her seasonal reappearance. Subsequently badly outpaced 3 furlongs from home when a disappointing last of five to Gussy Marlowe in the Group 3 Musidora Stakes at York (1m 2f 110yds, good), others make more appeal today.

8/5 JET SKI LADY: Kept on nicely to beat Classic Minstrel by 1½ lengths in a Listed race on her reappearance at The Curragh (1m 2f, good to yielding) but subsequently appeared to have her limitations thoroughly exposed when 4½ lengths 4th of 8 to Runyon in the Group 3 Derrinstown Stud Derby Trial over the same trip at Leopardstown (good to yielding). Looks one of the more unlikely winners this afternoon.

[handwritten: Ireland / Times]

The Gold Seal Oaks continued

10/20 MAGNIFICENT STAR: Relatively unfancied when 7½ lengths 5th in Umniyatee's Newbury (7f, good) race first time, the opposite was true next time out when she was an odds-on favourite at Warwick (1m, good to firm) but had to settle for 3rd, 3 lengths behind Fly To The Moon. Compensation was gained in the Listed Telecom Fillies' Trial at Newbury (1m 2f, good/to soft) last month, when again well backed (7/1 from 14/1), she was driven out to beat Positive Acclaim by 2 lengths in a slow time, but may struggle to trouble the principals here.

[handwritten: Un-raced 2-Y-O french fillies Sicambre '51 / Asmena 1950 – Ustaikhun 1932 most recent]

12/1 PEPLUM: A half-sister to Irish 1000 Guineas winner Al Bahathri, she comfortably accounted for fellow newcomer Ludina by 1½ lengths with subsequent dual scorer So Romantic 2 lengths 3rd on her Nottingham (1m 2f, good) debut. Contesting the Cheshire Oaks (1m 3f 70yds, good) next time, she had to be pushed along 4f out but prevailed nonetheless, beating Conor Lily by 1½ lengths. The merit of her form to date is not easy to assess but she looks sure to stay this longer trip and represents the stable who have won this race in recent years with Oh So Sharp and Diminuendo.

[handwritten: Infra 6000 –4000]

14/8 SHADAYID: Unbeaten in five starts to date, she enjoyed a lucrative juvenile campaign, culminating in a comfortable 2 lengths defeat of Caerlina in the Group 1 Prix Marcel Boussac at Longchamp (1m, good), a performance which sent her to the head of the ante-post 1,000 Guineas market. An impressive 3 lengths win over Silver Braid in the Group 3 Fred Darling Stakes on her seasonal reappearance at Newbury (7f, good, good) in April saw her strengthen that position. Odds-on in the Newmarket (1m, good) Classic, she duly obliged, running on strongly to see off the subsequent easy length 1,000 Guineas victor Kooyonga by 2 lengths. There is a small doubt about her ability to stay this trip, but she will be a warm order to repeat the stable's success in this race last year with Salsabil.

[handwritten: Kents £10,000 11/8]

15/1 SHAMSHIR: Reversed previous May Hill Stakes form with Majmu when beating Safa by 2 lengths in the valuable Group 1 Brent Walker Fillies' Mile at Ascot (good to firm) in September. Consequently having to concede 3lb to most of her opponents on her seasonal debut in the Group 3 Musidora Stakes at York (1m 2f 110yds, good to firm) in May, she put in a gallant effort to finish just over a length 3rd to Gussy Marlowe and Dartrey, both of whom had had the benefit of a previous outing. The additional 1½ furlongs today ought not to prove a problem and this Kris filly has solid claims to at least reach the frame.

[handwritten: £13,250 – 10,000]

PROBABLE S.P. Evens SHADAYID, 9-2 SHAMSHIR, 13-2 DARTREY, 12-1 JAFFA LINE, 14-1 AUSHERRA & PEPLUM, 20-1 MAGNIFICENT STAR & FRAGRANT HILL, 50-1 JET SKI LADY.

'Before' and 'after' racecards for the 1991 Gold Seal Oaks. On the left is the card used before the race, with several statistical nuggets neatly inscribed at the top: 33 favourites this century have won the Oaks, only once since 1846 has the same owner-trainer-jockey combination won both the Derby and the Oaks in the same year (relevant should Ausherra, with the same connections as Derby winner Generous, win), and so on. Betting moves for each horse are noted. Jet Ski Lady opened at 'double carpet' (33-1), was the same price at the next show, then went to 50-1. Note, by her, that Ireland has won the race four times. By Shadayid are recorded some of the bets laid about her: £6000 to £4000

with Taffy, £15,000 to £12,000, and £13,500 to £10,000 on the rails.

The 'after' card updates the statistical information on the 'before' to take account of different eventualities. Thus if Shadayid has won, she is the 34th successful favourite this century, the 47th filly to win the One Thousand Guineas and Oaks, and so on. Jet Ski Lady is the fifth Irish-trained winner. At the top of the right-hand page is information about the longest priced winners and the longest winning distance, both to become highly relevant in the case of Jet Ski Lady. The starting prices are entered on this card as soon as they are decided by the SP reporters.

The Gold Seal Oaks

FORM NOTES & BETTING GUIDE

3. AUSHERRA: Has produced her two best performances at courses with similar peculiarities to Epsom – finishing a never-nearer sixth behind Gai Bulga in the Group 3 Prestige Stakes at Goodwood (7f, good to firm) on the second of two juvenile starts, and, when beating Gai Bulga a length in the Listed Oaks Trial Stakes at Lingfield (1m 3f 106yds, good) last time – and thus looks unlikely to be inconvenienced by the track. Looked well suited by the trip on that latter start and has place claims at the very least.

5. DARTREY: An impressive winner of her sole juvenile start, when showing a good turn of foot to beat Diamond City in a Newmarket stakes race, her racing inexperience betrayed her when unable to match the principals' pace in the General Accident 1,000 Guineas at Newmarket (1m, good) on her seasonal bow, finishing a never-nearer 6th to Shadayid. She subsequently stayed on really strongly for a head second to Gussy Marlowe in the Group 3 Musidora Stakes at York (1m 2f 110yds, good to firm) and looks sure to relish the extra 1½ furlongs she encounters for the first time today. Trainer Michael Stoute has already saddled the first-past-the-post three times, and Dartrey has definite claims of making it four.

6. FRAGRANT HILL: Won a minor event at Newbury (7f, good to firm) last season, beating Exclusive Native and Silver Braid by ¾ of a length and the same, but subsequently ran well below that form when last of six to Crystal Gazing in the Group 3 Rockfel Stakes at Newmarket (7f, good). No excuses were given for that poor performance, but she reappeared better than ever, beating subsequently disqualified Sipsi Fach a neck in the Listed Lupe Stakes at Goodwood (1m 2f, good). Although that form is someway removed from a Gold Seal Oaks victory. She had been held up with a ricked back 10 days previously and is open to improvement.

7. JAFFA LINE: Bidden out to beat Ausherra a neck in the Group 3 Prestige Stakes at Goodwood (7f, good to firm) for the latter of two victories there last season, she stayed on well to finish a head 2nd to Hailsham in the Group 3 Thresher Classic Trial at Sandown (1m 2f, good) on her seasonal reappearance. Subsequently badly outpaced 3 furlongs from home when a disappointing last of five to Gussy Marlowe in the Group 3 Musidora Stakes at York (1m 2f 110yds, good), others make more appeal today.

8. JET SKI LADY: Kept on nicely to beat Classic Minstrel by 1½ lengths in a Listed race on her reappearance at The Curragh (1m 2f, good to yielding) but subsequently appeared to have her limitations thoroughly exposed when 4½ lengths 4th of 8 to Runyon in the Group 3 Derrinstown Stud Derby Trial over the same trip at Leopardstown (good to yielding). Looks one of the more unlikely winners this afternoon.

The Gold Seal Oaks continued

102. MAGNIFICENT STAR: Relatively unfancied when 7¼ lengths 5th of Umniyatek's Newbury (7f, good) race first time, the opposite was true next time out when she was an odds-on favourite at Warwick (7f, good to firm) but had to settle for 3rd, 3 lengths behind Fly To The Moon. Compensation was gained in the Listed Telecom Fillies' Trial at Newbury (1m 2f, good to soft) last month, when again well backed (7/1 from 14/1), she was driven out to beat Positive Acclaim by 2 lengths in a slow time, but may struggle to trouble the principals here.

121. PEPLUM: A half-sister to Irish 1,000 Guineas winner Al Bahathri, she comfortably accounted for fellow newcomer Midifina by 1½ lengths with subsequent dual scorer So Romantic 2 lengths 3rd on her Nottingham (1m 2f, good) debut. Contesting the Cheshire Oaks (1m 3f 70yds, good) next time, she had to be pushed along 4f out but prevailed nonetheless, beating Conor Lily by 7½ lengths. The merit of her form to date is not easy to assess but she looks sure to stay this longer trip and represents the stable who have won this race in recent years with Oh So Sharp and Diminuendo.

14. SHADAYID: Unbeaten in five starts to date, she enjoyed a lucrative juvenile campaign, culminating in a comfortable 2 lengths defeat of Caerlina in the Group 1 Prix Marcel Boussac at Longchamp (1m, good), a performance which sent her to the head of the ante-post 1,000 Guineas market. An impressive 3 lengths win over Silver Braid in the Group 3 Fred Darling Stakes on her seasonal reappearance at Newbury (7f 60yd, good) in April saw her strengthen that position. Odds-on in the Newmarket (1m, good) Classic, she duly obliged, running on strongly to see off the subsequent easy Irish 1,000 Guineas victor Kooyonga by 2 lengths. There is a small doubt about her ability to stay this trip, but she will be a warm order to repeat the stable's success in this race last year with Salsabil.

15. SHAMSHIR: Reversed previous May Hill Stakes form with Majmu when beating Safa by 2 lengths in the valuable Group 1 Brent Walker Fillies' Mile at Ascot (good to firm) in September. Consequently having to concede 3lb to most of her opponents on her seasonal debut in the Group 3 Musidora Stakes at York (1m 2f 110yd, good to firm) in May, she put in a gallant effort to finish just over a length 3rd to Gussy Marlowe and Dartrey, both of whom had had the benefit of a previous outing. The additional 1½ furlongs today ought not to prove a problem and this Kris filly has solid claims to at least reach the frame.

PROBABLE S.P. Evens SHADAYID, 9-2 SHAMSHIR, 13-2 DARTREY, 12-1 JAFFA LINE, 14-1 AUSHERRA & PEPLUM, 20-1 MAGNIFICENT STAR & FRAGRANT HILL, 50-1 JET SKI LADY.

Around to the CapGen van and hand over this information to one of the goddesses who prepare the captions – Sue Nicolle, Teresa 'The Delays' Wadeson or Dinah 'The Head Mistress' Quinnen: she's the one who looks after us and keeps the team in crocodile! With them are the genial 'JT' – racing history buff and author John Tyrrel – and Jo James: Jo (a chap even without the 'e') is a vital link in the transmission of betting news and results from the ring and the other courses in action that day: he receives information, via the Press Association, and my own updates, sifts them and passes them along the van to be typed into captions, ready for reading in the honeyed leading-man tones of JT, a former television 'Mystery Tipster' and noted theatrical actor.

An added complication on Oaks day is the presence of a film crew dogging our heels for my video accompanying this opus on the World of Betting. They are led by Colin Frewin, boss of Sunset & Vine, the production company responsible for Channel Four Racing's overseas coverage such as the Arc and Breeders' Cup, here swapping expense-account lunches and City wheeler-dealing for the real action at Epsom and remembering what it was like actually to produce programmes.

Ex-ITV soccer big cheese Jeff Foulser and 'Killer' (John Killeen) make up the team. Among the interviews we grab are with Timeform and Channel Four Racing's formbook maestro 'Jimbo', Jim McGrath, along with Newmarket trainer Welshman Ron 'Leek' Boss and 'GG'.

NOON

Calamity. No lunch! The 'chuck wagon' which serves the fifty-strong crew responsible for broadcasting that afternoon's racing aren't doing our midday nosh. Better find another bacon and sausage roll.

The remaining couple of hours before going on the air are spent checking round with on- and off-course firms for the latest market moves and picking up the tissue (the course bookies' betting forecast), recording video pieces and mugging up facts and stats. But nerves are taking over now, so a puff or two on a Lusitania cigar – being too poor to bet or have women apart from the Booby, a 'la-di-dah' a day is the one luxury.

Also remember to switch glasses. The on-air pair – nicknamed 'glasses for Phil' after Thames TV producer Phil King, who once insisted I take off my normal shades while broadcasting – are located by the Booby in my pink working hold-all.

Almost inevitably at around this time some optimist enquires, 'Backed one today, John?' To understand the game I've had to have been a 'sufferer' ever since running a book at Harrow. Punters are a breed apart. Nothing that life throws up can shock us – we've seen it all.

Nowadays, though, I try to avoid getting involved. Criticising jockeys, or blaming other factors on air when heated instant judgement is liable to be unduly influenced by personal betting, isn't fair.

That's not to say there aren't propositions too tempting to resist – such as 10-1 the French colt Toulon for the 1991 Derby immediately after he'd paralysed his Chester Vase opposition. Sent off 4-1 joint favourite at Epsom, Pat Eddery's ride never showed, lolloping in a distant ninth behind Generous. At least I beat the price!

And those with infuriatingly long memories will possibly recall that I was also quite sweet on another French colt, Machiavellian, 6-4 favourite, ridden by Freddie Head, when beaten by Tirol (9-1) in the 1990 Two Thousand Guineas.

True to type, viewers habitually hark back to such debacles and conveniently forget Reference Point, Ravinella, Slip Anchor, Nashwan, etc. And quite right too. The arm-waving blabbermouth is conceited enough as it is.

2.30 P.M.

Time to get rigged up. With the necessity of keeping both arms free to tic-tac prices (and pretend to admonish recalcitrant youngsters), a small microphone is clipped to the elegant lapel of the pink suit, with a wire running from it to a small box secreted in one pocket. Through the earpiece, discreetly lodged in the well-coiffed locks, comes a barrage of sound – from the programme itself, the director and producer, 'Blondie's' calm countdowns, and talkback from other presenters. Add to this a bombardment of noise from the public address along with the general babble at any busy racecourse, bookies shouting the odds, and the crowd's climactic roar at the finish. You can see why occasionally anyone caring to approach Channel Four's Man in the Ring is put off by a glazed stare into the middle-distance: he's not just listening to them – but maybe five or six others.

A small crowd often gathers and usually they are fine, adding to the bustling atmosphere. As I sometimes turn round and tell them: 'There's one moron allowed on Channel Four today and that's me – so no waving gestures or "Hi Mum!" placards, please!' Occasionally, though far less often than a few years back, some cretin starts gesticulating or worse.

Naturally racecourses don't like such unruly images being transmitted, and out of sheer exasperation a few tart words have been known to pass. A strategically placed Bobby (thanks, lads) is invariably enough to prevent any more serious disturbance.

Unique among all TV spouters, I'm totally unprotected – no studio, gantry, or even roped-off area during a two-hour live broadcast.

To get the 'feel' of the betting ring and be able to pass on the buzz, that's the way it should be. And, in reality, the forbearance and co-operation of racegoers is – with very few exceptions – amazing. After all, it isn't exactly a crime to wave to your mum!

One other vital piece of equipment – less technically wondrous but no less essential – is my pen tucked into the pen-holder strung round the neck, used to oblige the occasional request for a worthless autograph and for noting down constantly fluctuating market moves. These demand rapid annotation of the number one racecard. Frequent enquiries about 'that thing hanging round your neck' can only be answered untruthfully with: 'It's the only thing of mine that rises these days!'

2.35 P.M.

Down the earpiece comes 'Blondie's' countdown ('ten-nine-eight-seven-six-five-four-three-two-one'), and we're on the air. From then on the mind (or what there is of it) races to keep up with the swirl and nuances of information coming through the earpiece and bubbling up in the hyperactive jungle of the betting ring. Director 'Heart' Gardam (whose career, as he keeps reminding us on boozy evenings in distant hotels, goes back to when John Logie Baird covered Wembley Cup Finals) alerts each presenter to his next slot ('Cue John!'). But the hubbub doesn't stop while you're babbling on air, and to be able to carry on with as much sense as you can muster while all sorts of instructions, exhortations, exclamations and queries are invading your ear is one of the most challenging parts of the role.

HOW TO EMULATE YOUR HERO

'How can I become a racing hack?' So frequently the question is asked, and considering how appealing the life is, no wonder. (And the first rule of writing is never to start an article with a question – so there!)

Free racing is quite a perk for a start. But remember, as in all journalism, for those with bylines there are dozens toiling away in less glamorous parts of the industry.

On the plus side, you only have to know some (though not all) present incumbents of the plum jobs to realise that quality and dedication are not always essential.

There are so many more openings than ever before. Numerous radio stations and newspapers, specialist magazines and form books, plus extensive coverage in the nationals and the detailed reporting of the *Sporting Life* and *Racing Post*, mean that opportunities have never been greater.

So, apart from the proven, time-honoured and best path to the top, through hard graft and training at the local level covering council meetings, weddings and fetes, what short cuts are there?

Firstly, specialisation. When the Falkland Islands were invaded in 1982, anyone with a deep understanding of the area and able to write had it made. Similarly with any sport or activity that suddenly becomes big time, involving television exposure. In my case being

the only hack ever to have had practical experience in bookmaking, on course and in betting shops, proved an asset.

Reasonable competence then can lead on to permanent employment. Having compiled a detailed private handicap, firstly Formindex and then Racing Data, I wormed my way onto the *Sporting Life* as the coursing correspondent and branched out into doing 'returns' – the detailed results – and even features by Man On The Spot (known in house as – yes, you've guessed it – Man In The S**t!) and news reporting.

But not much subbing. Thinking up headlines to fit the allocated space and editing and rewriting copy takes proper professional skill.

Thanks to the *Life*'s former editor Ossie Fletcher, who wisely turned down my written applicaton for a job on leaving Harrow, and deputy editor Graham Taylor, I enjoyed the most absorbing but satisfying period of my career and also subbed on BBC TV's *Grandstand* behind David Coleman, Frank Bough (a smashing bloke on and off the screen) and super-cool gentleman Des Lynam.

That career 'in TV' was due to the old school tie influence of my fellow bookie at Harrow, BBC racing supremo Julian Wilson (thanks, Jules). And on ITV the late *Grandstand* editor Paul Lang, John Bromley, Trevor 'the Beast' East and the present Channel Four Racing bosses must shoulder most of the blame.

Luck, as elsewhere in life, plays a

huge part. But when you're determined, keep sending in those articles, tapes and applications. If you contribute a few well-written exclusive news stories, editors will soon take notice. And nowadays the requirement to be a union member thankfully no longer applies.

Once in, don't worry about hours or hard work or pay. Just be thrilled, as I was and still am, to be involved in any way with the sport with which you ideally must have been besotted since childhood. Avoid debilitating office politics (not easy), ignore setbacks – there'll be many – and treat disdainfully the inevitable sneers and jealous rivalry.

Put yourself about and you'll make it. There is, though, a surefire way to Fleet Street. Prove to any paper that you can tip fifty per cent of winners. Simple, really.

But if you could do that, there'd be no need to earn your living as a humble hack – like what I do!

Amateurs such as me are pretty hopeless, and I'm afraid it shows. Pros, like 'Thommo', Derek Thompson, with ten years' experience of radio sport, excel under such pressure. If in doubt, use the ubiquitous Thommo.

And that's why Franklin is finding it so hard to recruit a female member of the team. Having only men burbling away for two hours or more is totally unacceptable, and scores of potential performers have been screen-tested. Understandable nervousness hasn't been a problem. Nor, in most cases, has lack of racing knowledge. It is the absence so often of basic journalistic skills, concisely to put over news, that has been the main drawback. Several applicants, though, were amazingly natural, self-assured and skilled. Channel Four Racing needs a woman!

And when she joins us, one essential will be interpreting snappy, urgent instructions. A transmission up to three hours long can occasionally produce directions less than precise. With six presenters all waiting for Gardam's next cue, suddenly down the wire comes, 'Cue – [pause] – who?'. On 'Heart's' gravestone will surely be inscribed the words, 'Here lies "Cue – who?", the greatest director of his time'. 'Heart' revels in the off-beat, the unexpected, the telling picture. A former cameraman himself, he knows the pitfalls and skills involved at the sharp end, often exposed to foul weather. Initiative and alertness are essential, so that anything out of the ordinary can be picked up, followed and, if reckoned appropriate at the time, transmitted.

My aim during all this manic activity is to impart information, especially very early betting shows, that I myself would like to know, were I at the receiving end of the goggle box. We are guests in viewers' homes, pubs, and wherever they're tempted to watch. It is important that the banter and joking which goes on during each programme never descends into point-scoring or appears to do so. If you visit friends for dinner and the husband and wife are arguing or having a row, it becomes embarrassing. You feel uneasy and don't want to know.

Channel Four Racing, thanks to the leadership of Franklin and Scott, is a team effort. Yes, there are differences, but nothing significant. I recall an early Tuesday eve-of-Derby broadcast when I'd been allotted a minute for betting news. In rehearsal at the pub near Tattenham Corner where the programme was based, my rabbiting went on an extra 25 seconds. Brough immediately insisted the piece remained uncut and sacrificed one of his own slots. Typical of the man. No one on the box is more selfless or adept at 'passing the ball' to his minions than multi-award-winning hack Scott, also my boss on the *Racing Post*. (Interest declared, but the tribute is thoroughly deserved and deeply felt.)

We're fortunately a happy gang, and it seems to come over as such – though we can never match the infectious prep school humour of radio's *Test Match Special* team: no side could! We don't squabble over air time or being told what to do. There are disagreements about form, riding, or racing politics which crop up during broadcasts. But they only reflect differences among viewers. Discussion, conducted maybe with passion but without malice, often brings about a better understanding of issues.

As each race finishes SP reporters go into their huddle to agree the official returned odds. As soon as these are decided I call them down to Jo James, so that he can get the captions typed up by 'Neck', 'The Headmistress' or 'Delays' and screened. It is our intention that the winner's SP should be displayed whenever possible before the replay is shown, and for some long-distance races on the Flat and over jumps they are flashed up 'in running', thanks to the SP lads' cooperation, and even the 'Owl', in his brilliance, finds time to call the price of a horse clear a furlong out, if he's been given it.

Undoubtedly this has all helped defuse wild, baseless allegations that returns are 'fixed' once the result is known. I've been a witness at thousands of huddles and know they aren't. Such innuendoes, rightly, are deeply resented by SP reporters.

The Booby's a central part of many an afternoon's operation - and not only when it comes to holding an umbrella patiently over her dear boy's head. After the race she produces a tiny portable television set so that I can see the horses returning and gear relaying of SPs to the picture, though it may not often sound like it.

Here those stats come in handy. The complete outsider of the nine Oaks runners, Jet Ski Lady at 50-1 is the longest priced winner in 213 runnings, along with Vespa in 1833. And no Classic success has returned such a price since Snow Knight, also 50-1 in the 1974 Derby, and before that

WHY SHE'S MY BOOBY

In case you wondered, a Booby is a bird, found in South America and Hawaii, that cannot fly. Apparently it flaps its wings uselessly, squawks, and has been described as 'stupid and pathetically easy to catch'.

That's my gorgeous, sexy Booby!

66-1 Rockavon and Psidium in the 1961 Two Thousand Guineas and Derby. Jet Ski Lady is the fifth Irish-trained Oaks heroine, going back to silky smooth Noblesse in 1963, who like the 1991 winner coasted home by ten lengths – only Sun Princess in 1983 won by further, beating Acclimatise by twelve lengths.

Unscripted extras liable to occur unexpectedly include various interviews. Today I manage to grab the man himself – Michael Grade, boss of all Channel Four bosses – and give him the team's felicitations on air. One word from Mr Grade and we're all out of work. Thank you again, Sire, for your munificence.

Though no thanks to rails workman Teddy Driscoll. He observes loudly: 'McCririck looks more like a mobile tin of

Humiliating duty for a distinguished writer and Peer of the Realm, no less. Lord Ted Willis is obliged to grasp the clammy hand while dishing out the Television and Radio Industries Club 1992 Sports Presenter of the Year award at London's Grosvenor House Hotel. A Stewards' Enquiry followed immediately. But, through the alcohol-induced haze, it was accepted that the crop of '92 were way below selling plate class and the unworthy recipient, carrying far too much overweight, needed gelding anyway!

John West salmon.' Better though than the punter who shouts: 'You're just a pink turd!'

And throughout throbs that constant injunction to all broadcasters: if you don't know, shut up. Once, while awaiting the outcome of a desperate photo-finish, I called out on air in anguish: 'And what price a dead heat?' Down the earpiece came Franklin's tart – 'You damn fool, that's why you're there – to tell *us*!'

Naturally no one has ever even hinted that I'm loquacious, bombastic and repetitively guilty of indulging in didactic, obfuscating prolongation or tendentious verbigeration, but on the other hand, everything considered, and bearing in mind. . . .

5 P.M.

Off the air, and that sublime sense of relief. It's all over. Wires are removed, ear-bashing ends – except any that I care to dish out – and it's back to the control vans for quick post-mortems, tea with maybe a couple of icing-enveloped cakes and perhaps a relieving cigar.

6 P.M.

It's been a busy week. Ever Ready Derby Day on Wednesday is Channel Four Racing's most important single fixture. Nerves are tauter than usual. So the evening is given over to sheer relaxation. The Booby has long since departed for home. So 'Jacko', the video tape whizzkid also known as 'Mr Bicker' – he lives in 'Bicker Hall' and inhabits 'Bicker's World' – acts as chauffeur to Wimbledon dogs for the early Greyhound Derby heats.

We're on the Geoff de Mulder trained Fearless Mustang at 'double carpet' (33-1). Eventually, as it turned out, the brilliant 'Mustang' – a greyhound with that imperious look of eagles – went through to the final unbeaten. Starting favourite at even money ('levels you devils!'), Mustang, as invariably seems to occur whenever you've scooped the ante-post market, flopped, missing his break and running the worst race of his life. Ah well, back to work.

11.59 P.M.

Ensconced at The Trap. And so to bed.

But before energetically satisfying the Booby and drifting off, a few moments' contemplation. Whatever the criticisms and hassles, grumbles and stage-fright, there is time to reflect on the delights of racing in all its variety and moods the world over, and be grateful. 'Night 'night!

All right, Booby, just once more. . . .

A FAN AT LAST

Is there none of the old star quality left on the television screen? Yes, actually, but not on news and current affairs. The inheritors of the mantles of Dimbleby and Day are now found on the sports programmes. I don't think that any political journalist in the trade is more completely in command of his subject than Richie Benaud at the Test match or Peter Alliss covering the Open.

Racing is almost better, though it is one of the all too many areas where the BBC has lost its own natural superiority. The Beeb's coverage of Ascot this week has been mixed, to put it very politely.

But Channel Four Racing remains the best thing on television, the Johns – Oaksey, Francome and, yes, even McCririck – displaying that ease and expertise that thirty years ago we saw on the news and Panorama. Perhaps the three of them should take over ITN.

Geoffrey Wheatcroft, *Evening Standard* (21 June 1991)

NOBLESSE OBLIGES BEFORE MY DIZZY DATE AT EPSOM

One fleeting vision of Noblesse, Ireland's first Oaks winner, is the last racing memory I intend having on my deathbed. Her sublime athletic grace has been captured and stored, a treasured memory in the mind, and nothing again will ever match it.

All of us can instantly recall great deeds of the Turf we've been privileged to witness – a Classic triumph, a photo-finish that financially meant so much, or fear-provoking bravery of a horse or rider. All the stirring acclamations, the releases of tension, remain locked in our memories.

But for me, the pure, rhythmical elegance and seemingly effortless arrogance of that Empress of fillies, Noblesse, on 31 May 1963, transcends all else.

A group of mates and colleagues had wangled time off work and study to spend at Epsom. Being poor – nothing's changed much, I'm afraid – it was the free Downs in the centre of the course for us.

From there I'd seen Greville Starkey secure my each-way Derby bet on Merchant Venturer some way behind runaway Relko; those grand handicappers Passenger (ridden by 5lb-claimer Bruce Raymond) and Be Hopeful battling out a tight finish; a Lord Rosebery

favourite double with Gwen and Bivouac; and France's Exbury routing Hethersett in the Coronation Cup.

Come Friday, the final day of the meeting, just three of us remained solvent out of the original Derby Day dozen. It was time to rope in some girls.

Now fellas know what it's like taking a female to the races for the first time. They usually cling on, asking stupid questions all the time, or gush inane drivel. Unfortunately my choice, Sandra, a bit of a raver on the dance floor and elsewhere, was a combination of both and not the ideal partner for a serious day at the sports.

Nevertheless, being English gentlemen, we did try to make an impression. No free entry on the hill, mingling with the riff-raff. Instead we went for the Hyperion enclosure, the furthest ring down from the Grandstand, right opposite Tattenham Corner.

The girls arranged the picnic grub and we brought along some plonk and somehow found enough cash for rail fares and entry. How much that was I can't remember but, to our minds, it bought them body and all for the day.

Sandra must have been thrilled and grateful to be escorted by such a good-looking, debonair, man-of-the-world turfiste. She couldn't stop staring adoringly into my eyes while chattering away. Well, it seemed to me to be adoration!

Never can there have been a display of more profound ignorance of racing, betting and even horses. Rather than keeping quiet and trying to work out the basics like any sensible newcomer, she appeared to take a manic pleasure in flaunting her pathetic helplessness.

The four W's – 'why', 'what', 'where' and 'when' – took on a whole new meaning that sweltering afternoon. With machine-like rapidity questions assailed me from all sides. Anyone else would soon have wilted but, fancying my chances later, and being, as always, courteous and polite to ladies, the finer points were patiently explained again and again.

But when it came to betting we were sucked into a morass of misunderstanding. Trying to make Sandra comprehend that you win less than your stake when laying odds-on was a recurring nightmare. As for the difference between 6-4 and 13-8, it didn't add up to her.

However, as you've surely guessed by now, bubbly Sandra was destined to be the only one of us to leave the track in funds, though my best pal did manage to tap her for half the winnings!

Starting with 13-2 Miss Velvet she could do little wrong, except take under the odds: 'Oh, I love velvet! How much shall I have on her each-way? Does that mean I win if we finish fifth?'

An Australian link in her family was revealed on discovering the nationality of Scobie Breasley (two winners), Ron Hutchinson and Bill Williamson (one apiece). Winning became an easy game.

In the Oaks, the omens were particularly propitious: Aussie Garnie Bougoure aboard unbeaten, 11-4 on Noblesse, and Breasley on Pouponne. She went each-way on Pouponne, a 'double carpet' (33-1) chance, but offered by the books at 'special' place terms of around 2-1. There was no point telling her that the only thing 'special' about them was the convenient way they cut pay-outs.

Going for the thieving each-way, my modest interest was in Jeremy Tree's Spree, beaten a length in the One Thousand Guineas by Hula Dancer. The fact that she was returned at

Noblesse wins the 1963 Oaks. McCririck (arrowed, with Sandra) is At Large

what, for her, was little more than a canter. It was an unforgettable picture of power, harnessed to beauty. Up in the stands she will have been seen as one of the most impressive of all Classic winners.

Her ten-length rout of Spree and Pouponne equalled the race record, and was matched by Jet Ski Lady in 1991. This has only been eclipsed by twelve-length Sun Princess in 1983. But Noblesse's performance swept her beyond such mundane matters as statistics and money, though not for the nonplussed Sandra.

'Who won?' she asked.

'The favourite.'

'Which one was that?'

'Noblesse.'

'Did she have those pretty purple colours?'

'No dear.'

'What happened to my horse? What was it called?'

'Pouponne, dear, and it finished third.'

'Would it win if it tried again?'

'No, dear.'

'How do you know?'

'I do, dear, I do. Now, how about an ice lolly?'

100-7 – 11-10 'special' place odds – shows just how highly regarded Noblesse was.

Standing shirt-sleeved and not a little exasperated as the fillies swept around Tattenham Corner, I barely noticed Jimmy Lindley well up there on Spree along with the Queen's Amicable. Behind them, on the outside nearest to us, Bougoure had hold of the white-faced Noblesse. The reins were tight, he wasn't moving.

In full flight Noblesse, with her imperious, devouring stride, was an onrushing, unstoppable avenger, swooping down on her prey in

2 Punters – Life's 'Sufferers'

Anyone who bets has to be one of life's sufferers. Fate conspires with diabolical perversity to deprive them of rightful gain. Anything that can go wrong does go wrong for inveterate punters.

They come in all shapes and sizes. They use different methods and want different things out of the experience of betting. They bet in wildly differing amounts.

There are certainly plenty of sufferers:

- Around 70 per cent of adults in Britain like a flutter and some twenty million people do the pools, with Littlewoods' £2 million the top jackpot.
- One million people admit to betting every day.
- Britons bet about £5 per week per head of population, the highest amount in Europe, and lose around £100 a head per year.
- Half the betting population indulges at least once a week.
- Sixty per cent of people who bet claim they do it just for fun and/or wining a fortune.
- Around £6.5 billion a year is bet on horses, 57 per cent of the £12.2 billion total.
- Greyhound racing is Britain's biggest spectator sport after soccer, though in reality it is mainly the same hardened regulars turning up at meeting after meeting. Over £1 billion is wagered on greyhounds every year.

The 200-page report *Gambling 1991* carried out by Mintel listed the division of British gambling activities in order of the percentage of the adult population who engage in them (and of course some indulge in several):

	%
Football pools	37
Lotteries/raffles	28
Bingo	17
'Amusement with prizes' machines	15
Horse racing	13
Card games for money	9
Gaming machines in clubs/casinos	3
Greyhound racing	3
Gambling in clubs/casino	2
Other gambling	1
None	30

But never mind the statistics, how do they choose what to bet on? Few punters admit to taking their betting too seriously. For most, it is harmless fun, and they approach the business of selection with an appropriate lack of gravity.

If you do the pools, you probably forget any close study of the form and fill in the days of your family's birthdays, their favourite numbers and such variable figures as those to be found on your driving licence, car, passport, even DHSS number! Fair enough, but consider this: most people start at the top of the column and finish about three quarters of the way down. Other than on the most freakish occasions, to win a major dividend you must include some of the Scottish matches at the foot of the coupon. So why not halfway through filling in your draws, turn the column upside down and carry on from there?

Punters pick horses for different reasons, some of them more sensible than others. Sentiment, or simple popular support, is often behind a public fancy such as Desert Orchid. But bookies liked Dessie, for he always gave them a chance. When he ran

What would bookmakers do without greedy mugs? For the 1991 Budweiser Irish Derby (not 'Darby' as spelt on this Ladbrokes slip) a North London punter laid out £1100 cash tax paid on to win £1 million on 1000-1 'rag' Barry's Run. After Derby winner Generous had outstayed French Derby winner Suave Dancer, the judge remained long enough in his box to confirm that the hopelessly outclassed Barry's Run had finished last of six – beaten about two furlongs. Another easy 'grand' for the 'Magic Sign', who will lay a horse to lose £1 million – provided it hasn't got a prayer!

under huge weights in handicaps, punters wanted to back him because of who he was, but layers could afford to offer reasonable prices, as they wouldn't let sentiment cloud their view of the form. And at Cheltenham they could field against him with a reasonable hope of success – he won just once there in eight Festivals, that emotional 1989 Gold Cup.

Red Rum had won two Grand Nationals

Bookmakers liked to lay Dessie – but so often he proved the punter's friend

and been second twice by the time he lined up for the 1977 race. But the bookies were content for punters to back the people's choice at 9-1 and even better. Already a National legend, he won for the third time.

One of the most common, if completely irrational, ways of picking horses – or at least of giving their chance on the formbook special attention – is names. Until Snurge won the St Leger it was widely believed that horses with unattractive names don't win big races. All those appalling Arab-owned

Mujtahid, Mujaazif, Mu this and Al that. And Corrupt, 4-1 joint favourite for the 1991 Derby flopped. But good old Bog Trotter, with Doncaster's Champagne Stakes and Newbury's Greenham among his successes, hasn't done badly. Great name, the Bog Trotter! There certainly can be poetry in nomenclature, as Alan Ross pointed out in the *Independent* in 1990:

Although I never back a horse which, on any analysis, has no chance, I have certain attachments. Horses that have to do with ships and the sea, for example, horses with Indian, Japanese and Italian names, horses that the word 'night' is attached to, for example Nightshirt and Night At Sea, both profitable winners on several recent occasions. A lack of care in checking runners when there are several meetings can cost one dear. At Ascot this year I noticed too late that Pontenuovo was bottom weight in the Royal Hunt Cup. He won at Tote odds of 167-1 and it was the only time in his racing career that I had failed to back him.

Horses with poets' or painters' names do well: Baudelaire, Foujita, Causley. The latter I associate with Charles Causley, a wartime sailor who wrote excellent poems about naval life. He won twice in July. John Synge, until recently a director of the Redfern Gallery, backs horses with 'blue' or 'red' in their names (Red Toto, Lucky Blue), and 'march' (March Hare, Marching Song). ... Our mutual friend Freddy Mayor, who founded the Mayor Gallery and introduced Paul Klee to an unreceptive English public, used always to back horses 'napped' by only one tipster, or, alternatively, second favourites. He was totally indifferent to everything else about the animal: its name, breeding, form, habits. Perhaps it was a kind of mathematical sympathy related to abstract art.

Perhaps indeed, though it's the idea of backing a horse napped by just one correspondent which catches the eye. How about sticking to a horse napped by none of the hacks? The record of professional tipsters in newspapers makes you realise why the bookies take their holidays in St Moritz and Barbados. It's all very well trumpeting that this or that horse tipped has won at such and such a price, but very few consistently return a profit on their naps – their best bets – through a season. But under public scrutiny, and sometimes pressure from their editors, that accursed Naps Table makes the tipster's job one of the most exposed in Fleet Street.

And a special word here for my old comrade Cayton of the Communist *Morning Star*. He managed the remarkable feat in 1986 of napping fifty-seven consecutive losers, before finally coming good with a 9-4 on shot in a three-horse race. He did nap Beech Road, 50-1 winner of the 1989 Champion Hurdle, and has won the prestigious Naps Table several times, with winners like Russian Hero (66-1 in the 1949 Grand National) and numerous 'Reds' – all Marxist beauties!

Sadly the days of the colourful course tipster shouting his wares are virtually behind us, though you may be accosted in the car park by a seedy fellow who wishes to sell you a 'specially marked' card. Don't buy it.

There are many ways in which others tell punters what to back, and most will charge for the benefit of their wisdom. It's entirely up to you whether you choose to make your selections in this way. Often newspaper tipsters can add an extra dimension to the process of choosing, but following them blindly is no more guaranteed to bring a profit than supporting a jockey or trainer. A pound (tax free) on every one of Martin Pipe's 782 runners in the 1990-91 jumping season resulted in 230 winners, but an overall loss of £4.02. A pound (tax free) on each of the 505 runners of Arthur Stephenson, third in the trainers' table, would have brought 83 winners but an overall loss of £199.56. But the same stake on John Jenkins's 192 runners would have yielded 30 winners and a handsome £61.99 profit.

The *Racing Post* and *Sporting Life* offer an extraordinary amount of information and statistics. It is easy to spot trainers, and even jockeys, out of form and whether horses are being raised or dropped in the handicap. These are supplemented by *Timeform*, the national and local press, and a host of other authoritative form guides. Absorb them, and better still start your own form figures, but don't rely on other people to tell you what to back.

By all means listen to racecourse gossip and weigh it for what it is worth. Experience of past quality is the best guide, as you'll quickly find out. Treat with the same detachment all you hear on television. A jockey states he is very 'hopeful' (aren't they all?) or a trainer worries that the ground is too lively, 'but he'll run well'. And everyone associated with a horse always seems to tell us that he or she 'is very well'.

Today most trainers are candid with the Press, providing information about the well-being and future plans of their horses, which adds to the punter's armoury. Trade papers, and *Timeform*, regularly print stable interviews when the yard's top prospects are discussed in revealing detail.

Whatever the sources of your information, utilise them with care. Betting for the average punter is much more fun when making your own choice, for then you will have the added satisfaction, after your horse wins, of knowing that you did it *your* way.

Plenty of the big punters are mugs, the same as small ones. One bookmaker who caters for several of the higher-staking types

has been quoted: 'I can't believe some of my clients. Some of them, they're household names, running the government, you know, or huge companies. But when they come along to bet with me, they leave their brains at the gate.'

Professional punters, those who actually make a good living out of betting, keep their brains solidly in place, but even they are prone to the occasional slice of bad luck.

The late Alex Bird, perhaps the best known of the professionals, won vast amounts in a lifetime of betting, especially in the early days of photo-finishes. But the bet most

Even professional punter/trainer Barney Curley is not averse to taking advice from a real expert. (He would put it somewhat differently)

SNAPPING UP THE PRICES

Sandown's Friday Tattersalls patrons were astonished to see a pair of false teeth rolling down the slopes from the Dave Saphir pitch. 'Watch out, they've bitten two punters' legs and nicked a cheese sandwich already,' shouted one tic-tac as they rolled merrily on their way back to the line of bookies.

Their progress was halted without further damage to punters or themselves and they were tenderly returned intact to Dave's embarrassed clerk, who had bent down behind the joint to retrieve his pencil and had watched his spare set of dentures fall out of his top pocket.

(From David Smalley's column in the *Raceform Handicap Book*, 17 March 1990)

widely remembered from his legendary punting career is that in the 1954 Grand National on Tudor Line, whom he had backed to win half a million pounds. Tudor Line had a habit of jumping to the right, and he was usually fitted with a 'pricker', a small brush on that side of his bridle, to persuade him to keep straight. But trainer Bobby Renton decided to leave the pricker off for the National, and Tudor Line veered right at the last, forfeiting ground which he could not make up as he tried to peg back the Vincent O'Brien-trained Royal Tan on the run-in. At 10-1 he was beaten by a neck.

DOROTHY PAGET

Dorothy Paget, the famed eccentric who had inherited a vast fortune at the age of 21, was the owner of many famous horses – notably Golden Miller, five-times winner of the Cheltenham Gold Cup and the only horse ever to land the Gold Cup and Grand National in the same year (1934). She was also a punter on a huge scale, though not my sort of a girl if you can believe Ron Pollard's *Odds and Sods* (Hodder & Stoughton, 1991):

Dorothy was an enormous woman, a renowned lesbian and a fearful glutton who would eat twelve lamb chops for breakfast and still wonder what was for lunch. She always turned up at race meetings with two Rolls Royces, just in case one of them broke down, and if there was a place in the Guinness Book of Records for the person who set most beds alight with cigarettes in a lifetime, she would have claimed it.

Dorothy Paget's betting was, like her figure, stupendous. On one occasion she instructed her bookmaker that she wanted to back a horse to win £20,000. The beast went off at 8-1 on, making Miss·P's stake a mere £160,000 (approaching £2 million now). The horse won.

But perhaps the most remarkable fact about Dorothy Paget as a punter is that she was held in such esteem by the bookmaking fraternity – who knew her to be a gambler of complete probity and honesty – that one layer would allow her to bet by phone well after the race. This was necessitated by her curious life-style which involved sleeping through the day and being up and about at night. Upon awaking she would ring that trusting bookmaker and make bets on races which had taken place hours before.

If we could do that now, who wouldn't be tempted?

Alex Bird wrote in his autobiography: 'People never understood why I did not feel any emotion about losing. But winning and losing was my business just like buying and selling.'

Simon 'Dodger' McCartney is another pro. The son of a bookmaker, he has been backing horses (over jumps only) for a living practically since leaving school, though he claims that it took him twenty years to make it pay. For him, as for every other professional backer, the key is hard work and persistent study of the form book. 'I get every form book that's going – you can't skimp on that – you have to look at everything. There is no substitute for doing your homework.' He told Jon Freeman in the *Sunday Times* the key to his operation:

Value, that's what it's all about. I will never ever take under the odds I think a horse should be. I have losing days, of course I do. Sometimes it can go on for six weeks. But when it goes wrong I take a pull. I might have a day or two off. That should be the number one golden rule for any punter, never chase losses. And by the same token, if things are going well, crack away.

I wouldn't advise anyone to take up this game. There are only five people I know who I would call professional gamblers. Most bet-

Dorothy Paget with Golden Miller

ting-shop punters will tell you they win, but they don't. When you think about it, I'm not taking money from the bookmakers, but from punters who have backed the wrong horse.

And Paul Cooper, a professional punter since 1979, with the proud record of having forty-one credit accounts closed, explained to David Ashforth in the *Sporting Life* how he makes the game pay:

'People found it strange that I was prepared to have up to 60 Tricasts. Bookmakers normally rub their hands with delight when they see a bet like that, knowing that you've got 59 losers before you start.'

They rubbed their hands a bit prematurely in 1989 when Cooper capitalised on the huge advantage those drawn high in sprints at Thirsk sometimes enjoy. There were 23 runners for the Dick Peacock Sprint Handicap and the first three home were drawn 21, 23 and 22 at SPs of 20-1, 25-1, and 33-1. The Tricast paid £13,673 for £1 and Cooper pocketed £250,000.

A year later, the same race attracted 20 runners and the first three home were drawn 18, 19 and 16. (Three of those declared didn't run.) The fourth horse was drawn 17. Another six figures from the bookies' satchels.

SODS AND ODDS

This is what the nineteenth-century diarist Charles Greville wrote about my second favourite pursuit:

'Racing is just like dram-drinking – momentary excitement at wretched intervals, full consciousness of the mischievous effects of the habit and equal difficulty in abstaining from it.'

*

In London's Golden Horseshoe Casino in 1991 a female roulette player hit a fantastic winning streak: £100 stakes on the correct number kept coming up! At the end of the night she had won just under £627,000 – and naturally took her money in a series of cheques.

But the following day the fistful of £50,000 cheques were cancelled and police, along with Gaming Board officials, were called in. Something 'unnatural' had happened to the wheel. The casino commented: 'There was something wrong with the balance of the wheel but we couldn't stop the game while it was in progress.'

Sheer greed ruined that carefully plotted wheeze. Are others, more patient, getting away with it?

*

Yorkshire whizzkid Kevin Cooper made £25,000 in six months - playing fruit machines. Regularly he left pubs and arcades, his pockets bulging with coins.

He claims his success stems from having 'super-fast reflexes and memorising many of the machines' sequences'. Though he admitted: 'I'mgetting short-sighted from staring for hours on end at the reels and flashing lights.'

*

And two other youngsters, Andy Cattrell (21) and Mike Parry (20) in the summer of 1991 proved to the sceptical *Sun* newspaper how they could clean up on cross-channel ferry machines after being banned from clubs and casinos. In two hours 20 minutes they hit six £150 jackpots! But Parry admitted: 'It's bad for your health. Our eyesight is going and it can be incredibly tiring. The longest we played the machines was a 72-hour stint. We made more than £4000 so it was worth it.' And they're only beginners compared with pros in Las Vegas and Atlantic City!

*

Australian bookmaker Bill Waterhouse's philosophy is simple. 'I gamble on the punter rather than the horse. I don't care how good a horse's reputation, if I think the backer is a born loser I will stand their bet for a fortune. I never hedge. that game is for the weak.'

Cooper doesn't stop at horses. He will travel anywhere to back anything. 'I've raced in Thailand, Singapore, South Africa, Australia, New Zealand, France, Ireland and both coasts of the United States.

'I bet on cricket and golf and tennis and American football and financial indices. I've had £5000 on Essex for the county championship at 4-1 and I've backed Monica Seles for Wimbledon.' [Essex won but Seles didn't even turn up.]

It seems like the sort of approach that is doomed to disaster, but Cooper does have some rules – and he has one rule that rules every other.

- 'I don't bet on two-year-olds until Royal Ascot unless they have done a great time.'
- 'I don't like handicaps for three-year-olds only and I don't like three-year-olds early in the season.'
- 'I virtually never back a maiden.'
- 'I tend to home in on high-quality races and meetings. I love Group races and big events.'
- 'I'm thinking of a rule that I don't bet in races of more than one and a half miles. Longer than that and they tend to become diplomatic encounters between the jockeys – tactical events.'
- 'Apart from Cheltenham and Liverpool, I've stopped betting on National Hunt racing. It's too hard and if you want to bet to win £30,000 or £50,000, there is not much point going to Devon on a wet Wednesday.'
- 'There are a lot of trainers I never back, such as Peter Walwyn. I don't like Bill Watts. I'm not keen on Paul Cole. Alec Stewart has a lot of talking horses that are bad value. I don't often back Luca Cumani's horses because they are hard to assess. I like Elsworth and Stoute and quite like Hannon and Clive Brittain. I used to be

dynamite with John Dunlop. He got to August and suddenly realised that it was summer. Now he is an earlier man.'

It all seems a bit vague for a professional, but then there is Cooper's rule of rules. 'I'm a complete value punter,' he says. 'My life is about looking for value for money. I am constantly looking to diminish the bookmaker's advantage.'

Finding value means thorough research. 'I am not a whim bettor. I am not someone who just spends ten minutes assessing a race. There is always detailed research. I am a form student and a time student and an observer of trends.'

That's one man's methods. Cooper may be a maverick, but in the betting jungle he's a survivor – and there aren't many others.

And the best advice of all? A smart gambler never bets more when losing but does when winning. Take full advantage of a successful streak and contain losses while things aren't going well. Never quit on a winning run but bail out early otherwise.

Sufferers about to endure more agony – or ecstasy?

WHY WOMEN ARE CHASING ME

A woman's place now is as likely to be on the racecourse or betting shop as in the home. At last the days of being intimidated by hitherto male-dominated environs seem to be coming to an end. More women are gambling than ever before.

Today, the cosy bingo hall, ninety per cent of whose players are female, is having to compete with plush shops which ladies are finding almost as natural to patronise as they do their local crimper.

Smoke-filled lino and sawdust dens, full of sleazy blokes conspiratorially plotting crooked coups, comprise the far-fetched stuff of badly-researched screen fiction. Bright, clean, welcoming offices, with televisions, comfortable seating, refreshment facilities and toilets are the reality, some even being wholly or partially smoke-free zones. Only reactionary magistrates and moral bigots attach any stigma to taking on the bookies.

That furtive era when a lady guiltily sneaked in for a half-a-crown (12½ pence) each-way flutter has been overtaken by a marketing commitment to ensure she feels safe and totally at ease. Progressive layers have realised that there is a largely untapped potential in female custom.

In the vast casinos of Atlantic City, Las Vegas and Reno, predominantly middle-class and elderly women, often bussed in on 48-hour visits, plonk themselves down in front of serried rows of slot machines. There, hypnotically, they deposit coins, pull levers and squeal in uncontrolled ecstasy when the steel monster, lights flashing, spews out soon-to-be-returned winnings.

Potentially women are as susceptible to the timeless fascination of gambling as men. Blackjack, and especially roulette, in sedate gaming houses the world over bear this out.

But breaking down forbidding masculine barriers elsewhere has taken time; placing a bet can still be an unnerving experience. To aid nervous newcomers, especially women, through the mysterious ritual some firms set up information desks on Grand National and Derby days. William Hill even provide a phone line to answer queries and give advice (but not tips).

In a non-patronising way understandable difficulties, such as how to fill in a betting slip, are patiently sorted out. Ascot Gold Cup Thursday has been, on occasions, turned into Ladies' Day, in some enterprising shops with employees dressing up appropriately and gifts being distributed.

Apart from such gimmicks, the mainly female staff found in most betting shops can help turn a worrying sortie into a pleasant, fun experience.

Except in certain tough, inner-city ghettos, those soulless thick-glass grilles are being replaced by friendly, open counters. All offices hold only a few hundred pounds in cash at any time. Potential bandits are coming to realise that hold-ups just aren't worth the risks for little gain. And a lifting of restrictions on shop fronts, which prevent anyone seeing inside, would further deter potential armed robbers. Shouting impersonally back and forth through security cages, particularly daunting for women on either side, is less frequent. Firms, moreover, have slowly learned that women can

DAILY MIRROR, Tuesday, April 23, 1991   PAGE 3

HOT FAVOURITE LUCY SHOWS HER FORM

No wonder McCririck's wearing blinkers

DAZZLING: Well-bred Lucy gets into her stride   Pictures: ALAN GRISBROOK

DAZZLED: TV Tipster McCririck has seldom seen such a promising filly

By STEVE ATKINSON

★ SHE'S a classic filly. And as soon as Lucy Sangster stepped into the parade ring, she became a hot favourite of TV tipster John McCririck.

The cigar-puffing expert was so dazzled that he kept his dark glasses on while he studied her brilliant form.

★ As Lucy tossed her elegant head, McCririck noted her flowing mane. As she swung around, he admired her well-turned fetlocks.

Beautifully-bred Lucy, 23, had a head start on 13 other girls – all with racing links but novices in the catwalk stakes – who bravely took part in a fashion show in London which raised £50,000 for the Royal Marsden Hospital's cancer fund.

She was a professional model before she married Ben Sangster, whose father Robert runs a bloodstock empire.

★ Now she has a stable home life. And it's odds-on that she'll never again get into her stride for prize money . . . even though McCririck may mark her down as strongly fancied.

manage shops, areas, even whole businesses, just as effectively or more so than men. They realise, also, that with an all-female staff punters seem even less inclined towards anti-social, aggressive behaviour.

And much to my chagrin the first three Racing Post *Betting Shop Managers of the Year* have been men. I'm on the judging panel and have always plumped for a lady, but as usual no one listens to me.

But, despite all betting shop attractions, it seems ladies are less likely to stay and watch races screened by SIS (Satellite Information Services). Women, as we all know, have better things to do with their lives than become hardened betting shop regulars; their pattern is to have a bet and not hang about. They refuse to be sucked into the dramatic increase in grey-hound forecast wagering, so noticeable since SIS came on stream.

Nonetheless, at racecourses women are venturing down into the ring in far greater numbers than they used to. There principally is the magnetic attraction of my macho physique, and even United Racecourses' Girls Race Free promotions. They used to be called 'Girls are Free', but lewd minds conjured up connotations not appropriate to these, or any, occasions. But there must be other reasons.

Most bookies accommodate tiddly bets from women, for example, that would be turned aside if proffered by a man. Traditionally, however, most female racegoers opt for the ordered anonymity of the Tote. This trend continues, though it is somewhat eroded despite much of the machine's increasing on-course turnover still being down to women. Corporate hospitality, regularly maligned by the ignorant and snobbish, introduces thousands of ladies, including Hooray Henriettas, to racing. Invitations from companies to customers or their own workforce for a day out are usually for couples. During the past decade, wives, girl-friends, daughters and mistresses have become racegoers more than ever before.

Once there, few can resist a flutter; and, infuriatingly to men, who fancy their expertise with the form book, a number end up in front thanks to beginner's luck on the day.

So long as layers remain polite and considerate, women won't be apprehensive. Barriers shutting them out of riding, training and even administrating have quite rightly been breached to various degrees. Like bookmaking and betting shops that were almost exclusively male clubs for so long, such unjustified prejudice has mercifully become outmoded.

Nobody could ever accuse At Large of being sexist. The obedient Booby has been ordered to confirm this. Along with all reasonable thinking chaps, I want more women – in racing, I mean.

Emotionally exhausting – lusting over Lucy on the catwalk with diamonds

Back to Basics

WHY?

If people logically studied the mathematics and mechanics of punting, they wouldn't bet. The vast majority cannot win, and they know it. Yet they still gamble. Why?

For fun, yes, but the prime motivation, though not readily admitted, is simply greed – getting something for nothing rather than working for it. The quick buck.

Another reason, naturally, is sex. The experience of gambling (as has often been said) closely resembles that of love-making – a great deal of anticipation for a few moments of fleeting pleasure, and then (usually) awkward feelings of remorse and regret. Each finish is a separate orgasm. Betting gives you the opportunity to reach those heights and depths several times an afternoon or evening. No wonder the sex lives of most people in racing are a shambles – my own with the incredibly nubile Booby totally excepted!

For others, having a flutter is simply fun. The challenge of weighing up all the different clues which every single contest provides, of working out where the value lies, making your choice, striking a bet, watching its fate, and then analysing its performance, win or lose. Betting is enthralling and often infuriating. But you feel that it's also probably quite good for the soul. And for some, though they deny it, it's the masochistic relief losing gives them – the chance to indulge in sorrowing self-pity. As American gambler and pundit Wilson

Mizner wrote: 'The greatest thrill is winning a bet – the second greatest thrill is losing one.'

Whatever the motivation, for the great majority of punters betting is undeniably a mug's game. They understand that well enough. So do bookmakers. The individual skirmishes offer excitement and stimulation, but a mug's game it remains, for all but a select, dedicated few.

As evidence study how a book – a set of odds on a particular event – is constructed. Individual prices are tailored to the bookmaker's advantage, so that in the long run he is bound to come out in front of all but the most astute and patient of punters.

ODDS – THE MEANING

Odds themselves are simply a way of expressing the probability of a particular eventuality – be it the result of the Derby, the identity of the new Archbishop of Canterbury, or Elvis Presley turning up alive – and odds can be converted into a percentage probability. So a horse quoted at evens (1-1, or 'levels you devils') is deemed to have an exactly equal (or even, 50 per cent) chance of winning and losing. At 6-4 ('ear 'ole') against it is deemed to have a 40 per cent possibility of winning and a 60 per cent probability of losing. At 6-4 on (or 4-6) these are the other way round. At 3-1 ('carpet') against it has a 25 per cent chance of winning, at 9-1 ('enin') a 10 per cent chance, and so on.

ODDS PERCENTAGES

Odds on	PRICE	Odds against
50.00	**Evens**	50.00
52.38	**11-10**	47.62
54.55	**6-5**	45.45
55.56	**5-4**	44.44
57.89	**11-8**	42.11
60.00	**6-4**	40.00
61.90	**13-8**	38.10
63.64	**7-4**	36.36
65.22	**15-8**	34.78
66.67	**2-1**	33.33
68.00	**85-40**	32.00
69.23	**9-4**	30.77
71.43	**5-2**	28.57
73.33	**11-4**	26.67
75.00	**3-1**	25.00
76.92	**10-3**	23.08
77.78	**7-2**	22.22
80.00	**4-1**	20.00
81.82	**9-2**	18.18
83.33	**5-1**	16.67
84.62	**11-2**	15.38
85.71	**6-1**	14.29
86.67	**13-2**	13.33
87.50	**7-1**	12.50
88.24	**15-2**	11.76
88.89	**8-1**	11.11
89.47	**17-2**	10.53
90.00	**9-1**	10.00
90.91	**10-1**	9.09
91.67	**11-1**	8.33
92.31	**12-1**	7.69
92.86	**13-1**	7.14
93.33	**14-1**	6.67
93.75	**15-1**	6.25
94.12	**16-1**	5.88
94.73	**18-1**	5.27
95.24	**20-1**	4.76
95.65	**22-1**	4.35
96.15	**25-1**	3.85
96.55	**28-1**	3.45
97.06	**33-1**	2.94
97.56	**40-1**	2.44
98.04	**50-1**	1.96
98.51	**66-1**	1.49
98.77	**80-1**	1.23
99.01	**100-1**	0.99
99.60	**250-1**	0.40
99.80	**500-1**	0.20

A complete list of percentages is given above, and can be used for working out odds about any combination of possibilities. For instance, when subsequently disqualified Cahervillahow beat Docklands Express in that controversial finish to the Whitbread Gold Cup at Sandown in April 1991, Channel Four's burbling fatso in the betting ring pointed out that since both horses had started joint favourites at 4-1, the pre-race odds against *either* of them winning had been 6-4. How had he worked that out? Look at the percentages table: 4-1 against is a 20 per cent chance of winning, so two 4-1 chances between them have a 40 per cent chance – or 6-4 against.

Bookmakers ensure they will come out on top in the highly unlikely event of every horse being backed to win the same amount by betting to a list of odds which, when they are expressed as percentage probabilities, aggregate more than 100 per cent. (Mathematically, of course, the true probabilities actually add up to exactly 100 per cent.) The starting prices for the 1992 Ever Ready Derby at Epsom show this in action:

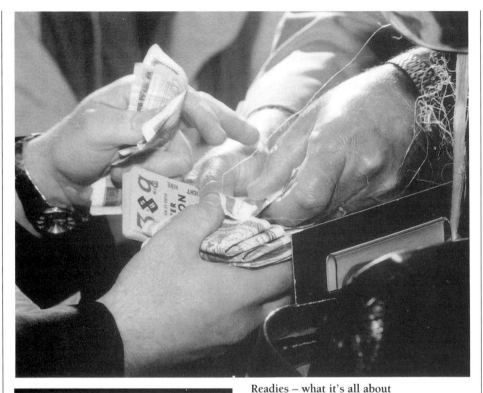

Readies – what it's all about

Horse	SP	%	Best price	%
Rodrigo De Triano	**13-2**	13.33	**15-2**	11.76
Dr Devious (1)	**8-1**	11.11	**10-1**	9.09
Assessor	**9-1**	10.00	**10-1**	9.09
Alnasr Alwasheek	**9-1**	10.00	**9-1**	10.00
Mutharram	**9-1**	10.00	**10-1**	9.09
Rainbow Corner	**9-1**	10.00	**11-1**	8.33
Great Palm	**10-1**	9.09	**11-1**	8.33
Silver Wisp (3)	**11-1**	8.33	**12-1**	7.69
Twist And Turn	**12-1**	7.69	**14-1**	6.67
Pollen Count	**14-1**	6.67	**16-1**	5.88
St Jovite (2)	**14-1**	6.67	**16-1**	5.88
Thourios	**50-1**	1.96	**50-1**	1.96
Young Freeman	**66-1**	1.49	**100-1**	0.99
Ninja Dancer	**100-1**	0.99	**125-1**	0.79
Well Saddled	**150-1**	0.66	**200-1**	0.50
Alflora	**200-1**	0.50	**200-1**	0.50
Lobilio	**250-1**	0.40	**250-1**	0.40
Paradise Navy	**250-1**	0.40	**500-1**	0.20
TOTAL		**109.29**		**97.15**

A book where the aggregate probabilities exceed 100 per cent is described as 'over-round', and here the book is over-round by 9.29 per cent. That is, the bookie may ideally expect to pay out £100 for every £109.29 he takes in. But on the very best prices available it was 'overbroke' by 2.85 per cent.

Everything's not quite as simple as that, of course. The bookmaker's liabilities for each runner will dictate whether the race is a losing or winning one, but by betting over-round and constructing the odds carefully it ensures that on average more is taken in than paid out. That £9.29 on the Derby is his margin. But if he laid the 15-2 Rodrigo De Triano, 10-1 Dr Devious, Assessor and Mutharram, 11-1 Rainbow Corner and Great Palm, 14-1 Twist And Turn and 16's Pollen Count and St Jovite, then the theory soon becomes cock-eyed.

The size of such a margin differs. In a race with a small field the over-roundness of a book is usually much less than in a big competitive handicap: the book for the 1992 Seagram Grand National, for instance, was over-round by 37 per cent, though not on the biggest prices actually laid at Liverpool. And in some big fields at minor meetings it can top a monstrous 150 or 160 per cent – or even worse!

Given bookmakers construct the odds, and are looking to build in their margin, it is rare indeed for a punter to be able to back every horse in a race and be guaranteed profit. Very occasionally by shopping around and grabbing the top of the market that idyllic possibility crops up, though you will need great powers of mental arithmetic and athleticism to be able to spot such a flaw quickly enough to take advantage!

Do not dismiss all this talk of percentages as too technical. A proper understanding of the maths of betting is an essential weapon in the punter's armoury.

THE MARKET – HOW TO READ IT

But the betting market is of course a very fluid affair, and its ebbs and flows offer clues to the likely outcome of a race.

Every event upon which people bet is a jigsaw of different pieces. Even if you are wagering on an apparently simple contest such as the next General Election, you still have different sorts and sources of information to weigh in the balance to arrive at a logical conclusion.

GETTING IT WRONG

Even SPs have been known to be overbroke.

At Yarmouth in June 1991 the returns on one race were 15-8 (34.78%), 7-2 (22.22%), 13-2 (13.3%), 7-1 (12.5%), 9-1 (10%), 25-1 (3.85%) and 50-1 (1.96%) – equals 98.4%.

And at the best odds available – 5-2, 4-1, 7-1, 14-1, 25-1 and 50-1 – 85.8%!

If prices are available at the off, to money (and not just an odd maverick 'fiddler'), they have to be the returns – overbroke or not.

The puzzle of a horse race contains more variants than other gambling mediums, and to arrive at a sensible decision you need to assess many different categories of information:

- how the horse has performed in previous races
- the class of those races, and the times
- the weight carried in relation to the weights of its rivals
- any preference for a particular sort of going
- current fitness, well-being and appearance
- its suitability to the nature of the track
- an ability to perform well over the distance or bred to do so
- the jockey
- the current form of its trainer
- the draw

and so on. Some or all of those small pieces of information make up the mosaic which provides a picture of any horse's chance.

The market before the race is just one more clue in the complex jigsaw, but it is the biggest single one, because ring moves take into account all others. So if a horse is apparently badly handicapped or is thought not to appreciate the going, it's very unlikely that a great deal of money will be invested on it. Betting encapsulates all the clues.

This is not to say, of course, that a horse drifting in the market will *not* win, or that a horse being heavily backed *will*. But the reasons for support or lack of it are invariably significant.

KNOW YOUR BETS

There is a baffling variety of ways in which the bookmaker can relieve the punter of money – or *vice versa*. Here are the most common (**with calculations excluding tax**: no tax is paid on course, but most off-course cash and credit bets are subject to 10 per cent deduction).

WIN

You bet on the horse (or dog, snooker player, soccer match or potential Miss World) to win. If you stake £10 at 5-1 and it wins, your return is £60 – £50 winnings plus your £10 stake back.

EACH WAY

You bet on the horse to win and to be placed. The notion of 'places' varies depending on the nature of the race and the number of runners:

2 to 4 runners:	no place pay-out
5, 6 or 7 runners:	first two
8 or more runners:	first three
16 or more runners *in a handicap*:	first four

These are the usual terms, but a book-maker's small print may deny you an anticipated pay-out. Outrageously and unforgivably, many bookmakers up till 1991 refused to pay out on the fourth horse in 16-runner plus handicaps. For instance at Liverpool in the 1986 Seagram Grand National Terry Ramsden's heavily backed 13-2 favourite in the forty-runner handicap, Mr Snugfit, ran past several tiring horses in the closing stages to snatch fourth place, and how there was not a public lynching of those grasping bookmakers I'll never know.

The odds for a place are normally one quarter or one fifth the odds for a win. Again, this can differ from bookie to bookie, so be sure to check. And remember all racecards will advertise the fractions of the place odds which bookmakers *must* apply.

An each-way wager is two bets – one to win, one to be placed, the place part being intended to offer some comfort if the win goes down but the horse is placed. So £5 each-way is £10. With the place odds one quarter of the win odds on a horse winning at 10-1 it returns £72.50 – £50 for the win, £12.50 a place, plus £10 stake. For a place only the return is £17.50: you lose the £5 win stake but get back your £5 stake on the place, plus £12.50 place winnings.

Even the most feeble mathematical brain should be able to work out there is no point in backing each way in betting shops a horse at odds of much less than 5-1. Though on course, in an eight-runner non-handicap when they bet 5-4, 5-2, 7-2, 20-1 and 'double carpet' (33-1) the rest, each-way one of the 5-2 or 7-2 chances enables you almost to guarantee at least half your win stake being returned.

PLACE

Virtually no bookmakers accept place-only bets. If you want a place only, go to the

Tote. Though if the beast happens to win at big odds you're in 'Why didn't I?' land.

COMBINATION BETS

Combinations, which can be win or each-way, involve predicting the winners of separate events, and you succeed only if they all do likewise.

Double

A double links two separate events. If the first succeeds the winnings and stake go onto the second. Say you have a £5 double on horses A and B, both at 2-1. A wins, so your winnings of £10 plus your stake of £5 – total £15 - goes onto B. When it wins the return due to you is £45 – £30 won at 2-1, plus the £15 stake. Thus your profit on the double is £40 (return of £45 less your original £5 stake).

A simple way of working out the odds about a double (and other combination bets) is to multiply the two odds together, then subtract one from the total. In the above example a double at 2-1 and 2-1 would work out at 3 × 3, less 1: 8-1, or (in this case) £40 to £5.

Bear in mind that you will not receive the full odds to a double if one event has a direct bearing on the outcome of the other. You could not, for instance, double Boris Becker to win his first-round Wimbledon match and the tournament overall. The first clearly affects the second. Nor could you, before the 1991 Two Thousand Guineas, have backed Generous to win that race and the Derby, expecting a multiple of the odds quoted for each individual event.

Treble

Combining three horses (or whatever). A £5 treble at 2-1 returns £135 if they all win. Work it out!

Accumulator

Combining any number of horses to win different races.

MULTIPLE BETS

Multiples combine different events in all sorts of bet, and, unlike a combination, do not fall down as soon as one of your selections fails. Below are described a few of the less mind-boggling.

Patent

Three different horses in separate races, in seven separate bets: three singles (A, B, and C), three doubles (A with B, A with C, B with C), and one treble (A with B with C). A £1 Patent costs £7, double that each way.

Trixie

Three horses combined in three doubles and one treble (four bets): a Patent without the singles. A £1 Trixie would cost £4.

Yankee

Four different horses are combined in eleven bets: six doubles, four trebles, one accumulator. A £1 Yankee costs £11. Double that for full each-way cover. If you add four singles (A, B, C, D) to your win Yankee, that is a Lucky 15 – 15 bets. If just one single wins, the odds for that winner are doubled by many firms.

Canadian

The Canadian, also known as a Super Yankee, combines five selections in 10 doubles, 10 trebles, five four-horse accumulators and one fivefold. A £1 Canadian costs £26.

Other multiples

You can of course construct multiples as big as you like, provided the bookmaker employs a patient enough settler. If a Canadian is too easy for you, you could try:

JUST TO MAKE IT MORE COMPLICATED . . .

Every punter should remember what happens with a few unexpected circumstances.

DEAD HEAT

In the case of a dead heat, stakes are divided and odds paid to each half. So £10 on a horse which dead-heats for first place at 3-1 brings back (excluding tax) £20, winnings of £15 plus the return of £5 (half the stake).

RULE 4

Tattersalls Rule 4 covers the eventuality of a horse being withdrawn from a race before the field has come under starter's orders but too late for a new betting market to be formed to take account of its absence. Rule 4 stipulates a table of deductions which can be made from winning bets on that race to compensate for the distortion in the market. Similarly, soon when a horse is deemed by the starter not to have taken part (such as when left in the stalls, unseating its rider at the start, whipping round as the tape goes up, or just stubbornly refusing to race) Rule 4 will apply. Naturally the withdrawal of a strongly fancied horse has a greater effect than the absence of a 'rag' (outsider): so if a long odds-on shot refuses to enter the stalls, the deduction is as much as 75p in the pound from winning bets.

RULE 4 DEDUCTIONS

SP	Deduction in the £
30-100 (or shorter)	75p
2-5 / 1-3	70p
8-15 / 4-9	65p
8-13 / 4-7	60p
4-5 / 4-6	55p
20-21 / 5-6	50p
Evens / 6-5	45p
5-4 / 6-4	40p
13-8 / 7-4	35p
15-8 / 9-4	30p
5-2 / 3-1	25p
100-30 / 4-1	20p
9-2 / 11-2	15p
6-1 / 9-1	10p
10-1 / 14-1	5p
15-1 (and over)	no deduction

HEINZ: 6 selections (15 doubles, 20 trebles, 15 fourfolds, 6 fivefolds, one six-horse accumulator): 57 bets. (Heinz 57 varieties – get it?)

SUPER HEINZ: 7 selections (21 doubles, 35 trebles, 35 fourfolds, 21 fivefolds, 7 sixfolds, one seven-horse accumulator): 120 bets.

GOLIATH: 8 selections (28 doubles, 56 trebles, 70 fourfolds, 56 fivefolds, 28 sixfolds, 8 sevenfolds, one eight-horse accumulator): 247 bets.

SPECIALITY BETS

Computer Forecasts

These require nominating the first two in correct order. The dividend, based on a complicated Einstein-defying mathe-

The problem for layers with Rule 4 is that its application – especially in small fields – can introduce fresh distortions. Hard As Iron was 13-8 on for the Headley Handicap Hurdle at Wetherby on Spring Bank Holiday 1991 when found to be lame at the start. His withdrawal meant a 60 pence in the pound deduction under Rule 4, which left the prices of the remaining three runners (7-2, 4-1 and 33-1) in effect reduced to 7-5, 8-5 and 13.2-1, a book of just 87 per cent (compared with 107 per cent before the favourite's withdrawal). Suggestion: carry a copy of the Rule 4 deductions with you when you come racing – you might be able to get one over those bookies!

Recently layers added a 5 pence deduction for 11-1, 12-1, 13-1 and 14-1 chances. Miserable skinflints!

No STARTING PRICE

Very occasionally a race will be such a foregone conclusion that no SP is returned. For example, when Dancing Brave had his 1986 Arc warm-up in the Scottish Equitable Select Stakes at Goodwood, the five opponents were such no-hopers that bookmakers did not bother to bet on the race, so no SP. In such cases all bets struck are void.

matical formula involving starting prices, is calculated by a bookmakers' centralised computer.

Tricast

This is another computer-calculated bet, requiring the selection of the first three in correct order in handicaps of eight or more declared runners (and no fewer than six actual runners).

THE TOTE

Totalisator betting is simply pool betting. All the money staked on a horse or dog race forms a pool of money which is then shared out equally between those holding winning tickets, after a deduction has been made for running costs, etc. With the Horserace Totalisator Board (the full name of the organisation popularly known as the Tote and sometimes still called the Nanny – nanny goat, Tote), the deduction includes contributions to racecourses and the Betting Levy. (Off-course Tote bets are subject to standard betting tax.)

Deductions in 1990-91 were:

Win pool: 16 per cent
Place pool: 24 per cent
Jackpot and Placepot pools: 26 per cent
Dual forecast: 29 per cent
Trio: 26 per cent

So to illustrate how the Tote works, imagine that a Win pool consists of £50,000, of which 2000 bets of £1 have gone on the winner. The Tote dividend is worked out thus:

Pool	£50,000
Deduction	£ 8,000
Payout	£42,000 – to be divided between 2000 winners
Dividend	£21 per £1 ticket

So here the 'Tote return' is £21, which includes the £1 stake. The winnings are £20, and the equivalent odds are 20-1.

The problem with betting with the Tote as opposed to a bookmaker – on-course or off-course – is that the very nature of Tote betting precludes the possibility of knowing, at the time the bet is made, exactly the odds you will be getting. Screens by Tote windows in racecourses will tell you the

In January 1982 Venture to Cognac (5-2) beat Great Dean (66-1) in the three-runner Fulwell Chase at Kempton. The previous year's Cheltenham Gold Cup winner Little Owl, sent off at 11-4 on, was pulled up.

With only six possible combinations the computer straight forecast, based on the starting prices, paid a whopping £14.27 to a 10p stake. The Tote Dual Forecast (Venture to Cognac coupled with Great Dean in either order), with three possible combinations, returned a more realistic 24 pence.

BOLA (the Betting Office Licensees' Association) immediately ordered an inquiry, and several bookies held up payment as thousands of punters couldn't believe their good fortune. Among them were some 'shrewdies' who took a chance and left out Little Owl – a faller on his only previous run that season and a reputed sufferer from broken blood vessels. Also it was well known that he had suspect legs.

It could have been even worse for the layers, as the final show before the off against Great Dean, pulled up on her last two starts, was 100-1.

There was nothing fishy about this result, though afterwards the computer formula, which even Pythagoras would have found incomprehensible, was 'adjusted'.

Needless to say, there aren't any 140-1 forecasts in three-runner races these days.

No 'adjustment' to computer dividends for horses and dogs – and there have been several – ever worked out in favour of punters.

You can bet on that!

likely return at any time, but it is not until the race is off that the pool can be complete – and thus the screens only give approximate information.

Overall the dividends are no better or worse than SPs. In itself that statistic isn't helpful. The times to keep an eye out for are when one or the other mode of betting becomes *significantly* advantageous. The Tote is rarely vastly better over an odds-on shot, and the weakness of the racecourse Tote market can give rise to some spectacularly poor dividends. On 29 November 1990 Serious Hurry won at Lingfield Park at 6-4 on, while the Tote dividend was their minimum £1.10 – 10-1 on (and the same for a place). Martin Pipe's Capability Brown, 14-1 winner of a handicap hurdle at Cheps-

tow on 21 April 1992, paid just £3.70 on the Tote – less than 11-4! It can work the other way, of course: on the same day at Wetherby, winners Couture Stockings and Pacific Sound returned starting prices of 14-1 and 16-1 respectively but paid £23.90 and £25.30 to a £1 stake on the Tote.

Key pieces of advice to punters about Tote betting are:

● Avoid small fields.
● Don't back obviously popular choices – greys, horses ridden by Lester Piggott, Pat Eddery, Steve Cauthen or Peter Scudamore, those owned by Royalty or showbiz stars (though the Queen's Colour Sergeant (20-1) paid £45.50 on the Tote after winning the Royal Hunt Cup in June 1992), those with impres-

The Tote – the simple way to bet on course

TOTE BETTING

Tote only bets are:

DUAL FORECAST

Pick two horses to finish first and second (in either order) in races of three or more runners.

JACKPOT

Pick the winners of the first six races at the Jackpot meeting. If the Jackpot is not won, the pool is carried forward to the next nominated fixture.

PLACEPOT

Select horses to be placed in the first six races (or to win in races of two to four runners). The Placepot operates at all meetings.

TRIO

Nominate the first three, in any order, on the day's selected race. The Trio on the 1992 Wokingham Stakes paid a record £10,137.20 to £1.

sive form figures and horses with appealing names such as Mummy's Darling, Good Looking or Romantic Night. Many small backers on racecourses – especially ladies – are intimidated by the prospect of approaching those 'fearsome' bookies in the ring and prefer the more homely touch of the Tote counter, manned, if that's the right word – by those courteous, efficient, Ladies in Red. And the Tote's on-course minimum stake (£2 win or £1 each way), while still too high in the opinion of many, is far preferable to some layers' £5 or £10 minimum.

- If there's a mighty gamble and you've missed the big prices get on with the Tote, which can be less responsive to sharp ring fluctuations.

- Keep an eye on racecourse screens for odds about any horse, particularly an outsider you fancy: bet late and you might beat SP in a spectacular manner.

49

When 50-1 Jet Ski Lady's 15½-1 Tote dividend made front-page news – 48 hours later. With £42,000 in the pool she was never shown as bigger than 24-1 on the course Tote screens and a late £1000 bet (not staked by a punter with much active grey matter as 66-1 was, in odd places, available in the ring) resulted in that derisory dividend. Most 'rags' pay more on the 'Nanny' but in a nine-runner affair, with betting figures already poor for bookmakers, it was crass stupidity to pour money into the official pool

WORDS OF WISDOM

There is a world of difference between the serious backer of horses (or of anything else) and the casual punter. Betting properly involves hard work, and adherence to a few sensible tenets.

MEANS

Under no circumstances bet beyond your means. This may be a cliché of betting advice, but it needs to be said time and time again. For most ordinary punters having a flutter is a hobby, and they expect to pay for it in just the same way as they would for an evening in the pub or cinema. But once you allow stakes to creep beyond the point where losses can be shrugged off, the enjoyment of betting evaporates. When the consequences of a bet are so important it leaves you hyperactively pumped up, sweaty, your stomach churning, heart pounding, a twitchy wreck unable to react coherently – that's the time to take a pull.

The more you can't afford to lose, the more you will.

SELF-CONTROL

To be a successful punter, the key words are *control, patience* and *discipline*. You do not have to bet every day; you don't have to bet on every race; you don't have to chase your losses; you don't have to make an attempt to wipe out the day's reverses by plunging desperately in the last race, the 'Getting Out Stakes'. Punters naturally want to walk away from the course or betting shop having made a profit. But there is always another day.

When deciding to back a horse you will, after weighing up the probabilities, have a notion of its correct odds. If quoted at such a short price that you no longer consider there to be value, leave it alone. The beast

---

THE TOP TWENTY

The twenty biggest betting races for Ladbrokes in 1991, in terms of turnover, were:

1 Grand National
2 Derby
3 Cheltenham Gold Cup
4 Eclipse Stakes
5 Two Thousand Guineas
6 King George VI Chase
7 Champion Hurdle
8 Welsh National
9 Oaks
10 Triumph Hurdle
11 Lincoln Handicap
12 Ayr Gold Cup
13 Cambridgeshire
14 Hennessy Gold Cup
15 Whitbread Gold Cup
16 St Leger
17 Scottish National
18 Supreme Novices' Hurdle
19 Ascot Gold Cup
20 Champion Stakes

Eight of the twenty are handicaps, and no two-year-old race nor a single Group Two or Group Three event makes the list. Twelve were run on Saturdays, when off-course bookmakers estimate their total turnover to approach the other five weekdays added together.

---

may or may not win. But central to the notion of discipline is to know when the odds on offer make any anticipated bet such an unreasonable proposition that it must be avoided. Perversely, many punters turn up at a racecourse or betting shop intending to back a certain horse, see that its price is much shorter than they had expected, and then lump on even more in the belief that because of support it must have a far better chance than they'd thought – even when it no longer represents a value bet! If a horse is not at least the price you anticipate, don't back it.

VALUE

You will often hear punters talk of 'value', but it is a difficult concept to define. A value bet is one when the quoted odds seem to the prospective backer to be longer than those which he thinks represent the true chance of that horse. So when the One Thousand Guineas and Oaks winner Salsabil went off at 11-4 for the 1990 Budweiser Irish Derby at The Curragh, such odds represented exceptionally good value for those who considered her real chance in that race to have been much closer to even money. Lycius was on offer at 40-1 on the morning of the 1991 General Accident Two Thousand Guineas – red-hot value for some punters: he started at 16-1 and failed by only a head to peg back Mystiko and reward his supporters' prescience. And in 1992, after Hills' morning line offer of evens the Oaks winner User Friendly for the Irish equivalent, and later 6-4 Irish Derby winner St Jovite in Ascot's King George, punters steamed in and backed them down to odds-on – and duly collected. But that, of course, is all after time, when it's easy! The search for value in betting is the hunt for a bargain. When you have weighed up all differing factors and believe bookies take a dimmer view of a horse's chance than you do, that is – for you – a value bet. For those wanting to study in more detail the notion of value and how to apply it, or even aspire to be a professional backer, Mark Coton's book *Value Betting* (Aesculus Press, 1990) is strongly recommended.

THE LONG AND THE SHORT OF IT

- Equinoctial won the Grants Whisky Novices' Hurdle at Kelso in November 1990 at 250-1, the longest ever SP winner in Britain.
- Theodore, the 1822 St Leger winner, returned 200-1.
- The biggest SP ever recorded in Britain was 3000-1 against Park Slave, unplaced at Wetherby in January 1988.
- The biggest price ever laid on a British racecourse was the 5000-1 about Countess Crossett at Kelso on 6 April 1992. She started at 500-1 and finished ninth of 17.
- The shortest priced winner of the Derby was Ladas, 9-2 on in 1894.

DISCRETION

The sort of race to look out for is one on which bookmakers are not keen. An eight-runner affair – the 'dead eight' – with the favourite odds-on presents gilt-edged each-way opportunities. For instance, if they bet 9-2 on ('on the shoulders on'), with 7-1 ('neves'), 10-1 ('net'), 20-1 ('score') and 33-1 ('double carpet') the four 'rags' (outsiders), it certainly is not odds against the 7-1 and 10-1 shots being placed. Yet the place returns on all races are arbitrarily based on a totally different book where win prospects alone are taken into account.

If you're looking seriously to win money, beware of betting in big handicaps – the very races which the bookmakers *do* like. That's why they sponsor them and prominently advertise prices so regularly. But hard graft can enable you to beat the handicapper – and the bookie!

Yet think of it. Would you reckon to have

Jeddah (1898), Signorinetta (1908) and Aboyeur (1913) all won at 100-1.

- Successful at 100-1 ON were Sceptre (winner of four Classics) in a race in 1903, and Ormonde (unbeaten in sixteen races) in 1886.
- The shortest-priced failure in the modern tax-free on-course era was Arum Lily, 14-1 on when beaten over hurdles by her only opponent Mrs Peopleeater (9-1) at Haydock in December 1988. There are other reminders that there is no such thing as a racing certainty. Royal Forest was 25-1 on when ridden by Gordon Richards in the Clarence House Stakes at Ascot in September 1948, with three opponents all on 33-1. One of the no-hopers, Burpham, beat the favourite by half a length. Markwell (also ridden by Gordon) was 20-1 on in a two-horse race at Chepstow in 1947, but whipped round as the tapes went up and dumped the 26-times Champion jockey on the floor.
- The most open race ever, according to the betting, was the Grand National at Liverpool in 1964, won by Team Spirit (18-1). Sent off 100-7 co-favourites were Flying Wild, Laffy, Pappageno's Cottage, and Time.
- At Hereford on 3 December 1985 the six winners were returned at 50-1, 13-8, 8-1, 33-1, 33-1 and 33-1. Going through the card would have landed an accumulator at odds of more than 47,000,000-1!

a better chance of collecting each-way over a 7-1 horse that's only got three serious rivals in an eight-runner conditions race, or an animal at the same price in a fifteen-runner handicap when they go 7-1 the field?

Try and learn to work out, however crudely, the margin at which the book-makers are betting. (This is explained on page 42.) If the book's over-roundness is stacked against the punter – say at 130 or 140 – simply don't bet. It takes practised skill to be able to look at a list of odds and rapidly calculate the margin, but soon it becomes instinctive.

RECORDS

Anybody aspiring to bet seriously must keep detailed records of their investments, day in and day out. Yet few follow this simple but so instructive policy. Write down every single bet. That way you can assess those races which prove a more profitable source of winners. So at the very least record:

- date
- stake
- selection
- price at which each bet was struck
- whether ante-post, board price, SP, whatever
- nature of the race
- result

At the end of each week, month and year you can see exactly the pattern of your betting. Our lives are full of records – bank accounts, building society and credit card statements – but most people treat gambling like shopping: they go out, spend the money and a week later have no recollection of how or what they won or lost. Keep detailed accounts. Bookmakers do!

'PRICEWISE'

'Pricewise' is a daily feature in the *Racing Post* which compares odds advertised by leading bookmakers on that day's major events, and highlights particularly appealing sources of value. It also calculates the best-price total percentage of a book compiled from the longest price on offer about each runner – thus occasionally even indicating ways in which by shopping around you could (assuming quoted prices held) be sure of beating the book, before 'bees' (beeswax – tax).   The point of Pricewise is not simply to indicate winners, but to highlight horses whose odds with some firms are disproportionately generous. In May 1991 the column enjoyed a particularly purple patch, pinpointing such bargains as:

Dry Point	16-1 (won at 8-1)
Run Don't Fly	16-1 (won at 6-1)
Amigo Menor	12-1 (won at 5-1)
Rocton North	16-1 (won at 17-2)
Darakah	33-1 (won at 11-1)

Pricewise is essential for all punters seeking value. No one intent on making betting pay can do without it. The highest recommendation is that bookies themselves dislike and fear it, yet cannot avoid reacting almost by reflex to discrepancies so shrewdly highlighted.

STEAMERS

A 'steamer' is a horse heavily supported on the morning of the race, and such market moves often prove highly instructive.

Backing the steamer at the best morning price provides the only infallible betting statistic down the years. Not one of hundreds of horses identified as a steamer on Channel Four Racing has ever started at odds longer than its top morning line price. Had you backed every steamer at that rate to a level stake you would show a profit. Not so however at its eventual starting price, the crumbs from the banquet.

So the trouble with steamers is that for success you need to get on at those fancy morning line prices, and often this is not possible. Take Daring Times, perhaps the most memorable and spectacular steamer of the last few years. This Lynda Ramsden-trained five-year-old won Doncaster's Shaftesbury Handicap on the Friday of the Lincoln meeting in 1990. That morning his price had been advertised by Ladbrokes as 'double carpet' (33-1), but who got on at those odds? Daring Times's owner, rails bookmaker Colin Webster, didn't, for one: 'I think the cleaning lady must have beaten us to the 33-1 at a minute past nine this morning,' he told Channel Four viewers before the race. He knew someone who very early that morning had tried to back Daring Times with Ladbrokes at 33-1 and was offered 14-1. Jack Ramsden, husband of the trainer, reacted vehemently to the advertised odds which disappeared so soon: 'That 33-1 is a lot of window-dressing for the bookmakers. They are whingeing window-dressers. I couldn't get that price and no one else could have tried because no one else knew about it.' Daring Times opened in the course market at 6-1 and ridden by Alan Munro (then still an apprentice) won by a grimly fought head at 5-1.

And the 'Mother of all Coups', as the *Racing Post* brilliantly headlined it, was landed by Father Hayes at Sandown Park in June 1992. A simultaneous *blitzkrieg* by on- and off-course punters at just after 10 a.m. shortened the maiden in a minor handicap from 16-1 and 14-1 to 5-2. On Channel Four from York I'd nominated him and

Willie Carson-ridden last TV-race winner Lucky Guest (5-2 favourite from 4-1) as the day's steamers.

Double carpet steamer Daring Times (right) cleans up for the cleaning lady!

Sent off at 4-1, Father Hayes roared in. Intensive Jockey Club inquiries followed, and tragically the gelding's trainer, likeable Will Pearce, died by his own hand forty-eight hours later.

With Father Hayes, the bookies never had a prayer!

Repeated complaints, constantly reiterated on Channel Four Racing, about the early prices not being available to anyone who actually wanted to back the horses led to some bookmakers finally guaranteeing their morning line until a specified time (such as 10.15 a.m.).

It isn't easy. Horses spotlighted in the 'Pricewise' column as being the day's value, or the medium of a developing gamble, are invariably seized upon, and when one of these steamers obliges the chastened firms reconsider their guarantees.

But the pledge should be consistently maintained to regulars up to a 'pony' (£25) each way. If the prices are wrong, sack the odds compilers – don't penalise the punters!

Hills, and others, sometimes guarantee to pay whichever is the bigger price – their 'Early Bird' or the SP. So if you suss out market moves early on, get going. Don't 'dwell in the box'. . . .

STATISTICS

Consider the 1991 William Hill Scottish National at Ayr. Favourite at 2-1 was Omerta. This Martin Pipe-trained gelding had won at the Cheltenham Festival and then beaten Cahervillahow a short head in the Irish National. That epic victory had put him in line for a £50,000 bonus if he could land the Scottish equivalent. In terms of form Omerta was a worthy 2-1 shot, and the market confirmed confident support.

But one factor against Omerta was the statistics. Just three favourites had won the Scottish National since 1935. The race had been held twenty-five times at Ayr, and only one of those runnings went to the market leader – Red Rum at 11-8 in 1974 (with the Noble Lord second on Proud Tarquin at 16-1). So the stats were stacked against Omerta. This was not to say that he couldn't win, and one day the favourite will land the Scottish National leaving people with short memories to pooh-pooh this stat. But not Omerta in 1991! He finished runner-up to 40-1 shot Killone Abbey, the second longest priced winner ever. So the statistical record of the favourites worsened a notch, and then another when 'exes' (6-1) jolly Tom Troubadour pulled up in the 1992 renewal: still just Red Rum after twenty-seven runnings at Ayr, and at the now closed-down Bogside, Fincham (9-4 in 1960) and Wot No Sun (2-1 in 1949) in fifty-seven years.

Stats are yet another clue in the jigsaw, but they are a fascinating one. Only a nutter would bet with any confidence on the 'jolly' (favourite) in the five-furlong handicap for three-year-olds on Doncaster's opening day of the Flat, run in 1991 as the Raceform Update Handicap but lovingly known to traditionalists as the Batthyany Handicap. The last forty-six runnings have produced just two successful favourites, both at the defunct Carholme at Lincoln during the

CAN'T PAY, WON'T PAY!

Forecasts within racing that off-course credit betting, the spine of the sport up till the advent of cash-only shops in 1961, will have virtually ceased by the end of the century are already being borne out.

When punters don't have to 'reef up the readies' the temptation to fire away is always there and since betting on credit began seriously in the 19th century, firms have had to write off millions in unrecoverable debts.

That they aren't subject to the normal laws of trading date back to a time when young bucks 'did' their

1950s. Be so careful of the Ladbroke Ayr Gold Cup – just two winning favourites in the thirty-seven runnings up to 1992 (one of those joint). And Jack Berry's So Careful, at 'double carpet' (33-1) in 1988 certainly wasn't one of them!

On the other hand, the Derby is an excellent race for fancied horses. Of the thirty runnings since 1963, twenty-two have gone to the first or second favourite.

The fact that the Derby and the Ayr Gold Cup produce such widely divergent statistical patterns so far as the market leaders are concerned is no surprise. The former is run at level weights by three-year-olds whose form has usually been as exposed as is possible at that stage of their careers, whereas the latter is a highly competitive sprint handicap in which anything can happen.

Stats can be invoked to throw light on all sorts of possibilities. When Seagram ran in the 1991 Whitbread Gold Cup he was attempting to become only the fourth soon-to-be-inherited estates and fortunes, often through bets sent by telegram.

Bookmakers preferred putting on the squeeze for payment in their own sometimes crude ways and even in the computer age there has been no pressure for legislation to bring gambling into line.

The worst that can befall a defaulter is to be 'taken to the Rooms' – Tattersalls Committee – and if staying away, or showing no sign of attempting to pay, the ultimate penalty is to be 'warned off Newmarket Heath'. Effectively that means a ban from all British tracks, and there is a reciprocal worldwide agreement between national Jockey Clubs to enforce such a ruling.

Recurring bad debts have eroded profit figures and make credit betting an abnormally risky undertaking despite much tighter modern safeguards and financial checks.

With the deposit option not catching on, latest technology, via 'Switch' or 'Delta' cards (where credit is guaranteed by banks and building societies almost instantly if the funds are there) have started to do away with the need for offices just to hope they'll be paid some time.

Switch cards are a boon. At least the worst excesses and misery of gambling will soon be no more.

National winner of thirteen to have tried since the war to win a race that season following Liverpool glory. The others were Mr Frisk, bold winner of the 1990 Whitbread, Red Rum, in 1974 that sole Ayr Scottish National favourite, and Quare Times back in 1955, who won a small hurdle race in Ireland. Finishing fourth at Sandown, Seagram failed to join this elite bunch.

And if you're a favourite backer, how about the seven-furlong Krug Superlative Stakes for two-year-olds at the Newmarket July Meeting (formerly the Bernard Van Cutsem Stakes)? When the following year's Derby winner Dr Devious landed odds of 5-4 in 1991, it was the twelfth time in sixteen runnings that the market leader had won. But when Stagecraft, backed down to 6-5 on, was beaten in the 1991 Juddmonte International Stakes at York, he became the eighth odds-on loser in twenty runnings.

Use stats wisely, and don't dismiss their significance because they're spouted at you by Channel Four's fatso in the betting ring. There is good reason why Derby favourites fare better than those in the Ayr Gold Cup, why so few National heroes win again that season, and two-year-olds and novice hurdlers in non-handicaps are the best medium for favourite backers. You may ignore statistical signs, and sometimes rightly so. But at least pay them attention.

SYSTEMS

Put not your faith in systems. If there were even one that consistently worked, whether at the track or in the casino, everyone would have cottoned on to it by now. A number are more logical than others:

● Backing a horse which won the same race last year. There is a lot going for you in such cases: the animal likes the distance, the course, the timing, etc.

● The dear old 'outsider of three' can pay handsome dividends, as these races are often run at a false pace. With punters concentrating almost exclusively on the front two, the outsider can provide very decent value. Similarly, you could argue, in matches (two-horse affairs) and even four- or five-runner races.

● In an apprentice or amateur riders' race ignore horses and instead back the best and most experienced jockey.

● Winners running again within seven days are at the peak of their powers, as the enigmatic Spinning showed, winning twice in 48 hours at Glorious Goodwood in 1992.

● In sprints run on extremes of going over courses where the draw has traditionally had a pronounced effect, concentrate on the favoured numbers for all bets, including various forecasts.

● Stick to the top weight in nurseries (two-year-old handicaps). It is on form the best horse in the race, and being a youngster is usually more enthusiastic than a wary old, cunning campaigner.

● Pick an up-and-coming apprentice (a 'bug', as they're dubbed in America) and follow him. If you go along with a highly talented lad, the allowance will prove invaluable.

● In maiden races, study future engagements. Animals entered up in top-class events later on in the season are clearly considered above average by connections.

● Follow champion jockeys riding in handicaps at weights below 8 stone: for instance, the late Doug Smith off 7.9, and nowadays Willie Carson at around 7.10.

● Follow top jockeys riding at their absolute minimum weight.

● Horses weighted after winning their only previous race. So often it turns out that the handicapper, lacking enough evidence, underestimates true ability. In the old days all horses had to run three times before being allowed in a handicap. The change affecting winners has benefited punters.

● In handicaps, keep to horses running off their old mark but whose rating is higher in future handicaps.

● Back horses blinkered or visored for the first time.

● Stick to geldings on the Flat. The late George Todd, one of the shrewdest of all trainers, said: 'Give me a stable of geldings and I'll put the bookmakers out of business in six months.'

● Support the stable with runners who've travelled the longest distance.

● Opt for a stable's second-string runner. Winners are infrequent but the odds are usually big.

● Back the sponsors' horse in their own race. Often laid out for the sponsors' big day, they are usually 'buzzers'.

● In a seller, back any horse owned by a lord.

● Watch for the horse with most connections in the paddock. Though the proliferation of syndicates somewhat negates the logic!

● Wait for the horses to leave the paddock for the 'last out, first back' theory.

● In roulette, study the faces around the table. One player is likely to be desperate to win. Perhaps stolen money is involved. Whatever the reason, bet against him.

Popular systems with *no* logic include:

● Couple horses or dogs with the same initial in forecasts. Or the favourite with the complete 'rag' (outsider).

● Back any horse with the same racecard number and draw.

● Follow throughout the day the horse or dog carrying the same number as the winner of the first race. (With dogs at least you could be going along with in-

FLOAT THE TOTE

That betting on the Tote remains less than 5 per cent of that with bookmakers is scandalous. Plans harboured by racing's 'good and great' to take over the Nanny are outrageous.

Just as so many nationalised industries were privatised under Margaret Thatcher, there is no reason why the Tote, with around 160 shops – and hopefully more – as a financial base, shouldn't be floated on the free market.

Individual bookmakers would be prevented from owning more than one per cent of shares and no group or individual could hold more than 2½ per cent. The Tote's contribution to racing has to be guaranteed.

With a free, swashbuckling management the privatised Tote – offering special 'no deductions' terms on certain races, improved computerisation bringing in enterprising pools and genuine competition to bookmakers – could revolutionise betting habits ingrained for generations.

Shareholders – thousands of them – would be the Tote's salvation.

---

side or wide runners possibly favoured by the going.)
● Back trap 3 in the first race and do a reverse forecast 5 and 6 in the last.
● Stick to horses with seven letters in their name. (Any system based on nomenclature is illogical.)
But always remember the telegram wired by the roulette aficionado: 'System working well – send more money!'

THE LANGUAGE OF BETTING

Betting is a secretive business, and from the coded world of wagers struck and odds quoted has grown an intriguing parlance. It baffles most outsiders, so here is a brief glossary of the most common slang terms.

BAR a betting show which ends '33-1 bar ten' indicates that all horses not quoted in that show are priced at 33-1 or longer; in a race with a short-priced favourite you might hear a bookie calling out 'six bar one', to indicate that the shortest price of the rest of the field (i.e., bar the favourite) is 6-1

BEESWAX (BEES) betting tax

BOGEY the outstanding loser in any book

BOTTLE 2-1

BURLINGTON BERTIE 100-30 (also 'scruffy and dirty')

CARPET 3-1

CENTURY £100

COCKLE £10 or 10-1

DOUBLE CARPET 33-1

DOUBLE NET 20-1

DOUBLE TAPS 15-8

EAR 'OLE 6-4 (and 'bits on the ear 'ole' is 13-8)

ELEF 11-1

ELEF A VIER 11-4

ENIN 9-1 (nine spelt backwards)

EXES 6-1

FACE 5-2

Rails bookmakers braving the elements at Sandown Park

FACES so-called shrewd or 'live' punters

FIDDLERS bookmakers prepared to lay only small bets

FLIMPING giving under the odds, or underpaying

GRAND £1000

HAND 5-1

HEDGING bookmakers lessening the potential liabilities by themselves backing the horse

JOLLY the favourite (the favourite is occasionally known as the 'splonk')

KITE cheque

KNOCK owe

LAYING OFF bookmakers giving to another firm all or part of a bet they've laid

LEVELS even money (also 'levels you devils')

MACARONI 25-1 (also 'pony')

MONKEY £500

NANNY Tote (nanny goat)

NAP a newspaper tipster's top bet of the day

NELSONS cash (Nelson Eddies, readies)

NET 10-1 (ten spelt backwards)

NET AND BICE 12-1

NET AND ROUF 14-1

NET AND EX 16-1

NEVES 7-1 (seven spelt backwards – pronounced 'nevis')

NOT OFF perceived not to be trying to win

ON THE SHOULDERS 9-2

OVER-BROKE betting with no profit margin for the book

OVER-ROUND betting with the profit margin in the bookmakers' favour

OVERS overpaid

PONY £25 or 25-1

RAG an outsider – not, as I keep telling owners, that their precious creature is useless: a 'rag' in the Derby could be the 'jolly' next time out in a handicap

RAILS BOOKMAKER layers are not allowed to bet within the members' enclosure on racecourses (though the Tote do), so a select group of bookies bet over the fence (the 'rails') dividing members from Tattersalls, or grandstand enclosure, which contains the main betting ring. At present they are prevented from displaying odds on boards, but in time that will change. Cash bets are accepted with credit and Switch card arrangements available to known clients.

READIES cash

RICK error

ROCK CAKE small bet

ROUF 4-1 (four spelt backwards – rhymes with 'loaf')

SAIS A CHING 6-5

SATCHEL SWINGERS bookmakers

SCORE £20

SHOULDER 7-4

SKINNER a horse unbacked – if it wins the bookie 'cops the lot' and pays out nothing

SKY-ROCKET pocket

SLEEPER uncollected winnings

STEAMER a horse gambled on in the morning whose starting price will be shorter than the morning line (see page 54)

TANK reserves of cash

T.H. 8-1

THICK 'UN a big bet

TIPS 11-10

TISSUE a forecast of how the betting will open, prepared by bookmakers or a form and ring expert for them

TON £100

TOP OF THE HEAD 9-4

UP THE ARM 11-8

VILLAGE all the bookmaking fraternity

WITH THE THUMB the odds are being taken and will not last

WRIST 5-4

ON THE SOAP-BOX: SUNDAY RACING

Politicians have many uses – no, I'm not asking you to nominate any – but interfering with basic freedoms isn't one of them.

What business is it of Parliament if betting shops open in the evenings and on the Sabbath? And why shouldn't racing go ahead on the Lord's Day as happens in far more religious nations than ours, such as several in strongly Catholic Europe, and in the United States with their Moral Majority?

But, as the Home Office has repeatedly made clear, Sunday racing without betting shops being allowed to open is quite rightly a non-starter. For one day a week, except for better off credit clients, it would be back to the bad old temptations of illegal betting.

Let the people decide. If they don't patronise shops or courses then market forces will soon ensure closure.

Staff rights need to be protected in law. Overtime, even double time, is a must, and no one should be forced to work on Sundays or forfeit career prospects if they don't.

Stable staff, subjected to appallingly long unsocial hours, already cover seven days a week. But for betting shops problems will be acute, especially at managerial level, though longer opening hours mean greater employment, much of it part time, more turnover and increased choice.

Gone forever are the days when I used to do odd jobs in betting offices and racing was all over within three hours or less. Now non-stop activity makes huge demands on underpaid employees with little time for more than fleeting lunch breaks.

Evening greyhound racing will soon learn to compete with betting shops by offering its specialised coverage and hopefully tax-free betting facilities, run by themselves if Westminster agree, for 'away' horse and dog meetings shown on SIS.

Already in the Channel Islands, where betting is tax free, shops stay open until after the last race. And SIS have started transmissions into Jersey's 29 shops (nine run by Coral), though they can't take bets at the local Les Landes meeting.

On 26 July 1992 the Jockey Club initiated an historic experimental Sunday meeting at Doncaster. It was a family occasion. There were no bookmakers, and off-course betting was at prices offered by individual firms or quasi-Tote odds, but the ball of Sunday racing had been set rolling.

In the wider context of life racing is a minor triviality – a frippery. That being understood there is no reason it should be constrained.

Freed from artificial shackles brought about by our rulers' refusal to trust the people, the whole game would face a new dawning of opportunity.

Only Parliament is delaying the challenge and prosperity that lies ahead for the betting industry.

Kindly get off our backs!

MCCRIRICK AT LARGE

WHY SOL WAS NATIONAL DAY'S UNLUCKIEST PUNTER

Any betting shop settler on the 'missing list' on Grand National day had better not expect a heartfelt welcome back the following Monday.

Having once been landed right in it on the nation's gambling day of the year, there's no sympathy from At Large for any of them suddenly taken poorly or, even more improbably, mourning at some distant relative's funeral.

Back in 1968 Joe, one of those quiet knowledgeable old-timers with a lifetime on the fringes of racing, did most of the settling in our local independently-owned betting shop, just off London's Edgware Road. At weekends, and other odd hectic afternoons, my part-time job was to take care of smaller bets.

Now, in this precise computerised age, no youngster can possibly imagine how basic were working conditions and practices then. A packed, cramped, grubby, smoke-filled, first-floor office without a carpet or toilet, let alone printed betting slips, nevertheless had a magic atmosphere and camaraderie lost in today's centrally-heated, creature-comfort SIS era.

Fellow keen form students, mates, shrewd 'judges', naïve interlopers, perpetual skint merchants, unemployed loudmouths, villains and local workers, comprised a fluid bunch of 'sufferers'. Daily it was a joy to plod up those creaky stairs, full of hope, to partake in the latest gossip and commiseration.

To be paid to spend odd spare afternoons settling, in what had become virtually a second home anyway, became a pleasurable but necessary luxury in a season decimated for six weeks, from the end of November, while fatuous Home Office bureaucracy closed racing down during a foot-and-mouth epidemic. But when, at 11 a.m. on Grand National Saturday, Joe's missus rang to say the old boy's chest was playing up, At Large wasn't too kindly disposed to either of them.

Already, a forbidding heap of ten bob (50p) bets and less had piled up in my secluded corner. Not, of course, all written on neat duplicate slips but rather envelopes, scraps of paper, cigarette packets, even bits of toilet roll, anything that could be clocked up on the till. With the guv'nor rarely more than a glad-handing overseer, the wretched At Large, a mathematical dummkopf, nervously faced the horrendous prospect of alone having to work out literally hundreds and hundreds of wagers.

Joe had no time for settling machines. Even if there was one, its intricate workings, like today's incomprehensible word processors and pocket calculators, would have been quite beyond his and my limited intelligence. The good old diary, with charts of how much various singles or doubles came to, was the life-raft upon which an undistinguished filling-in career had precariously floated for many years. Wading through small bets it normally sufficed, though to be a penny short on a pedantic pensioner's pay-out was often the cause of disgruntlement.

None, that I recall, after being overpaid, ever returned any of those 'overs'!

Anyway, coming up to the big race we badly needed a 'result'. Following 100-1 Foinavon the previous year perhaps four 'rags' would fill the frame and the afternoon could be spent contentedly putting a line through almost every bet. We had no TV, even under the counter, and relying on Extel's commentary it was amazing how rarely a fancied runner fell or no-hoper even got a fleeting mention. The outcome just could not have been worse:

1st Red Alligator (100-7) – third a year earlier
2nd Moidore's Token (100-6) – winner of his past five races
3rd Different Class (17-2 fav) – owned by film star Gregory Peck
4th Rutherfords (100-9 2nd fav) – in front when brought down by a loose horse at the 23rd in 1967, which had let in Foinavon.

It seemed not a slip, many with up to a dozen horses brought in from numerous offices, shops and families, didn't have an each-way bet on at least one of the first four, from 6d (2½p) to a few pounds and more. At that time, it was still three years before bookies cottoned on to the simple wheeze that has saved them, and cost us, millions – shaving 100-9 (11-1), 100-8 (12-1), 100-7 (14-1) and 100-6 (16-1).

Soon it was pandemonium at the pay-out window. The guv'nor, not as pathetically inept as me but no candidate either for any rapid settler award, buckled down. As we were grafting away, a shop habitué called Sol, who had

rushed in after watching the race on the box, bluffed and pushed his way to the front of the queue. Perspiring and red-faced he begged: 'Quick, John, do mine. They're all on Sutcliffe's in the next. It's the business.'

'What did you have, Sol?' I asked.

'£7 each way Different Class, £2 each way Rutherfords and a quid on the winner. Won't take you a second John,' he said.

'Leave me out, Sol. Look at this lot. Anyway yours will be over there with the guv'nor. Could you find it amongst all that bumph?' I replied

'I used lined paper. You know my writing, come on, come on!' he pleaded.

Frantic flicking through masses of bets, now alarmingly spreadeagled across the desk with others falling to the floor, proved hopeless and while Sol vainly tried to get on by promising to pay later, or even raise a loan on his winnings, they were off in the mile handicap at Liverpool (a mixed meeting in those days). Inevitably John Sutcliffe's went in, Venture Boy (5-2 fav from 9-2) under claimer Tony Murray, and by four lengths.

Not surprisingly, Sol was beside himself with rage. Pounding the counter in utter frustration he cursed the fates, the system, everyone and particularly me. And silently I was similarly berating old Joe. He would have sorted out the mess in no time. But the last thing we all needed, with tempers boiling up anyway, was aggravation and a ruck just now from Sol, whose sportsmanship in the face of frequent adversity had been known to disintegrate before.

Eventually, to everyone's relief, his tatty bit of paper was located and paid. (No, I won't work out again how much it came to!) Immediately Sol lumped his 'case' (last) £40 on the favourite in the following three-year-old handicap, a beast who had a week before won the seller at Doncaster's opening meeting, ridden by Geoff Lewis.

Penalised 10lb, it started 11-4 and went past the post neck and neck with a forlorn 20-1 shot. Liverpool didn't have a photo-finish in those days and when, amazingly, the 'rag' was announced the winner, by only a short-head as it turned out, from his Lester Piggott-partnered jolly, Sol snapped.

Whining incoherently to anyone who would listen about injustice, crooked heats, filthy bookies, incompetent odd-job settlers, in between beseeching the heavens for a reprieve through an objection, he finally, after the weigh-in had been routinely called, blundered blindly down the stairs into oblivion.

We never saw or heard from Sol again. What happened to him nobody found out. But he was truly unlucky for more than one reason.

Old Joe would certainly have worked out his bet in time for Venture Boy. And that other horse he backed, which a year earlier had dead-heated in the juvenile seller at the Grand National meeting, was to become Aintree's greatest hero. In the 1970s, few punters at Liverpool ever lost money again . . . on Red Rum.

In the Shops

Oh yes, I remember it well. On 1 May 1961 I climbed the rickety wooden stairs to Jack Swift's first-floor betting office in Dover Street, off Piccadilly in London's West End. On that first day of legal betting shops, this tiny emporium was glorious bedlam, packed out with punters shouting their horses home. The place was filled with smoke, but that day a breeze of fresh air wafted into the lives of Britain's punters.

I crammed in there as Jim Joel's Black Nanny, the 2-1 favourite in the first at Nottingham, duly obliged, and realised beyond doubt that this would be the Promised Land. Spread out before me was the future of betting in this country, and if I'd had any brain and business initiative at all I should have turned that recognition to my advantage. Clearly here was a bandwagon to jump aboard, yet I just stood and stared as it moved off out of my reach, leaving the poor miserable humiliating existence as a hack I have to eke out now. This was the once-in-a-lifetime insight – the great opportunity granted to most of us to grab the future – and I did not have the nous or drive to take advantage of it. No wonder I'm such a piteous pauper!

But on that magical May Day a new era was dawning, dragging gambling out of the Dark Ages when the only legal bets were those made on the racecourse or on credit. Street betting had been rampant and everyone knew it. Bookies' runners ferried bets between punters and bookmakers, collecting in pubs and clubs (commonly in the urinals) and on street corners. In Redcar it was said that a stranger would be directed to an illegal betting shop by the local policeman, if he asked nicely, and generally the police paid no more than lip service to enforcing a law widely regarded as obsolete and pointless. Benny Green's recollections in the *Guardian* of his Uncle Henry's activity as a street bookmaker recalled how

in his eleven years as a bookie, my uncle was arrested only seven times, and there was a good reason for this: our six local street bookmakers were arrested in strict rotation at regular periods, and were informed in advance of the event.

The details are hazy, but I can still see the police sergeant arriving outside my grandfather's house on Saturday mornings, looking suspiciously innocent and on business bent. My uncle would go out to greet him by shaking his hand – the least conspicuous way of performing the ritual known as 'bunging a film'.

The Betting and Gaming Act of 1960 swept away all such traditional rituals and paved the way for betting shops, and the architect of that Act, Home Secretary Rab Butler, gave a special message on the front page of the *Sporting Life* on 1 May 1961:

Today the betting provisions of the Betting and Gaming Act, 1960, come into force and it will become possible for cash bets to be taken by bookmakers off the course without breaking the law.

The old law had fallen into disrepute and in

IMMORTALITY DENIED

Modern technology has destroyed my one claim to immortality.

In 1978 in the *Sporting Life* I revealed how clever crooks, by delaying actual Extel commentaries and results for a minute and then relaying them into a betting shop, were defrauding bookmakers.

Then off times of dog races, which usually last thirty seconds, were given to the nearest minute. To counter electronic whizzkids Extel introduced 'off Hackney 12.49 and 37 seconds' instead of just 12.49.

Sensibly SIS have brought in automatic digital timing, so no longer can you blame me for that boring 'and 37 seconds'.

After-time betting

A punter in a Mick Dines betting shop near Manchester spent half an hour one day poring over the form and working out two each-way Yankees.

Not one of the eight selections was even placed but he got his money back.

He'd been studying the previous day's paper! Though you might well ask what chance does the fellow ever have when he can't pick winners nearly twenty-fours hours after the races?

It's as bad as the chap in an Edgar Wallace short story who picked up the paper and amazingly found it was tomorrow's! All the results were there, so he had an accumulator at the day's meeting and one by one they all went in.

But he was never paid. The last winner, given in the late news Stop Press, was disqualified after a stewards' enquiry!

Small money

The days of having sixpenny (2½ pence) bets are long gone. Tiny wagers simply aren't economical to accept. Bookmakers estimate each one going across the counter costs them around 15p for the slip, service, etc.

But nothing has so infuriated numerous punters as high minimum stakes, such as Ladbrokes' £1.

Commercially it makes sense – National Savings Bonds, for instance, can only be purchased £100 at a time. But managers ought to use discretion, especially with long-term regulars. Similarly on course, where £5, £10, even £20 minimum signs proliferate, and where the Tote's £1 each way minimum is still resented.

Firms should never forget: today's 50p or £1 punter could be tomorrow's . . .

---

many parts of the country there have been book-makers who have taken cash bets in one way or another in defiance of the law. The Act provides a means by which, by setting up licensed betting offices, these men can now conduct their business without fear of infringing the law.

From what I have heard, they have been ready to take this opportunity and are anxious to comply with the various controls and regulations which remain.

TALKING SHOP

Only one newspaper column gets inside betting shops and keeps the issues and personalities bubbling away. That's the forthright Jim Cremin's 'Talking Shop' in each Thursday's *Racing Post. Habitués* and staff are catered for in quite the most readable, incisive and thought-provoking grassroots feature in print.

Loath as we all are to laud another hack, I have to accept that my weekly visit to Cremin's 'Talking Shop' is a compulsive delight.

If the new laws are to work well, the co-operation of everyone concerned will be required. I am convinced that this will be given willingly and that the new social experiment will be successful.

Those 'controls and regulations' included making betting shops as uncomfortable as possible, in order to prevent punters loitering: no television, radio, nor refreshments. And customers were not to be 'encouraged' to bet – so the outside of the shop could not afford passers-by a view of the enticing world inside: windows and doors were glazed or net-curtained.

The stigma of betting shops as somewhere not quite wholesome still lingers, despite the best endeavours of the bookmakers to reduce their mystique. New legislation promoted by Tory MP Sir Ian Gilmour and passed in 1986 allowed for a general brightening up of betting shops – they were, for instance, permitted to sell light refreshments, the restriction on which previously had been a gratuitous insult to customers – and, most significantly, at last they could show live races on television. No more furtive glances at a set hidden under the counter. An end to standing around staring vacantly at the wall and listening to usually charmless Extel commentary ('Shergar going clear at Epsom, Shergar by six lengths, Shergar by eight lengths, they're in the traps at Hackney'). Early on you could watch Channel Four and BBC action live as it happened. Then, starting in May 1987, pictures were supplied by Satellite Information Services (SIS), who were soon providing a full technically magnificent, accurate and highly informative ser-

vice to the majority of shops around the country.

Just as the rich had their London clubs, like the Beefsteak, Boodles, White's and the Turf, so now we poor folk have our betting shops.

The atmosphere and ambiance had been transformed, a transformation furthered (for better or worse?) in some shops owned by big companies with an audio service direct into each from their head offices. There are now just over 9000 betting shops in Britain, with a turnover of nearly £5 billion per year.

Betting shops are (on the whole) bright and cheerful, friendly and welcoming. If you don't know what to do, staff will show you. They need your business and want you to enjoy yourself while you are in there, so never be shy of venturing in. You'll be quite safe. The natives are usually quizzical but friendly!

However, rumours, put about by owners, that betting shops are branches of

The only sensible one is the dog!

(continued page 72)

HITTING OUT AT THE HACKS

Journalism can be a tacky, undistinguished and at times disreputable profession where trust so often turns into betrayal and confidences, between fellow hacks or with members of the public, usually mean nothing. No wonder polls show their esteem to be on a par with second-hand car salesmen, just below estate agents – though perhaps my being awarded 'very substantial' libel damages in the High Court in May 1986 against the *Daily Star* editor Lloyd Turner (soon to lose a £½ million case against former Tory Party chairman Jeffrey Archer) and reporters Frank Curran and Peter Hooley has warped my objectivity.

Maybe. But anyone who hasn't experienced at first hand the depth of deceit and sheer subterfuge of which Fleet Street is capable can possibly realise how ruthless and devious the reptiles can be.

A free press is essential. But in order to bring about more responsible reporting and comment, a law ensuring that journalists themselves, out of their own pockets and not of those of their papers' proprietors, must meet all libel damages would immediately rein in the worst excesses.

As one of the few hacks to sue and to have been sued, I am more acutely aware than most of the pressures, judgements, deadlines and agonies involved.

Anyone glibly countering that journalists dish it out, as they do, and should therefore be able to take it, ignore intolerable libels.

If a newspaper headline untruthfully blazons that you, whatever your occupation, are a child molester or fraudster, what else can you do but go to m'learned friends for redress and public vindication, whatever the cost? One irresponsible or malicious article is capable of destroying lives and reducing victims to shamed, reclusive pariahs.

But if the allegations are true and the reporter has the necessary evidence to back them up, then fine – such criminal behaviour ought to be revealed.

Writers prepared to destroy reputations and jobs have to operate realising their own mortgages and employment are on the line. Insurance cover would be prohibitively expensive for hacks known to be prepared 'to take a chance'.

In my particular case, Turner was fired soon afterwards because of the Archer debacle (I was in the High Court and couldn't resist the odd gloat as the *Star*'s subterfuge was ruthlessly exposed – well done, Jeffrey!). But seven years on Curran and Hooley, their careers totally unaffected by inflicting on me a trauma the scars of which will never heal and which cost their paper tens of thousands of pounds, still regularly write front-page stories for their employers Express Newspapers.

Reform wouldn't put a stop to essential investigative articles and exposures. But any story, printed or spoken, has to become subject to personal responsibility for content. False bylines, or none at all, would put the livelihoods of editors themselves at risk.

As a former British Press Awards Campaigning Journalist of the Year, I know that newspapers have nothing to fear from enforcing individual necessity to be accurate. Far better such self control than any imposed government restrictions reminiscent of a totalitarian regime. How far have we come from the journalistic ideal: 'To comfort the afflicted and afflict the comfortable'?

Few hacks, when they think about it, can have much pride in what they do. And I'm no exception. The only difference is that, unlike the rest, I freely admit to being ashamed. Having failed as a bookmaker no one else will employ me, so I'm reduced to journalism.

And in racing, though standards in the 1980s improved with so much extra competition, principally the *Racing Post* taking on the *Sporting Life*, my description of most (though not all) of my fellow hacks as being 'supine' many years ago stands.

That, as you may imagine, has ensured my in-house popularity! But almost without exception – one being the *Life's* incisive columnist Jack Logan (*nom de plume* for former Tory MP and Home Office minister Sir David Llewellyn) – the racing press believe massive increases in prize money are essential. (Some actually have advocated increases in off-course tax or even charging entrance fees to betting shops!) Consequently any proper writing is flawed by that basic erroneous proposition. Tipping isn't taken seriously by most of them. With praiseworthy exceptions, so many rely on the admirable *Timeform* and guesswork rather than keeping their own detailed form figures which, admittedly, are hard work to maintain. Having for six years from 1965 single-handedly produced ratings for Formindex and Racing Data, no one is more aware than I am of the sheer graft involved.

But looking back, one story of mine, splashed in the *Sporting Life*, did some good.

In October 1983 BOLA director-general Tom Kelly had only been in the job two months, following his editorship of the defunct *Sporting Chronicle*, when penning a 'discussion paper' on the alternatives to starting prices, whose inconsistencies and compilation, often from weak, unrepresentative betting rings, still so infuriates and worries betting office chiefs.

Read again, word for word, one option put forward by Kelly as the time approached for the renegotiation of the whole SP system:

Although the present method of returning SPs has stood the test of time, recently the weak on-course market and the 'knock out' have exposed flaws which may be difficult to eradicate as long as off-course bookmakers depend on the racecourse for their prices.

As some change is inevitable at the end of next year (1984) BOLA may wish to consider whether the opportunity should be taken to break this dependence on the racecourse.

In other words, has the time come to create a separate system of Off-Course Prices unrelated to the racecourse market and reflecting only the weight of money in the betting shops?

Probably the simplest and most efficient method of establishing such a system would have a number of carefully selected betting offices feeding information into a central computer in order to produce an Off-Course Price (adjusted for duty and levy) which would be a more accurate reflection of the off-course market.

The betting public is quick to believe the worst of bookmakers and some type of watchdog would be desirable.

Another difficulty could be the reaction of the Sporting Life which would not appreciate being excluded from the SP operation and which could use its columns to foster resistance.

It has been suggested that should Off-Course

Prices ever be introduced, the old method of SPs might continue alongside, at least until the public became accustomed to the new system.

This, however, could create problems. What would happen, for instance, if the punter felt that the new prices offered him reduced value? And who would pay for the continuance of the racecourse operation? Certainly not the Sporting Life *in its present perilous financial situation.*

Any substantial change in the traditional method of creating SPs must be made with the greatest care, and the aim of this paper is not to recommend but to help discussion and create opinion.

What a cunning wheeze, and how plausibly it was to be foisted on an unsuspecting public.

With off-course bookies making up prices after the results were known, or at any time, instead of the free racecourse market, imperfect as it is, imagine how punters would be ripped off mercilessly. By publishing parts of the leaked 'discussion' paper, I ensured that the subsequent uproar killed off the suggestion.

Someone, somewhere in the higher echelons of bookmaking must have been so disgusted at his colleagues' intention to manipulate returns that he passed on the document.

Whoever you are, thanks, old chap. By listening to your conscience you did more for the game than many in far more exalted positions. Punters aren't able to show their appreciation, but on their behalf I can – and willingly do. That revelation, which scuppered a nightmarish off-course bookies' dream and left it dead in the water, somewhat helps to salve my conscience at being a hack.

the local DHSS doling out money, can be safely discounted – though they do provide a valuable social service.

This is all a far cry from that May afternoon off Piccadilly when I had my vision of the future. Pity me my wretched lack of brain!

At least I didn't happen to be alone. The great William Hill himself, whose credit business dominated the market, was a late convert. Others were shrewder and accumulated fortunes. As the 'King of Glasgow' John Banks avowed at the time: 'Betting shops are a licence to print money.' For the mercurial, flamboyant JB they certainly were.

BETTING IN A SHOP

Having overcome shyness and sidled through the door, you will usually be confronted by vast displays of information on banks of television screens and in sporting newspapers displayed around the walls. If not already convinced about what you want to back, this welter of advice will offer the most detailed of clues.

Having decided on your bet, simply take a slip from the dispenser (different sorts of bet require different slips, but all are clearly marked), fill it in, and present it to the counterhand behind the desk, who will photograph and time-stamp the slip, returning the lower copy. This is your receipt and must be presented for payment if you win (as you surely will!).

But bear in mind a few gems of advice about off-course betting:

- You can bet at starting price (SP) (and in most shops at Tote odds) or at the 'board price' displayed on the screens or on the shop's board at the time you place the bet. If taking a board price make this clear on your slip: it will be authorised by the clerk at the counter, and those are the odds at which (if on a winner) you will be paid.
- Be careful to fill out the slip accurately and clearly. Too many disputes about bets arise from confusing or ambiguous instructions and, most frequent of all, mis-spelling. And beware horses with similar names. At Stratford on 27 November 1990 the field for the Whichford Novices' Hurdle included a horse called It's Nearly Time (10-1) and Nearly Time (100-1). On 2 May 1988 Whitewash (20-1) won a maiden at Warwick and Whitewash (USA) (12-1) finished sixth at Doncaster – both trained by John Dunlop! Write down the wrong one and you won't be paid if your choice wins. Other examples: at Kelso in 1990 The Builder (9-1) beat The Maltkin (8-1) with The Langholm Dyer (9-1) third, while at Newmarket in 1947 Ladycross (9-2) won, with the 'Burlington Bertie' (100-30) favourite Lady Mary Rose third, Lady Angela (4-1) fourth and Lady May (25-1) tailed off.
- Be careful to stake your bet properly, especially in a complicated multiple. A £2 each-way Yankee, tax paid, for example, requires the payment of £48.40. If you get your calculations wrong stakes on each bet in the multiple will be adjusted proportionally.

WHO'S UP?

From 1992 jockeys in Britain have been declared overnight. Regrettably the system, initially at least, is voluntary. Nevertheless, backers know that – barring late injuries, ill health or tardy arrival – those 'jocked up' will ride. Hopefully there will be no more deceptions of off-course punters – such as in July 1991 when gambler-trainer Barney Curley's Threshfield, backed from 9-1 in the morning and 6-1 at Sandown into 3-1 favourite, was ridden to an easy victory in a twenty-runner handicap by leading rider John Reid, replacing unknown, winnerless seven-pound claimer Tony D'Arcy.

Curley, founder of the Independent Racing Organisation, commented: 'The Government says we've got to help ourselves – so I have!'

And in August 1991 at Pontefract, Threshfield had no rider down in the papers but won, at 11-10 favourite, ridden by one L. Piggott!

- Familiarise yourself with the bookmaker's rules. They are not the same in every shop, and ignorance could prove very costly. In 1984 Edward Hodson, a Wolverhampton punter, had a 5p Yankee in which all four horses won, at aggregate odds of 3,956,748-1. But instead of a return of not far off £20,000 for his 55p investment he received just £3000, his bookie's payout limit. Limits vary from £1000 to £¼ million.
- Remember the implications of backing an unnamed favourite in a race. If there are joint favourites, your stake is halved and placed equally on both, and like-

wise is divided between co-favourites. Backers of the unnamed favourite of the Law Society Legal Handicap Hurdle at Hexham in April 1991 had their fingers crossed, but in the event there were *seven* co-favourites, who went off at 6-1. Six of them filled the first six places, the seventh – who gloried in the name of Irish Flasher – was a tailed-off last. A £7 win single on the unnamed favourite in that race would have been a loser off course – the £7 return from the £1 bet on the 6-1 winner, less 70p tax.

● Take heed of the implications which betting tax has for your returns, and decide whether to bet 'tax paid' (that is, with the tax paid at the time of the bet being struck and the amount being added to your stake) or not. A £10 bet tax paid costs £11, but you will not be taxed on the payout. It is only marginally preferable mathematically to pay tax on. A better reason could be that, for their own tax reasons, bookies prefer you to have the 10 per cent deducted from winnings. Whichever way you play it betting tax ensures, as everyone professionally engaged in the game agrees, in the long term you simply cannot win. Margins for the most successful of backers are so tight that only by investing tax-free on course have you any hope of consistently coming out in front. So the moral is clear: *think* about your bet and the consequences of striking it in a betting shop rather than with an on-course bookmaker, though if in any doubt pay tax on.

But of course even the most naïve of punters don't bet long odds-on in betting shops unless perhaps coupling them in doubles, trebles, etc., to 'pay the tax'. The animals still have to win – as, for instance, Henry Cecil's unraced Intent forgot to do at Thirsk in August 1991 when backed down from 3-1 on to 13-2 on!

For many people the soul has gone out of betting shops. They have SIS and high-tec processing of bets and information, but many punters yearn for the good old days of fug, babble and genial boardmen, that increasingly rare species of betting shop personnel who would write up the odds and results on a huge board on the wall of the shop, and would double as father confessor or agony aunt (in drag) to the mentally tortured punters. No one was a better judge of form, or at least reckoned he was, than the charismatic boardman. In my days with the chalk, the regulars soon learned to take no notice of me – just as on Channel Four Racing now!

In the *Guardian* in 1991 Chris Hawkins had a go at the big firms, with their individual audio service supplementing SIS:

Spending an hour in the local betting shop yesterday afternoon, it was uncomfortably clear how drastically things have changed from the old pre-SIS days when punters were left in peace to ponder the form and place their bets.

The only sound to disturb their reverie was the crackly old radio commentary offering results and betting changes. Those days are long gone.

The punter is now assailed, both verbally and visually, by a constant stream of information-cum-propaganda propounded by a double act seemingly hell bent on advising the customers of the quickest route to Carey Street.

Thankfully not all punters are taken in and one old die-hard was singularly unimpressed.

'What a load of bloody rubbish that bloke talks,' said the grizzly punter.

Not everyone is so discerning, however, and there will no doubt have been a few mugs around the country persuaded into parting with their 'hard earned' on a horse which is still running.

No doubt the well-intentioned duo do occasionally tip a winner but is it right that they should be giving opinions from which there is no escape?

I say 'well-intentioned' because I am sure they would never deliberately try and mislead, but the more cynical will say the bookmakers, who employ them, are quite happy for them to be wrong.

Newspaper correspondents are sometimes accused of being in the pay of bookies, of keeping the real information to themselves and giving the public the duff stuff.

This is arrant nonsense, of course, but even if it were true would it be as unethical as feeding advice to a powerless, captive audience as happens in the modern betting shop?

A newspaper reader ultimately exercises choice – whether he buys the paper or reads what the racing correspondent has to say – but the betting shop punter is deprived of this. His mind is being made up for him.

SIS as originally conceived sounded wonderful, but while unquestionably providing a bigger service it is not necessarily a better one.

The punter, denied any official representation, cannot be blamed if he sees himself these days as mere betting fodder.

For maximisation of turnover, read exploitation of punter.

Some truth there. But the direct SIS factual service during racing, as arguably distinct from 'extras' put in by the major chains, is quite superb. Possibly the audio greyhounds are 'a race too far', but SIS swiftly and accurately report the news, and to say it is a bigger service 'but not necessarily a better one' has to be very unfair.

No one yearns for the good old days more than I, a founder member of Nostalgia Freaks Inc. But if shops went back twenty years, they'd soon be empty.

And what has not changed is the human side of betting shops. Most punters operate in solitary fashion, studiously making their choices by themselves rather than engaging in a general discussion of prospects with other customers. But come the off, and the entire band are subjected to a communal anguish, from which only a few will emerge as winners.

During the race different punters react variously. Some yell advice at Pat Eddery or Peter Scudamore (so much easier these days when they can see what those champions are doing 'wrong'), others huddle in corners, desperate for the agony of the race to be over, or pace the floor like expectant fathers, while some just stand or sit impassively. They are all united in the exquisite anxiety and suffering of betting.

That's one thing you can be sure of. Everyone who gambles is a sufferer. Stoically they endure travesties of fortune. Bad luck, or so they believe, is never far away.

Sufferers divide into two different breeds. The first strides into his, or her, betting shop, looks up at the screen or board, and if the horse they've backed isn't in the frame (usually first, second or third), simply cannot believe it. Quickly they scan the non-runners: no, it ran. So did it fall, was it disqualified by the Stewards, or even did the wretched jockey forget to weigh in? Their own judgement can't have been at fault – or so they kid themselves.

The second kind of sufferer, the more sensible (can there be such a breed?), glance up at the results and are incredulous if their choice has won.

All the misfortunes that could have befallen it have been overcome. A miracle indeed!

CREDIT BETTING

About 10 per cent of the off-course bookmakers' business is betting on credit. Ladbrokes, for instance, have some 15,000 credit clients. On an ordinary weekday the firm's credit room might receive around 10,000 calls, but this figure multiplies before the big occasions such as the Grand National and the Derby.

Credit bookmakers come in all shapes and sizes, but usually offer various ways of betting. You can open a simple credit account (once the firm has been satisfied about your solvency, by a reference from your bank or another bookmaker with whom you do business). This will allow you to bet to a certain credit limit. Or you can open a deposit account, whereby you deposit a certain sum of money with the bookmaker (probably not less than £100), and bet until this is used up. Or you can open an account based on a 'switch' card, that new banking wizardry which directly debits the cost of your bet from your current bank or building society account. (This was pioneered by forward-looking North-west firm, Mawdsleys.)

The mechanics of credit betting are simple enough. The client phones, states his or her name and (with the bigger firms) account number, and the clerk then calls up on to the screen in front of her (or him) the details of that person's account – and woe betide any in arrears with payments! The punter names the bet, which is then read back to the client for confirmation, and that bet appears on the client's next account. Settlement is usually required every two weeks.

But the big bookmakers didn't get where they are today without realising that the course of true business between layer and punter doesn't always run smooth, and to

avoid altercations over whether a bet was struck or not, or the exact nature of what was said during the phone conversation, calls are recorded.

At racecourses credit clients can bet with course representatives of firms with which they have accounts. The largest credit betting organisation in Britain, Wigan-based Tote Credit, has special offices on racecourses for the use of its 50,000 customers.

Credit betting comes into its own when watching racing on television at home. Remember, except for those on steamers and at top *Morning Line* prices, that it is the mug punter who bets early. 'Shrewdies' wait until the last minute, in order to study all those myriad clues in the great jigsaw, notably by this stage the way in which the horse moves in the market and to the starting post. Once they're at the post, few off-course punters have time to belt down to the betting shop and have a bet. But the ease with which the phone can be picked up and a wager made is very tempting.

Also tempting, though, is staking more than you intended. Actually handling cash or a switch card reminds you of how much you're having on. Barking instructions down the phone may be *too* tempting for your own good, so go easy!

ANTE-POST BETTING

Ante-post betting – wagering on an event well in advance of its taking place – happens mostly off-course, though on-course representatives of major bookmakers will lay an ante-post bet tax free.

Early prices produce an amount of publicity quite out of proportion to the business they generate (which is a very small part of annual turnover), but none the less it is an intriguing and potentially very

The Ladbrokes Credit Room – betcha get on?

profitable form of wagering – if you are careful.

Bookmakers maintain they lose on ante-post betting. Think of some ante-post favourites for the Derby in the last couple of years who never got so much as a whiff of Epsom on the first Wednesday in June, and you might query such a claim. But there is no doubt that ante-post betting is fun.

It's more fun for some than for others. Owner Raymond Guest backed his then unraced two-year-old Sir Ivor for the 1968 Derby with William Hill at 100-1, and the colt duly obliged at 5-4 on. Derek Powley, manager of the Cliveden Stud, backed an unraced two-year-old who had been foaled at the stud for the 1987 Derby: he got odds of 500-1, and the colt – Reference Point – powered home at 6-4. Even dear old Brough Scott has had his moments, and goes dewy-eyed at the mention of Nashwan and the 1989 Two Thousand Guineas and Derby, pointing out that the miles of paddock railings encompassing the Scott acres (which stretch as far as the eye can see, and beyond) were installed courtesy of Hamdan Al Maktoum's strapping chestnut.

The biggest ante-post races are the first four Classics (on which betting commences during the previous year), the Grand National, Cheltenham Gold Cup, Champion Hurdle and Triumph Hurdle. There is ante-post interest in the major Saturday handicaps on the Flat – notably the Lincoln (along with the Grand National the traditional Spring Double), the Cambridgeshire and the Cesarewitch (Autumn Double) – though in terms of overall betting turnover the weekday big handicaps are not as significant as you might think. In Ladbrokes' list of their fifty biggest races in 1991, the Royal Hunt Cup (run on a Wednesday) and the Stewards Cup (Tuesday) – both traditional major ante-post events – were respectively thirty-fifth and twenty-second.

Ante-post betting is great for the ego. When you have 'double carpet' (33-1) and the beast goes off 'top of the head' (9-4) favourite, that voucher is testament to your perspicacity: it doesn't mean the nag is going to win, though!

A few points to keep in mind about ante-post:

- The risk inherent in any long-odds bet – you lose if your creature doesn't run – will be reduced if you are privy to reliable inside information about connections' intention to aim the horse for that race. The more you know, the better placed you are to take advantage of the value ante-post undoubtedly offers.
- A horse known to be able to act on any going will be a better ante-post proposition than one whose chances might be scuppered by extremes – though there are of course exceptions, as Desert Orchid's Gold Cup in 1989 showed. Assumptions about the going on a day weeks or months ahead can prove wide of the mark. Who, for instance, could have safely predicted that the 1990 Gold Cup would be run on firm ground, with 11-10 on Dessie only third this time to 100-1 Norton's Coin?

Quite the opposite happened in an amazing 1977 Champion Hurdle. Night Nurse, 2-1 favourite when taking the title a year earlier, was thought to be ineffectual in the mud. It poured at Cheltenham, bookies pushed the champion out from 5-2 to 15-2, and ante-post supporters, at much shorter odds, were in despair. But no one told Night Nurse, who battled on up the hill to hold off Monksfield and Dramatist at the longest price he'd been since before Christmas.

- Be especially careful about races where your fancy's chances may be affected by the draw. The obvious example is the William Hill Lincoln Handicap. Some question the sanity of anybody who strikes a serious bet for the Lincoln before the draw is known on the day before the race, but then opinions about the effect are themselves often suspect. 'It's the low-draw Lincoln', trumpeted the *Racing Post*'s front-page headline on the day of the 1991 race, above a story which stated that 'it is widely expected that the curtain-raising cavalry charge will be won by a horse drawn on the far side of the course' – that is, drawn with a low number. What happened? The dishy Alex Greaves won on 22-1 shot Amenable, drawn 23 of the twenty-five runners.

It is a fundamental maxim of book-making that 'you can't go skint taking a profit'. If a layer has accepted a bet for a horse at 10-1 and can lay off at 12-1, he will not go broke. But legally only licensed bookmakers can lay off bets. So if you've backed a horse at 40-1 and its odds come down to 6-4, it would be nice to think you could then lay that horse yourself at 2-1 in order to guarantee a profit. Legally you cannot do this. The only way to take advantage of a long-priced ante-post voucher when the odds come down dramatically is to cover yourself as much as you can by backing other horses in the race – unless, of course, a 'friend' is willing to take that 2-1 from you.

Look round for those 'with a run' ante-post bets which give you your money back if the animal is withdrawn. Often one bookmaker will offer a horse 'with a run' while another has it at the same odds, or marginally bigger, without that proviso. Don't ask which is the better proposition. . . .

Don't throw away an ante-post voucher as soon as you hear your horse has been withdrawn from the race, particularly an event such as Newbury's Tote Gold Trophy (previously the Schweppes) in February which was abandoned because of the weather eight times between 1969 and 1986. In that case, or a race being declared void for any reason, all ante-post bets are refunded – even those when the beast had been withdrawn weeks ago!

Reference Point (Steve Cauthen) winning the 1987 Ever Ready Derby at 6-4 favourite. One punter backed him at 500-1!

ROBIN HOOD IN REVERSE

Ever since a levy on betting – approximately one per cent on all off-course bets – was introduced in the 1960s the racing industry has squabbled about how the money should be spent.

It came to around £40 million in the early 1990s, and few were prepared to accept that this largesse represented Robin Hood in reverse.

The poor – that's we betting shop regulars – are being robbed mainly to benefit the rich. Eighty per cent of prize money goes to the top ten per cent of owners, among whom are the most affluent on earth, such as The Queen, the Sheikhs, scions of the Jockey Club, American billionaires and the latest saviours of the bloodstock industry, the Japanese.

One argument is that higher prize money will enable more money to 'filter down' to those at the bottom of the heap, like stable lads. Nonsense. The wealthy have never been renowned for largesse. Paul Hayward in the *Independent* quoted this advertisement for a stable lad in the early nineteenth century:

He must, God willing, rise at seven in the morning, and obey his master and mistress in all commands. If he can dress hair, sing psalms, and play at cribbage, the more agreeable.

NB – He must not be familiar with the maidservants, lest the flesh should rebel against the spirit, and he should be introduced to walk in the thorny paths

of the wicked. Wages 15 guineas a year.

Things have improved – if not with the maidservants! – but racing's shame is the millions spent on Thoroughbreds and the comparative pittance paid to a workforce who work long, split hours with little social life.

As Lord Wigg, the twentieth-century equivalent of Admiral Rous, the great reforming administrator of the nineteenth, said in 1972: 'The death knell of racing will be labour trouble. You've got to have well paid, contented staff. You haven't got it.'

Yet owners, instead of being grateful for the Levy – along with the BBC licence fee almost the only instance in Britain of money being extracted and going directly to the beneficiaries rather than via government handout through such as the Arts Council (and you can guess what I think of *that*!) – ask for more.

Sir Ian Trethowan, the late Levy Board chairman, put it succinctly in 1987: 'No one is forced to own racehorses.'

Like everyone else, I would love to own racehorses. But, being impoverished, I can't afford it. Just as I don't expect anyone to subsidise my gluttony, frequent sexual adventures or cigars, why should I indulge racehorse owners?

There are too many of them and their charges anyway. Numbers could fall by a third and racing wouldn't be affected one jot except for regrettable but inevitable unemployment.

When horses are dying of

Warwick, then there will be a case for subsidy. Until that becomes stark reality, owners, by the very nature of their hobby or business better off than most of us, should be grateful that 16 per cent of racing's income is provided by ordinary punters.

And the bursting, at last, of the bloodstock bubble, proving yet again that market forces cannot for ever be defied, means Thoroughbreds are comparatively cheap. You can still purchase a horse for a few thousand pounds and it could – I repeat could – end up worth a million. This is rich folk's equine version of roulette.

Until the Levy Board is superseded by an overall racing body having full authority to negotiate with bookmakers in the free market, one fact is clear. Punters cannot and will not pay more. Off-course ten per cent deductions are too high as it is. Ireland imposed a grotesque twenty per cent – the tax paid on with all bets – but illegal gambling flourished and in the late 1980s rates were slashed.

In the Budget prior to the 1992 General Election (coincidence?), Chancellor Norman Lamont ingeniously clipped 0.25% off the government rake-off, releasing around £13 million to the industry. For the first time greyhound racing, scandalously without its own levy (thus leaving bookmakers to 'cop' around 1% on dog bets), was targetted by Mr Lamont in alliance with Home Secretary Kenneth Baker. Such sweeteners were all part of the election-winning formula.

The only other source of revenue are bookmakers. An improved fixture list, to include a Wednesday to Gold Cup Saturday (or better still Thurs-Sun) Cheltenham Festival, seven-race cards ending with a handicap, and big events on Saturdays rather than (as now) often in mid-week, would help by boosting turnover. It might reverse the trend that saw nearly 15,000 betting shops in the early 1970s reduced to just over 9000 twenty years later.

But bookies have never been renowned for their generosity, except as individuals, and short of legislation they won't give a farthing more than they have to, claiming, with some justification, that profits of around three per cent overall cannot be considered excessive.

So the obscene spectacle of the wealthy grumbling that everyone else isn't giving them still more will go on.

Few outside the game and one or two of us inside it are impressed. And of the thousands of punters – providers of the money – whom I've spoken to down the years, not one has ever complained that prize money – an insatiable false god – is too low.

The voice of the punters must be listened to.

And so should the Duke of Devonshire, owner of that super mare Park Top. His Grace blew the gaff in the House of Lords in February 1991 by telling his fellow peers quaintly: 'One does not expect to make money out of one's yacht or one's grouse moor, so why should one expect to make money out of one's horses?'

Quite.

McCririck AT LARGE

FROM THE PERILS OF 'WINGY' TO THE JOYS OF TODAY

Back in the 1950s, if you didn't have a credit account or send off bets by letter, illegal street bookies were the only off-course outlet. And dominating the lucrative patch around London's Edgware Road was shabby, one-armed, unshaven, slightly sinister 'Wingy', shuffling around his mini-fiefdom surreptitiously accepting grubby bits of paper and cash from regulars.

Whether the right arm had indeed been lost serving his King on the Somme, as he said, or in some gangland feud, as seemed more probable, you didn't cross 'Wingy'. It was whispered that he could kill a man with one blow from his remaining upper limb – or even that he had in fact done so.

But as the pockets of his torn, dirty overcoat bulged with evidence of his calling, the ever-present fear of arrest, £5 fine – 'fourteen days to pay, m'Lud?' – made Wingy one of those characters forever glancing suspiciously over their shoulders. And that nervous-ferret look became accentuated by the perennial ill-made roll-your-own forever teetering on the tips of his nicotine-stained lips.

On mornings when you couldn't find him in the egg and chip cafe or sawdust-floored pub haunts, you knew which beak he had been up before on his return by the foulness of his temper and muttered oaths.

During racing hours he used to commandeer a side street's solitary red phone box and relay prices, garbled commentaries and results to a core of loitering hard nuts eavesdropping intently on every mumbled word. God help any unsuspecting granny nattering away on the phone when Wingy opened the door to requisition it each quarter and half hour. And as his occasional part-time hanger-on, my job on busy afternoons was to guard the booth and repel potential users. Disgruntled members of the public were far less fearsome than an enraged Wingy denied access to 'his' blower.

His office had to know the bets taken and if what he termed a 'polite request' to vacate wasn't speedily adhered to, that powerful left arm proved very persuasive. And during rainlashed afternoons Wingy took refuge in 'his' call box, transacted business as usual with a menacing contempt for aspiring interlopers that was his trademark to clients.

Of course, you must understand that At Large was at this time barely a teenager, and observed all this merely as an intrigued onlooker, though the odd shilling each way did pass between us.

At least settlement was within twenty-four hours, unlike those alternative letter bets to McLaughlins in Glasgow, whose tell-tale brown envelopes invariably had to be intercepted from the understanding postman at dawn lest my housemaster at Harrow cottoned on to the regretful reality that the only maths his dim-witted pupil was interested in involved working out cross doubles and trebles.

Poor old Wingy would have been lost in our new-fangled computerised age, though the way 100-9 has become 11-1, 100-8 12-1, and so on, and the slashing of many place odds, would have earned his incredulous approval. Pulling strokes on punters was all part of the game, but in fairness, come rain or shine, Wingy never did a runner and was always around the next day paying out. What percentage of business he turned into a sideline earner, and how much went to his guv'nor in a dingy backstreet office, we'll never know. But Wingy and thousands like him were the precursors of plush betting offices. Without the need to legislate against his ilk, today's facilities would never have come about.

Having lived to witness the transition from the perils of Wingy (who faded out of my life in 1961 when licensed shops opened) to the marvels of SIS has been a joy and a privilege. Though whether the Promised Land has turned out to be too much of a money-making accountancy operation for bookmakers is an argument which will go on and on.

Yet those of us who dealt with Wingy and his like still cannot believe that out of it all we have the finest betting service for punters with a free market of Tote, ante-post, board prices or SP.

In their selfish greed overseas racing establishments, led by owners and breeders, treat off-course punters with a take-it-or-leave-it pool monopoly disdain. Here we enjoy the best of creature comforts, more national and satellite TV, wider choice and, for the discerning, better value than anywhere in the world.

5 *If It Talks, Bet on It*

Bookmakers don't like betting on anything that talks. None the less, there are plenty of mug punters around, and bookmakers will quote you a price on virtually anything.

You can wager on the outcome of almost any sporting contest. The 1990 World Cup Soccer Finals in Italy produced a turnover in Britain of over £12 million. Big events in snooker, athletics, cricket, rugby, golf, boxing, tennis and American Football generate tremendous interest and a wide range of possible bets.

And then there are the fringe areas, which grab an increasing amount of headline space and provide a mind-boggling array of possibilities for the backer.

In politics, odds about the outcome of the next General Election are bandied about before all the votes have been counted in the previous one. Between General Elections, punters are offered by-election odds, and on those occasional political upheavals which can pop up almost without warning – most notably, in recent memory, the pulsating Conservative leadership election in 1990.

There are also wider-ranging political bets, such as the 5-1 quoted in February 1990, three months after the collapse of the Berlin Wall, that German reunification would take place before 1 December. East and West Germany united that November.

Then there are the other competitions which can be spiced up by a bet: the dear old Eurovision Song Contest, Miss World,

the Oscars and the Booker Prize. Odds were quoted on the World Hairdressing Championship in September 1990, with the winners Great Britain going off at 5-4: they didn't miss the cut! (Ouch!) And were a real snip (even worse).

And for something completely different, there are the more bizarre bets:

- verification of the existence of the Loch Ness Monster
- weather predictions (most common, will it snow on Christmas Day, or heatwaves take over the summer?)
- which record will top the pop charts at Christmas
- is Elvis Presley (contrary to most reports) alive?
- whether aliens will land on the planet by a given date

and plenty more.

Daftest of all is the bet about whether the world will end by a nominated date: a nice wager, no doubt, at a million to one, but if you're right and the world *has* ended, how will you be paid out?

SPORTS BETTING

The level of wagering on sports other than horse and greyhound racing has increased significantly over the last few years: the big companies report a doubling of interest since 1987, and attribute the growth to a variety of factors, notably increased media coverage of the betting possibilities of sports events.

A person who regularly bets on horses or dogs is exposed to fresh opportunities to pit his or her wits against bookmakers figuring that the same principles will apply: a rigorous study of form, whatever the event, will point to the winner. At the same time, bookmakers are looking to encourage betting from followers of non-racing sports but not habitual punters.

The top ten sports in terms of betting turnover are:

1. Horse racing
2. Greyhound racing
3. Soccer
4. Golf
5. Snooker
6. Rugby Union
7. American Football
8. Cricket
9. Tennis
10. Boxing

Horse racing apart, the top three individual events which would generate the most betting money in a year without a global competition such as the World Cup or Olympic Games are the F.A. Cup (and Scottish Cup), the Open Golf Championship and World Snooker.

SOCCER

You can bet on your team to win one of the major competitions, including European Leagues such as Germany's Bundesliga, and bookmakers supplement their League books with other betting possibilities – for instance, promotion or relegation, whether one team will finish above another or odds about managers keeping their jobs till the end of the season.

League odds can alter wildly as the season progresses. Before the start of the 1991-92 season, Manchester United could be backed at 9-1, Leeds United at 14-1. By the end of the year, with Man Utd two points clear of Leeds at the top with two games in hand, the Manchester team had shrunk to 7-2 on, Leeds 13-2. As the end of the season approached and Manchester United's title seemed ever more inevitable, the odds went as low as 8-1 on – before Alex Ferguson's team fell apart in the closing stages and finally handed the title to their rivals.

And scarcely had the League season reached its sensational finish before the next big soccer betting bonanza was under way, the European Championships in Sweden. England were a best-priced 7-1 before the start, with Scotland the rag at 33-1. But the Scots turned in a much more spirited effort than Graham Taylor's lads, whose spineless exit after the group matches left patriotic fingers burnt. Tournament winners Denmark – who only got in after the last-minute political exclusion of Yugoslavia – touched 80-1 during the group stages!

In televised games bookmakers advertise odds for:

NINETY MINUTES: Which team will have won (or whether the game will be drawn) at the end of the first ninety-minute period. (Credit bookmakers bet 'in running' during the match.)

WIN OUTRIGHT: This takes account of the possibility of the game being drawn at ninety minutes and decided during extra time, a penalty shoot-out, or a replay.

Three days before the 1991 F.A. Cup Final a punter walked into a Ladbrokes betting shop in Central London and had

£80,000 in cash on Tottenham Hotspur, at even money. The *Racing Post* described this as 'the behaviour of a complete moron', pointing out that he would have saved himself £8000 in tax by striking the bet on a racecourse (had he been able to get on). He could have earned almost £70 by leaving the money in a building society until the day of the match, or, as it turned out far better still, had the winners Spurs at 11-10 with other firms!

CORRECT SCORE: Predict the exact score over ninety minutes.

HALF-TIME/FULL-TIME DOUBLE RESULT: A double on the outcome of the first half coupled with that at ninety minutes. In the 1992 Cup Final between Sunderland and Liverpool, the half-time/full-time odds for a draw at half time and Liverpool to win at full time – which is what happened – were generally 4-1.

FIRST GOALSCORER: Which player will score the first goal, whenever it comes. For the European Cup Final in May 1991 Hills introduced the notion of betting on the *last* scorer of the game – a bet for which there had been numerous calls from punters looking to sustain interest. If persisted with, this tantalising tempter could catch on.

Soccer betting is big business, and offers exceptional opportunities for value if you are prepared to eschew jingoistic partisanship. ('Ignore patriotism', advises Derek McGovern, brains behind the *Racing Post*'s coverage of sports betting: it can distort your assessment of the value.) One punter who clearly let his heart rule his head was the fellow who in March 1991 staked £100 on non-league Colne Dynamoes to win the F.A. Cup before the end of the century. He was quoted odds of 5000-1 by his bookie

(must have been Scrooge's great-great-grandson!), but soon knew his fate, as the club folded shortly after the bet had been laid! But what happens if the Geordies, Newcastle United, my team, change their name to Colne Dynamoes and win the Cup? Howay the lads!

SNOOKER

With a generation of younger players outpotting long-established stalwarts, betting on snooker is booming, and for McGovern it offers 'the best value, without a doubt'.

For ranking tournaments, where Coral usually offer on-site facilities, you can bet on the eventual winner, individual matches, and frame scores.

To sustain interest during night after night of bleary-eyed viewing of the cueing, study the draw. Some knock-out events – soccer's F.A. Cup is the most obvious example – proceed on the basis of a random draw being made after each round. But in snooker, except for the British Open, it is constructed at the beginning of the competition, with the best players seeded. Mark Coton, the instigator of 'Pricewise' in the *Racing Post* (see page 54), highlighted the exceptional value of 80-1 against Doug Mountjoy winning the 1989 Mercantile Credit Classic. Careful consideration of the draw made it possible for him to calculate the 'true' price of Doug's beating each of the possible opponents who awaited him: these odds were much shorter than the 80-1 quoted at the start of the tournament, and Mountjoy did his bit to land Mark a spectacular piece of tipping.

Favourites don't always win. Joe Johnson was 150-1 before winning the 1986 Embassy World Championship. The 1989 and 1990 British Open champions, Tony Meo and Bob Chaperon, started out at a top price 200-1 and 150-1 respectively. Steve

COME COURSING!

Coursing's classic Waterloo Cup was as big a betting event in the nineteenth century as the Derby. Even up to the Second World War it attracted huge crowds to the traditional running grounds at Altcar near Liverpool – and some of the biggest names in bookmaking, like William Hill and Joe Coral, were coursing stalwarts.

Things are far more restrained now, though Newmarket trainer Sir Mark Prescott revived interest spectacularly in the 1980s. But ante-post betting on the sixty-four greyhounds in the Waterloo Cup, with the draw made at the outset so that the winner of the first course goes through to meet the winner of the second, etc., is still lively.

Match betting in coursing, though bookies ask for 'bottle on' (2-1 on) about each on occasions, can be rewarding. Knowing your dogs, their handlers, and 'reading' each course knowledgeably is the key.

And don't bleat on that coursing is cruel to hares. If you want to see hares in Britain go to a coursing meeting. There they are protected all the year from the bullet, poison and traps. Hare shoots, with wounded gangrenous animals taking days to die, can be grisly affairs.

The object, scored on points by a mounted judge, is to test the speed, skill and stamina of the pursuers -- not to kill hares. Maybe three hundred in a season (September to March) die, a fraction of those run over on the roads or destroyed by farmers, who know these voracious eaters of crops are pests they simply cannot afford to tolerate. Walt Disney has a lot to answer for in portraying hares as cuddly, lovable fellows. They aren't. And before condemning man's oldest field sport, go along and see for yourself.

Gruesome tales of hares being 'ripped to pieces' are emotive claptrap. Just as it's virtually impossible to tear off a human limb, so dogs cannot mutilate hares. Let's have a referendum of hares. They'd vote unaminously for the good life, on farms owned by coursing fans.

James, winner of the 1990 Mercantile Credit Classic, also could be backed at 150-1. Events where the early rounds comprise the best of nine frames are most likely to produce upsets. The longer the match, the more likely the 'form dog' is to win.

Individual game betting can be profitable if you keep a careful eye on different firms' prices. McGovern explains: 'One bookmaker will make one player favourite, another bookmaker will make the other player favourite – it's a bonanza for the punters.' Indeed. In the betting for the fourth round of the Rothmans Grand Prix in October 1990, one layer had Tony Knowles at 5-4 on, and another priced his opponent Ken Owers at 11-4. A quick sum with the percentages table on page 41 shows that this is a book of 82 percent: you could have backed both players and been certain of making a profit, even after tax, whatever the outcome. A licence to print money! But who actually got on both players at those prices?

HOLING OUT

The 'Hole-in-One Coup', which caused such a fuss in the spring of 1992, was four years in the planning.

Essex lads Paul Simmons and John Carter, former betting shop managers, hatched a scheme to capitalise on the ignorance of some small businesses over the true odds of a hole-in-one being scored in any major golf tournament.

Think about it for a moment, and you'll realise that with a hundred or two of the world's top golfers teeing off at up to 72 holes, the chances of a single hole-in-one during such a competition are not very remote. Indeed, statistically it's around even money that at least one player will hole out from the tee, but Simmons and Carter, by concentrating on independent, locally owned betting shops, were able – quite legally – to take advantage of the naivety of managers who thought a hole-in-one to be some sort of freak occurrence.

They drove over 200,000 miles to place their bets on a variety of different events, visiting a thousand bookies and managing to get on with 135 – who offered odds of up to 100-1! The big chains – over whose eyes it is not easy to pull the wool – were more on the ball when quoting marginal odds against, but the intrepid duo managed to get on £30,000 in singles and doubles.

Not every tournament on which they bet produced a hole-in-one, of course, but several did: in the 1991 British Open, during which one mug layer had accepted a bet at 100-1, Brian Marchbank holed out with his first stroke at the twelfth in the opening round. A total pay-out of half a million pounds accrued – before some of the layers cried foul and refused to pay. Eleven firms, with a liability of nearly £85,000, dug their heels in.

The *Sun* highlighted the cunning plot. Bookies squealed and protested that they'd been duped. Legal action was threatened. Betcha, though, that now there's no 100-1 available against a hole-in-one – even in your local club's Medal round!

Bookies too rise early, and 'sharks' are usually 'knocked back' when going for the stand-out prices.

Firms offer odds over who will make the highest break in a tournament and on what it will be: the best price quoted for a maximum 147 in the Embassy World Championship at The Crucible, Sheffield, in April 1992 was 14-1 – and Jimmy White became only the second player ever to achieve the maximum in the world's top tournament, following Cliff Thorburn in 1983.

Other novelty bets included nominating the two finalists, players to win their respective quarters of the draw, the nationality of the winner, 16-1 against picking twelve losers in the first round, and sets of odds for the round in which some of the top players will be beaten.

At the end of some sessions during the three ITV snooker tournaments I'm sometimes able to pinpoint the top odds available the next morning – so stay up late. I admit there are more pleasant images than

GOLF

Most bookmakers offer a variety of prices on big events here and in America, which are revised round by round and, during live coverage, hole by hole. Also popular is handicap betting, with less fancied players receiving shots from the market leaders, head-to-head 'matches' (one player against another), how many shots the winner will take, and naming the top British, European, American, Australia or Australasian player. Some firms offer up to ten places each way (a tenth the odds).

Hills bet on-course at a minimum of six European Tour events, and as Jeremy Chapman pointed out in the *Sporting Life*:

All the homework in the world, all the hours spent poring over which stars play which courses particularly well, which ones tend to come out of the traps fast in the spring and which ones come with a long, late run in the autumn, will not necessarily pinpoint one single outright winner in a year's betting.

However, golf does usually give the punter a good run for his money through a number of sensible each-way investments . . .

With the number of first-time winners and outsiders like 250-1 shots Michael McLean, Gavin Levenson and Andrew Sherborne winning, virtual unknowns like Stephen McAllister going in not once but twice in 1990, and Yesterday's Men like Hale Irwin taking on a new lease of life to win the US Open at 100-1, any punter who can honestly say he makes a profit out of golf has to be admired.

It ain't easy, but then making money was never meant to be.

And when rookie John Daly, the ninth reserve and only called up overnight to complete the 151 field, won the US PGA in August 1991 bookies enjoyed their ultimate 'skinner of skinners'. Two rounds went by before they even laid a 'rock cake' (small bet) about Cinderella man Daly and, to top up everything, the three places went to 100-1 (twice) and 125-1 chances. Golf's fairytale was, for punters, a wicked fairy.

But in the 1992 British Open at Muirfield Nick Faldo, controversially labelled a 'bottler' by the *Racing Post*, slammed the bookies when rallying to counter-attack America's unknown John Cook after being laid at all prices from 9-1 down to 7-1 on.

RUGBY UNION

Betting on Rugby centres around the World Cup, every four years, and the annual Five Nations championship involving England, Ireland, Scotland, Wales and France. Here you can back a team to win the championship, Triple Crown, or Grand Slam and can bet on individual matches, the first try-scorer, or winning points margin.

The 1991 World Cup, which reached its climax in that pulsating England-Australia at Twickenham on the day I was trying to earn a crust covering the Breeders' Cup at Churchill Downs, attracted over £5 million of betting turnover.

Readers of Sports Betting in the *Racing Post* had been alerted months previously to the value of 4-1 against the Wallabies, but the layers' biggest losers once the tournament got under way were New Zealand (best priced 13-8 at the off) and the surprise package Western Samoa (top price 300-1). They beat Wales 16-13 — what would the score have been if Wales had taken on all of Samoa?

AMERICAN FOOTBALL

There has been a steady increase of interest in gridiron betting since Channel Four started screening the National Football League in the mid-1980s: the more people become familiar with its intricacies, the more confident they will feel about punting. Ex-*Racing Post* Bob Leder's regular guide in the *Sporting Life*, along with Pricewise, are indispensable. You can compare the 'line' (odds) in Las Vegas with the prices widely advertised in Britain. When there are major differences, which can occur, be guided by the Vegas line – their skill in 'handicapping' teams is legendary. Literally their jobs depend upon it in the cut-throat gambling Mecca of the world.

In each NFL game you can bet 11-10 on either side with the 'spread' – that's a points advantage given to the underdog. So the San Francisco 49ers, at say -8½, would be 'tips on' (11-10 on) against the Los Angeles Rams. If you were on the 49ers, they would have to win by nine clear points. But the Rams – the 'dogs' in this instance – could lose by eight points or, of course, win, for a bet on them at 11-10 on to be successful.

On no event on earth are larger sums gambled than the Super Bowl. Far more than major league baseball (boring) or basketball (even more mind-numbing, being played at the top level by freakishly tall men), let alone a horse or trotting race.

How the Booby and I (or should it be Me and My Booby?) got into Super Bowl XXII in San Diego in 1988 when the natives, real dedicated fans, couldn't beg or even steal a ticket, was – I admit – shameful. But, like the Kentucky Derby and World Heavyweight title bouts, Super Bowl is a sporting extravaganza of hype and spectacle which remains indelible in the memory.

And a handy bet on the Redskins to beat the Broncos in the cauldron of the Jack Murphy Stadium – the only live NFL game I've ever seen – made it specially so.

CRICKET

Prices are regularly offered on Test series, the County Championship and knock-out competitions. In individual matches, betting on the result is often supplemented by nominating such as the top batsman on either side. Ladbrokes operate betting shops at Test matches, updating odds – hence the famous 500-1 quoted against England in the 1981 Headingley Test before Ian Botham tore the Australian bowling apart and Bob Willis thundered in to grab eight cheap wickets. Aussies Dennis Lillee and Rodney Marsh had some compensation, having availed themselves of a little of that 'monkey'.

The 1992 World Cup in Australia stimulated an estimated £5 million in bets, with eventual winners Pakistan touching 100-1 after losing three of their first five games. But Imran Khan's men were best-priced 5-4 for the final, with Graham Gooch's England just favourites at 6-5 on.

On-site betting shops also offer novelty bets (for instance, on how many wickets will fall before lunch, or a recalled Ian Botham to take a wicket with his first ball (100-1)). To cover 'expenses' there is a 5 per cent tax, which also applies to horse and dog bets laid at cricket and soccer grounds, snooker venues, and so on. Bookies don't do owt for nowt!

CYCLING

Over the fifteen days of the Tour de France odds fluctuate continually. Inside knowledge of ailments and team schemes are a decided advantage.

TENNIS

Wimbledon fortnight accounts for about

seventy per cent of turnover on tennis. You can bet on the outcome of tournaments, individual matches, and winning margins.

In 1987 tennis was the medium for one of the largest individual bets ever placed. A businessman staked £120,000 (tax paid, making a total investment of £132,000) at 6-5 on about the holder Boris Becker retaining his men's singles title at Wimbledon. Winnings would have been £100,000, but Becker was knocked out early in the tournament by 500-1 outsider Peter Doohan. Jonathan Sparke, Director of City Index, the London bookmaker who laid this mammoth bet, reported that the punter took his setback calmly. 'He phoned me during the closing stages of the match and asked me to give him 10-1 about Becker still winning Wimbledon. I refused. He listened to the last few points with me and said at the end, "You win some, you lose some".' You do indeed!

But you simply couldn't lose on the Jeremy Bates versus Javier Sanchez second-round game in 1992, had you been able to get on at the 11-4 against quoted by Victor Chandler – compared with anything from 5-2 on to 11-8 on from other layers! Sanchez was a best-priced 7-4. But this licence to print money had a rapid expiry date, as punters who tried to get on with Chandler soon discovered: those who called bang on 9.30 a.m., when the firm opened for business, were quoted 7-4 on – though regular clients had allegedly been accommodated to small amounts before that point. Bates won in straight sets. No medals for VC!

In the second round of the Ladies Singles in 1991, bookies priced Amanda Grunfeld at 'double carpet' (33-1) against nine-times champ Martina Navratilova. Layers could never remember bigger odds being offered in a sports match (boxing has the draw as the third 'runner'). Navratilova won.

And in the 1991 Men's Singles Germany's Michael Stich, pinpointed in the *Racing Post*'s Sports Betting section at 40-1, delighted layers by overcoming hotpots Stefan Edberg and Boris Becker in the semi-final and final to floor virtually every double coupling Graf.

BOXING

Prices are regularly given for the big bouts, on the outright winner and the round in which it will finish.

Big hitters – not boxers but gamblers – plunge on the outcome of a fight. When Mike Tyson faced Buster Douglas in Tokyo in February 1990, one Vegas gambler put down $100,000 on Tyson at odds of 35-1 on. 'This was like Secretariat against a Clydesdale,' said Russ Culver, the manager of The Mirage, the only legal Las Vegas sports book to give odds on the bout. By the opening bell, Tyson's odds had contracted to 42-1 on. 'People still bet Tyson,' said Culver: 'They thought we were giving money away. A lot of people bet because, even at those odds, they figured they could make three per cent interest on their money in just a day or two. That's a lot better than you can get in a bank.' No it's not. Tyson lost.

But he didn't in June 1991 when rapper superstar M. C. Hammer, a successful racehorse owner, bet $250,000 on 'Iron Mike' at 5-1 on to beat 'Razor' Ruddock. Then Tyson was comprehensively knocked out by the courts in Indianapolis.

Also highly popular in Vegas is predicting how long a fight will last. When the durable, cagey 'Bonecrusher' Smith fought Tyson in 1987, it was 11-10 on the fight going under or over four rounds. Tyson won the twelve-rounder on points and the 'shrewdies' paid for their trips by going for the 'over' – saying it would last at least into the fifth round.

Similarly, when lovable Frank Bruno, the 9-1 'dog', survived (just!) the fourth round in 1989, his large contingent of Brits were spraying dollar bills in joints along the garish strip for days afterwards. It was the one way of backing 'their' man and still 'copping' in defeat. Pragmatic chauvinism!

DARTS

For major competitions, odds are quoted for the tournament, individual matches and game scores. Phil Taylor, winner of the 1990 Embassy World Darts Championship, started at 100-1.

GRAND PRIX MOTOR RACING

Betting on the following year's Formula One drivers' championship starts as soon as one season's champion is garlanded. Odds fluctuate after each of the fifteen Grand Prix, on which win and each-way bets are widely available, as they are on each race and different events such as the Indianapolis 500.

And for other sports and events, from the Boat Race to bowls and hurling, just ask your friendly neighbourhood bookie!

POLITICS

Non-sporting wagering, mainly in betting shops, really began with politics. Ladbrokes' Ron Pollard, the grand old PR man of bookmaking, relates how the start of non-racing betting came in the Tory leadership struggle following the resignation of Harold Macmillan in 1963.

I thought: what a golden opportunity to get the name of the company on the front pages, rather than the sports pages. And I sat down and did the odds (because I'd always been a political animal). I went

5-4 Butler
7-4 Hailsham
6-1 Maudling
10-1 bar three

The Evening News *that night came out with a magnificent banner headline: '10-1 BAR THREE FOR NUMBER TEN.' . . . We took the measly amount of £14,000. Sir Alec Douglas-Home won it – he had said he was a non-runner very early on – and we won £1400. But we had millions of pounds' worth of publicity, and the next General Election had to be held within one year – and on that General Election we took £650,000, which was more than four times what we took on the Derby of that year.*

In that 1964 General Election, Maxwell Joseph, boss of Grand Metropolitan, staked £50,000 – described at the time as the world's largest ever recorded bet – to win £37,500 if Labour won: they did so, with just three seats to spare.

Betting on politics naturally concentrates on General Elections and by-elections, and few events have ever illustrated the volatile nature of political betting more dramatically than the General Election in 1992, on which Hills and Ladbrokes took in excess of £4 million out of a total of £6 million.

When the Prime Minister announced on 11 March that the election would be held on 9 April, the Tories were apparently sitting pretty at 9-4 on, with Labour 13-8. You could name your own price about the Liberal Democrats – generally put in at 500-1. At that stage the odds for a hung parliament were around 6-5 on.

Then the campaign started, and the odds began to fluctuate in response to the latest batch of opinion polls. Within a couple of weeks the parties had flip-flopped. On 26 March, Ladbrokes went 6-4 on Labour, 11-10 Conservatives. Gradually Labour, like Mike Tyson and Arazi, began to look

Tories stayed
loyal to the grey
– and despite
flip-flopping it
was a Major
result

unbeatable – and remember, these were odds for the greatest number of seats, not for any party to gain an overall majority! Those who had backed Neil Kinnock's lads at 13-8 now waited patiently as the Tory odds lengthened, bringing in that ecstatic situation of being able to back both sides at odds against and guaranteeing a profit.

A week before polling day Corals priced Labour down to 4-1 on, Conservatives 5-2, and Hills tried to liven up a rapidly dying betting market by introducing odds on who would be Conservative leader by the end of the year (evens Major, 2-1 Heseltine, 5-2 Kenneth Clarke).

Two days before polling Corals saw Labour at 6-1 on, Tories 7-2, but those who had heard rumours of a late swing against Labour put their money where their ears were and brought the Conservative price back to 11-10, and a sensational flip-flop right at the eleventh hour had Ladbrokes

restoring the Tories to favouritism – then, with Labour apparently rallying at the death, quoting 5-4 on each of two, while Hills went 11-8 on Labour, evens Tories, and Corals 13-8 on Labour, 11-10 Tories.

What no one had really considered was that the Tories would get an overall majority – when one firm quoted them at 12-1 early in the campaign to do just that, there was little interest – but they did, by 21 seats.

Even before Neil Kinnock had announced his resignation, John Smith was installed 6-4 on favourite to be Labour's next leader. (Soon he was 9-1 on, and duly routed solitary rival Bryan Gould in July 1992.) John Major became an even-money chance to remain Prime Minister until 1 January 2000. Not much more than a year and a half before the Election, Hills had offered 5-1 against Margaret Thatcher; now a noble Baroness, still being Prime Minister on her seventieth birthday in 1995. Hope you weren't tempted!

There is also the occasional bonanza of political punting such as that brought about by the fevered Conservative leadership election in November 1990, on which around £1.5 million was wagered. For both ballots of the 372 Tory MPs prices were quoted on the candidates winning (and fluctuated wildly as different signs, rumours and speculation emerged from the campaigns). In addition, bookmakers offered odds about the number of votes each candidate would poll, and the *Racing Post* was rightly pleased with itself for directing its readers to take 8-1 Heseltine to get between 141 and 160 votes on the first ballot: he polled 152. (When Mrs Thatcher herself had taken over from Edward Heath way back in 1975, she had been the 8-1 outsider of three before the first ballot behind Heath and Willie Whitelaw.) For the second ballot, John Major started at 5-2 before shortening to odds-on: one punter had £20,000 with Ladbrokes at 6-4. (Mr Major had been a 66-1 shot earlier the same week when his candidature seemed unlikely.) Douglas Hurd, the third contender in the second ballot, went from 10-1 to 13-8 and back out to 10-1 as mercurial prognostications emanated from the corridors of power. The result: Major 185 votes, Heseltine 131, Hurd 56. The beaten pair conceded.

Another example of the see-saw element in political betting came during the Monmouth by-election in May 1991. The day before the poll, Dominic Chapman in the *Racing Post* wrote:

Politics has again proved another money-spinning winner for the bookmakers with a turbulent market stimulating considerable interest in tomorrow's by-election in Monmouth.

We nailed our colours to Labour [who won

the seat] at 6-4 last Thursday when Hills and Ladbrokes were at odds in naming the favourite.

The topsy-turvy contest went completely haywire on Monday and yesterday with the publication of a poll showing Labour some eight percentage points ahead of the Tories.

A rapid reappraisal of the situation saw Ladbrokes cut Labour from 3-1 to 1-2 while the Tories went from 1-3 to 6-4. Inside just 24 hours punters could have snapped up odds of 2-1, 3-1 and 20-1 about the only realistic contenders for Monmouth. That means a book showing an incredible 63 per cent.

Such a disparity in pricing over such a short time allows big-money punters to move in and this was illustrated yesterday by activity at Ladbrokes. They reported several hefty wagers, including £1000 on Labour at 1-2 while a £5000-£250 was placed on the lagging Liberal Democrats.

We were surprised to see Labour drift so badly in the market as one statistic sticks out like a Monster Raving Loony Party candidate: the Tories have not won a by-election in Wales since the war.

Ron Pollard, that wise old bird, was spot on when he realised that betting on politics would bring in millions of pounds' worth of publicity for the bookies, as 1992 demonstrated so vividly. Not the least amount of public attention focuses on those daft bets which are endemic to politics. Screaming Lord Sutch, that standing dish in elections for so many years, backed himself at 50,000-1 to be prime minister. And Richard Meacock of the Quality For Life Party staked £500 at 500-1 against his overturning the Tory majority in the Richmond and Barnes constituency. He didn't quite manage that £250,000 pay-out: Tory Jeremy Handley polled 22,894 votes, Mr Meacock garnered 62.

If you had just one wager every year during your lifetime – under-18s legally cannot bet – and 'copped' once at 100-1, profit would be assured.

That 100-1 was the price laid by Hills against one spot of rain landing on the London Weather Centre roof every day during June 1991.

Amid mounting hype and hysterical headlines, the odds tumbled as surely as the rain. With opening week of Wimbledon thrown into chaos, the 'thirty days hath September, April, June . . .' appeared to give punters a twenty-four-hour edge, but on 29 June, while it spotted down in north London, the crucial roof remained dry – though it was sodden again on the 30th!

Hill's Graham Sharpe observed dryly: 'We've been saved from a real soaking.'

EXOTIC BETTING

Sport and politics provide high-profile gambling opportunities, but you can dabble in any sort of contest provided there is a bookie prepared to price up the possibilities. Over the last few years the growth of non-sports betting has led to an explosion of interest in the weirder areas of punting, and though turnover for such events is minute compared with that on horses, greyhounds and other sport, it generates tremendous public interest and fun.

Back in the days when televising Miss World was the bright point of gloomy November, this annual parade of pulchritude generated enough betting interest to keep major credit bookmakers open throughout the evening.

In 1980 the *Sporting Life* devoted a whole page (page 3, as it happened) to a complete form guide, compiled by the paper's sexiest reporter, a handsome, rotund and bewhiskered fellow. His preview apppeared on the *Life*'s front page.

Viewers of the flesh extravaganza will be amazed how some of the contestants come to be tottering along the catwalk at all.

Rating them, as the phrase goes, in reverse order isn't too difficult. It is safe, I think, to eliminate the big-nosed Miss Cyprus, the so-ordinary Miss Canada and the gap-toothed Miss Isle of Man.

But splitting the finely chiselled features of Miss Jamaica, the class of Miss Israel, Miss Dominican Republic's eye-swivelling bearing, the crimper's crumpet Miss New Zealand, those dazzling molars of Miss Switzerland, the Amazonian Miss Germany and the best from East of Suez, Miss Guam and Miss India, could come down to how each performs under pressure.

Page 3 gave form figures, odds, and an 'expert' summing-up by the hairy expert:

'Argentine: tall, flabby rear, bony shoulders, flat-chested . . .
Austria: the most generous thighs of all . . .
Denmark: protruding rear . . .
Italy: has that man-eater look, enjoys horse racing . . .
Mauritius: plenty of meat on her . . .
USA: Miss Debbie Freeze leaves me cold . . .'

And so on. Sexist and disgraceful! But all the major bookmakers gave prices on the event. Betting was part of the fun. Now it's been scrapped from network TV (feminists triumph?).

So it is with some less obvious contests. Pollard describes how in 1974 Ladbrokes' efforts to increase the range of their business (and thus heighten public awareness

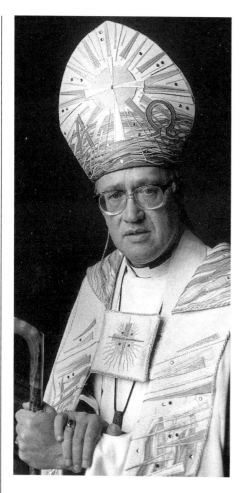

He opened as a rag but became a steamer: George Carey, who succeeded Robert Runcie as Archbishop of Canterbury in 1991

the interviewer said, "Archbishop, when did you first know you were going to be the next Archbishop of Canterbury?" And the Archbishop said, "Have you heard of a firm called Ladbrokes?"' Divine assistance – or as near divine as you are likely to get – in spreading the gospel about betting.

The nomination of the next Archbishop of Canterbury in 1990 caused a considerable ruckus – and brought proportionate publicity to the bookmakers. In early shows the Bishop of Bath and Wells, George Carey, was a 20-1 'rag'. He remained steady at that price, and near the off started attracting several £50 bets. Ecclesiastical shrewdies were at work, and odds tumbled. Ladbrokes had not seen a penny for Carey until, on the morning of the announcement, they took more than £2000 on him. Someone somewhere knew something and Carey was duly named the new Archbishop. Bookmakers grudgingly paid up. Hills' Don Payne complained that inside information 'got to persons who were prepared to use that knowledge and exploit poor, unsuspecting bookmakers.' It just shows that God and Mammon can mix.

God presumably knows more than most about the weather. Specialists in this area are Hills, who have a contract with the London Weather Centre. To help pay for it one punter lost £1000 backing the temperature in the UK to reach 100 degrees Fahrenheit in 1991. And the self-proclaimed betting specialist is astrophysicist and amateur weatherman Piers Corbyn, who claims to have won several thousand pounds on such bets as whether it will

of it) led to the suggestion that they offer odds on the new Archbishop of Canterbury. Though at first reluctant to get involved in an area he knew nothing about, he was encouraged by Ladbrokes chairman Cyril Stein, who helped Ron set about making a book: 'I'll give you a start – the Chief Rabbi is 500-1.'

For more authoritative information Ron contacted the editor of the *Church Times*, who marked his card. Donald Coggan was installed 7-4 favourite and duly became the next Archbishop. 'He was interviewed on the television that night', recalls Ron, 'and

PREVIOUS PAGE: A quick lick

BELOW: A gamble thwarted: 'bottle' (2–1) favourite Dancing Brave (Greville 'Dogbarker' Starkey) agonisingly fails by half a length to overhaul 11–2 second favourite Shahrastani ('The Choirboy', Walter Swinburn) in the 1986 Ever Ready Derby.

Something always pops up to save those wretched bookie chappies!

RIGHT: Las Vegas sports books bet 'with the spread' on the NFL

FAR RIGHT: Boris Becker cost one punter £120,000

BELOW RIGHT: Backers of Tottenham's Paul Gascoigne at 'net' (10–1) to score first in the 1991 Cup Final against Nottingham Forest were doomed – Gazza was stretchered off after 15 minutes

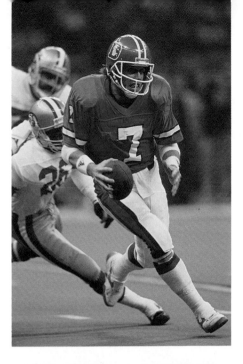

ABOVE: Chips
with everything

RIGHT: Life's
sufferers

be sunnier in London in the first week of May than in the last, or if rainfall in Birmingham will be more than 40 per cent below normal during the same month. However, when I challenged the redoubtable Piers live on BBC TV's *People Today* programme to forecast the 1991 Derby Day weather five weeks in advance, he chickened out. Generalities are easier to guess at than specifics.

Extremes of hot weather always give rise to betting about how long it will be until rain falls, and the traditional weather bet is about a white Christmas – whether one snowflake falls on the roof of the London Weather Centre during the twenty-four hours of 25 December. The odds usually open at around 10-1 – though punters might get cold feet about such a bet if they realised that it has not snowed in London over Christmas since 1981. That year it snowed on Christmas Eve, stopped on Christmas Day, and started again on Boxing Day! And one Londoner would have collected £5000 if a snowflake fell in the capital during August 1991. It didn't.

You can bet on the outcome of the annual Hollywood Oscars. *The Silence of the Lambs*, Best Film in 1992, was a 2-1 chance (from 7-4), while Anthony Hopkins was backed from 4-1 to 9-4 before securing the Best Actor award. Best Actress was Jodie Foster, always favourite at 13-8 on and 6-4 on.

For the 1992 Eurovision Song Contest rumours that the programme had been prerecorded with Yugoslavia the winner brought that country's odds plummeting to even money, but as so often the rumours were unfounded, and Ireland won with Linda Martin singing 'Why Me?' – an anthem for losing punters if ever there was one!

Truly zany bets generate an amount of media attention quite unrelated to actual turnover. (For example, you can get 100-1 against Boris Becker marrying Steffi Graf before 1995.) And Ladbrokes bet on who would land the plum role of the *Eagle* comic's Dan Dare in an upcoming TV series. Nigel Havers and Clive Owen were 4-1 favourites with Jason Donovan and Frank Bruno 50-1 and Gazza 500-1. Bags I get the part of the Mekon!

Perhaps the most famous of such bets was struck early in the 1960s, when a farseeing punter asked the price against a man walking on the surface of the moon before the end of that decade. He was quoted 1000-1, made the bet, and Neil ('one small step for a man . . . ') Armstrong landed him the wager with over five months to spare.

Nowadays outlandish betting has spread even more incongruously. In spring 1992, these were some of the odds quoted by Hills against happenings within one year of striking the bet:

1000-1 (from 500's a year before) Elvis Presley proved to be alive (though Ron Pollard has talked to the man who cut Elvis's hair before he was laid in his coffin, and thinks the odds-layers are on safe ground)

250-1 (from 500's) Conclusive proof of UFOs

500-1 Positive sighting of the Loch Ness Monster

1000-1 Any named British tennis player to win either of the Wimbledon singles titles. Even better, Hills will lay

1,000,000-1 against YOURS TRULY winning the Men's Singles – double those odds if I beat Screaming Lord Sutch in the final. Come on: now is the time to bet like men!

Another popular flutter is on the naming of Royal babies. This started back in 1964, when the Queen, Princess Margaret, Princess Alexandra and the Duchess of Kent were all expecting. According to Graham Sharpe's book *Amazing Bets* (The Sporting Life, 1988), the odds about the name of the monarch's offspring ranged from 10-1 against George to 50,000-1 Nikita. For the Duchess of York's first-born to be called Beatrice was rated a 100-1 shot, a positive steal compared with the value given to the lady in London who had £1 on the Duchess having twins named Jason and Kylie. A variation on Royal baby betting is the weight of the child at birth.

And on that subject, betting to produce twins is fairly common among members of the public who request odds about particular personal happenings: the usual odds are 20-1, and plenty of expecting parents invest as an insurance policy, though advanced pre-natal scans have curtailed opportunities. And when the little horrors are born, they're at least useful for a few more betting opportunities:

● A golf-mad Birmingham punter staked £20 on his son to be British Open Champion before the year 2015 – odds 10,000-1.

● An Edinburgh man has backed his infant daughter to win an Olympic medal at any sprint distance by 2016 – odds 100-1.

● A London father pockets £1m if his son ever wins Wimbledon and a Reading dad has had £5 on his three-year-old son to win in the year 2010 – at 20,000-1!

Even weirder:

● One Leicester punter has £50,000 to £50 (1000-1) about the Archbishop of Canterbury confirming that Christ has appeared in public during 1991.

● A Leeds man regularly accepts the 5000-1 offered him by Ladbrokes

FANCY A FRANCHISE FLUTTER?

In 1991, when the ITV franchises were up for renewal and subject to secret bids, betting – especially from those involved in the media hothouses – was intense. Everything depended upon the deliberations of the Independent Television Commission in October, and there were some tight races according to Ladbrokes, who closed their book in June (leaks, you know, old chap . . .).

At the close the incumbents were all favoured:

LONDON WEEKDAY
Thames 11-10
Carlton 5-4 (won)
CPV-TV 9-4

LONDON WEEKEND
LWT 2-1 on (won)
LIB 11-8

BREAKFAST
TV-AM 11-10 on
Daybreak 5-4
Sunrise 5-1 (won)

against aliens landing on earth and taking over government of the planet.

● Unarius, a sect based in El Cajon, California, is so convinced of an alien invasion that it has built a landing strip to accommodate the extra-terrestrials. Over the years they have staked more than £30,000 at varying odds that their visitors would arrive.

● A few punters have bet on the Prince of Wales renouncing his right to the throne, bringing the Hills price down from 100-1 to 25-1.

NORTHWEST ENGLAND
Granada 5-4 on (won)
North West TV evens

SOUTH AND SOUTH EAST
TVS 6-4
CPV-TV 9-4
Meridian 5-2 (won)
Carlton 7-2

YORKSHIRE
Yorkshire 3-1 on (won)
Viking 4-1
White Rose 9-2

EAST OF ENGLAND
Anglia 5-2 on (won)
3 East 9-4
CPV-TV 6-1
(A bet of £50 at 5-2 on, subject to 10
per cent tax, means you'd win just
£13 – true odds of almost 4-1 on!)

Feverish activity in shares and
betting shops, while awaiting
judgement from the ITC, ensured it
was a toss-up between gambling in
the City and down at the bookies.

But a line has to be drawn somewhere, and most bookies refuse bets on the grounds of taste. You would be hard pushed to find any firm to lay odds about the Queen's abdicating in favour of the Prince of Wales. Nor will bookies bet on questions of life and death or on tragedies: Pollard was once approached by a man who wanted odds about there being a disaster at the new Forth Road Bridge near Edinburgh within six months of its being opened. He declined. In infinitely worse taste was the enquiry to Hills about it being proved that rumbustious actor Oliver Reed has a tattoo on his genitals. Now who'd want to authenticate that – even in a pub?!

Another bizarre problem of authentication would have awaited Pollard had he accepted what he considers the strangest bet ever: 'A gentleman phoned me up to ask me what price it would be that Mae West, when she died, was found to be a man.' Having no authoritative way of finding out, Ron declined.

Bookmakers don't like betting on anything that blabs. Unless, that is, the oddsmaker should be in the perfect position of already knowing the result. One time I dubiously made money was as school bookmaker at Harrow, when discovering the identity of the next Head of School twenty-four hours in advance of the official announcement. This was a popular betting medium, and I was able to clean up by taking bets on all other candidates at 'generous prices' and refusing them on the chap about to be named. The old conscience still twinges occasionally, though!

Having been of the last generation trained to administer the Empire, which was rapidly disintegrating, I didn't bother to study. How I scrambled my miserable three O-levels remains an obscure mystery. And, though enthusiastic, I was useless at 'eccer' (games) except in 'ducker' (the outdoor swimming pool where for the first two years juniors bathed nude) and 'pingers' (table tennis). Regular beatings at Harrow made me what I am today – though I learned the fundamentals of bookmaking, far more important than Latin and Science. No wonder I ended up in the kitchens of London's Dorchester Hotel and being a useless commis waiter!

But I digress. For a final example of how people will bet on anything, what about the one that got away? In February 1965 an

Well, is this a man? Mae West, object of the bet that had Ron Pollard declining to come up and see her (him?) some time

African Golden Eagle in London Zoo made a break for it and attracted a huge amount of public attention before being recaptured. Then on 15 December Goldie popped out again, and this time Pollard saw an opportunity. He offered 12-1 against the bird being recaptured before midnight on Christmas Eve. Perched in a tree in Regent's Park and watched by a crowd which on occasions numbered five thousand, Goldie imperiously stayed above such frivolities as betting on his fate. But just before midnight on Christmas Eve the temptation of a rotund rabbit left on the ground proved too much for him, and down he came. Ladbrokes paid out £14,000.

If it screeches (or whatever African Golden Eagles do), bet on it!

MCCRIRICK AT LARGE

FORGET THE RUMOURS – SNOOKER ISN'T FIXED

At the first sign of a possible snooker coup, the dreaded word 'fix' invariably surfaces.

It's bad enough on the racecourse when beaten favourites are 'hooked up' or 'not off', according to aggrieved punters. And you can't count the number of winners who 'weren't trying' on their previous outing. On occasions, no doubt, they have a case.

And press coverage nowadays ensures that sensationalism haunts snooker at almost every tournament. Prior to the World Championships especially, the tabloids usually manage to rake up some sort of sex, betting or drugs scandal.

In seven years of close involvement on the circuit with ITV's tournaments, meeting players and witnessing the pressures they're under, allied to the importance of winning, I can avow that no match, to my knowledge or that of anyone who would know, has been 'arranged'.

Players have been below par on occasions for various reasons but none, I'm convinced, has ever 'thrown' a game. If time proves me wrong it will show how naïve I've become as I approach middle age. But there is still a belief in my ample gut that it won't happen. Players, watched intimately by millions on the box, are desperate to win not only for the money but for vital ranking points and prestige.

Snooker 'insiders' more clued up than bookies, who use their own individual judgement based largely on televised snippets, enjoy a big betting edge. Especially as Pricewise repeatedly reveals opinion so varied that it is often possible to back both players in a game and make at least a pre-tax profit.

There are a number of shrewd judges close to the players who understand the game so well that they come out in front most seasons. Apart from form, they get to know if a player isn't 100 per cent for whatever reason, or maybe has personal or emotional problems, and 'go to work' accordingly.

Once, I remember, a star turned up at the venue following a three-week holiday in the sun during which he'd never practised or even held a cue. Wise guys wised up and cleaned up as the bookies' favourite went down 5-0.

How a single bet can 'snowball', especially in snooker, is simple.

A 'face' comes in to a betting shop with £100 on a 5-4 frame score. His bet is noted, either by a gambling employee or nearby punter, who reckons there is something to it and trolls off to another shop for a slice of the action. This occurs several times and soon all round the area the fever develops. Those original £100 punters, placing between them £2000 worth of bets, could be copied to ten times that amount.

There will always be cynics who reckon the game is crooked and that, for instance, whenever there is a last-frame thriller, it's all a fiddle laid on for TV.

Conveniently forgotten are numerous one-sided matches which evoke despair among TV executives, for example the 1988 British Open Final. That day Stephen Hendry rolled over Cuemasters stablemate Mike Hallett 13-2, virtually wiping out Sunday's audience, potentially the largest of the ten days.

That, and so many other examples, do nothing to placate cynics convinced the whole thing is a ramp. In reality snooker is hard and relentless, being played out under the merciless glare of TV lights. You can safely carry on enjoying a wager. It isn't fixed.

The On-Course Jungle

The on-course betting ring is the hub of the world of betting. It is the wellspring of prices on which millions of off-course bets are settled, and the lure of its magnetic appeal never fails to entrance.

Odds were first called on a racecourse by William Ogden at Newmarket in 1790. The earliest betting ring was at Doncaster in the 1850s when starting prices, which varied, were regularly returned. The system was unified in 1926.

Tatts is the essence of the jungle – on big days a seething mass of excitement and activity, and even on quiet occasions at smaller courses a source of constant fascination. For here is the battle between punter and bookmaker in the raw, face to face, eyeball to eyeball. Here are the mechanics, the mathematics and the scheming marvel of the betting world in their purest form. Above all are the characters which make the betting jungle such an extraordinary habitat.

Bookmakers, quaintly alluded to as 'Satchel Swingers' by cricket's master commentator Richie Benaud, make the racecourse atmosphere. Go to Longchamp, Santa Anita, Tokyo or Woodbine – wonderful courses all – and something will be missing. Return to Cheltenham and you'll know what that absent ingredient is. The noise. The sound of scores of bookmakers calling the odds, the buzz of frenetic activity makes British and Irish racecourses unique in the din they generate.

(I know, they have on-course bookies in Australia, but they make a different clamour.)

And then there is the movement. Punters weaving in and out of bookmakers' joints in a mad scramble for the best value, thrusting wads of banknotes towards their chosen target in a desperate, lemming-like rush to get on before the price goes. Layers themselves deftly adjusting odds, and every now and then wiping the whole lot off and pricing up the complete field with a breathtaking assuredness. And tic-tacs, seemingly wildly semaphoring bets and price changes from one part of the racecourse market to another.

For sheer throbbing atmosphere, there's nothing like it. But what exactly is going on in this seething hubbub?

The main betting ring is in Tattersalls – on some courses called the Grandstand – enclosure. (Bookmakers are not allowed in the members' enclosure – hence their presence on the rails (see page 61)). Bookies also operate in the cheaper rings, but Tatts is where the dynamic action is.

Layers line up in rows, their position ('pitch') decided according to seniority. The pole positions are those in the front row nearest the entrance to the members' enclosure and the rails.

Boards bookmakers need a 'joint' (board, on which to chalk up prices, and the steel frame which supports it), a 'hod' (the bag or satchel) which will soon be groaning (they hope) with 'readies' (cash), the 'captain' (clerking book in which bets are registered), a 'mush' (umbrella) and 'briefs' (betting tickets).

Employees usually comprise a clerk, who stands at one side of the joint and enters every bet on a huge ledger as it is struck: each horse occupies one column, so that the clerk and bookmaker can assess at a glance liabilities on that runner. Then there is the 'floor-man', who acts as the bookmaker's ears and eyes in the rest of the ring, scurrying around to discover the prices others are betting at, listening to see what bets of significance are struck, and hedging at the top prices nearby when required. In this way the layer builds up an essential picture of who is backing what, and (if possible) why. For many that information is crucial, though others know nothing of

LET'S HAVE A LOOK!

When you visit the theatre or most sporting events, the whole spectacle is set before you. There is no moving from place to place. Not so on the great majority of racecourses.

Paddocks ideally should be sited in front of the stands, as at Doncaster or Newcastle. There jockeys ought to weigh in and presentations take place.

And instead of the horses – the stars of the show – charging haphazardly down to the start, they should always be paraded in racecard order (as occurs for Group One events) so that the paying spectator can obtain a proper view on offer without having to trek back and forth.

YOUNG AND OLD

By Spring 1992, only ten of Britain's fifty-nine racecourses regularly provided a creche! Channel Four Racing highlighted this absurdity at a time when tracks professed to be attracting families.

And there isn't even a universal policy of cheap entry for young people up to the age of 25, the racegoers of tomorrow (an obvious comment but short-sightedly not fully appreciated).

Most shameful of all, what about pensioners? Many have spent a lifetime 'coming racing', and it's about time courses recognised this by

form or gossip and simply aim to 'play the game', ideally make the favourite and second best losers, the third in 'takes the book' (ensuring no profit or loss on that race) and the rest are winners.

A bookmaker may take in a large amount of money over a single bet and often will reduce liabilities by 'laying off' (backing that horse himself) to other bookmakers in the ring – or, if betting in one of the cheaper enclosures, to the bigger firms in Tatts or on the rails (known as 'inside').

Staff will often do this betting with other layers through the intricate sign language of tic-tac, the basic signals of which you can learn on pages 114-17. The mass of signs being extravagantly waved throughout the rings, incomprehensible to the casual observer and even those who follow that cack-handed exponent of the art on Channel Four, conduct the flow of money around and between bookies. In order to give these transactions a degree of necessary secrecy time courses recognised this by offering substantial concessions – such as half-price entry, or less, and so on.

Scotland, in particular, has taken the lead. But managements failing to encourage youngsters and older folk (I've already applied for my bus pass) not only lack a social conscience but, far worse, fail to recognise the potential market. They may not be affluent big spenders, but in these hard times every bit helps.

Another disadvantaged group – literally – are the disabled. Sandown Park leads the way in facilities, but generally these are minimal afterthoughts even in many betting shops. At a time when all new public buildings have to be designed with the obligation to make life easier for the handicapped, racing lags well behind. Perhaps if all of us – including stewards and track bosses – had to spend just one day wheelchair-bound, action involving ramps, easily accessible entrances, toilets and viewing areas in front and behind stands, etc., would miraculously appear.

Those are three campaigns I won't drop: crèches, at least half-price entry for pensioners, and vastly improved facilities for the disabled.

Let's have action this day!

firms work off special cards with numbers different from the racecard, so that only those in the know can always be aware which horses are being backed.

Literally hundreds of millions of pounds are transmitted by signs alone. No words, nothing in writing, and yet provenly far more effective than walkie-talkies, time-wasting portable phones or any other modern short-distance communication. Trust and honour constitute the core of racecourse transactions.

Professional tic-tacs like Mickey 'Hokey' Stuart, Johnny Mack ('Whitenob') and Freddie Deverson ('Pink Card') act as inter-mediaries, brokers between one book-maker wishing to 'stand' a horse punters nearby won't come for, and another trying to put money on it, either at a bigger price than he has just laid or to cut down his lia-bility. And even just to back it like any other racegoer.

Course bookmakers must be aware of liabilities on each runner, in order to lay off when necessary – so that any particular out-come will not result in abnormal losses.

So there are two separate but related acti-vities going on throughout the often fre-netic minutes before any race: punters bet-ting and layers balancing books.

But what starts all this activity in motion? How do the bookmakers know the odds to price up soon after one race has been run?

It all begins with the 'tissue'. As I remind Channel Four Racing viewers early during each transmission, the tissue is the course bookmakers' forecast of how the market will open. Some firms do their own but generally it is compiled for them by a form and betting guru, who for each race has made a detailed analysis of the likely chances of each runner, allied to morning office moves, likely weight of money, public trends in the press, and 'informed' gossip. On this basis and an intuitive feel for the market, bookmakers receive odds, with around twenty per cent in their favour, so they can price up 'safely'.

Thereafter it is up to them. If especially keen to 'get' a particular horse because they reckon it will not win, or the odds seem too short, they will seek to attract money for it by offering a longer price. When wary of taking money for the opposite reason, they will keep its odds below the available rate to dissuade punters.

And operators everywhere, though more often in prime front pitches, are never averse to laying under the current odds to slapdash punters.

You can't blame them, but the principal reason for contracting prices is simple volume of money. If large sums go on, odds shorten. How much it takes to reduce any price varies according to its market position, source of the bet, and type of meeting. In the strongest rings – the Cheltenham Festival, or Royal Ascot – bets of several thousands of pounds are liberally struck, and have little effect. (In the 1991 Norfolk Stakes at Royal Ascot, bookmaker Stephen Little laid £100,000 to £50,000 (2-1) the winner Magic Ring – and it still went off 7-4 favourite.) At minor meetings, with weak markets, even small sums can have a significant influence on the odds. At Southwell in August 1991 a measly £200 office money resulted in a price plummeting from 7-1 to 3-1 favourite. As the money ebbs and flows, so do prices, as in any free market from the Stock Exchange downwards.

A big factor, of course, is just who is placing the bets. Bookmakers are familiar with 'faces' and 'shrewdies', whose investment has much more meaning than that of an ordinary punter. 'Faces', backers with that extra level of insight or inside information, know what they're doing (or reckon they do), and bets are treated with some respect.

The on-course jungle

Usually most important of all is money coming into the market from off-course bookmakers. When Ladbrokes send it down, their identity in tic-tac is like drawing a circle over the head – the 'Magic Sign' which alerts layers that this is Ladbrokes money. Immediately, like magic, prices are wiped off boards in anticipation – just like that!

Much fuss has been made about this practice of off-course bookmakers – and especially Ladbrokes – shovelling money into the racecourse market in order to shorten up certain horses' odds. How is it that often a very small amount of Ladbrokes' money can shrink the price of a horse which they know to have been well backed in their shops to reduce the SP, and consequently diminish returns? Aren't punters being deprived of

their full rightful gains by manipulation of the market?

Of course not! The essential point is that it is a *free* market. Anyone is able to invest, and if more off-course bookies emulated the 'Magic Sign' the whole system would be infinitely stronger. It would be ludicrous for the amount of money taken off-course not to be reflected in the ring and hedging is entirely legitimate though can be grotesquely abused when rushed down late.

But usually, though not always, heavy support for one horse results in others getting bigger in price. No complaints from their backers when they win!

Although illegal, there are still 'private layers'. They go racing and want to 'take money out of a horse', in other words act as bookmaker. To 'get' it they have to offer a bigger price than generally available. So if an animal is fluctuating between 'wrist' (5-4) and 'up the arm' (11-8), a tic-tac might

show 'ear 'ole' (6-4) *once*. That means one bookmaker, or perhaps a 'private layer', will lay 6-4.

Whether that's snapped up immediately (often by bookmakers who've already laid the shorter price) or is soon emulated indicates the current strength of that horse in the market.

As betting on a race progresses, moves are being monitored by at least two and sometimes four pressmen whose responsibility it is to return the official starting prices. From the *Sporting Life* and the Press Association, they liaise just after the 'off', comparing their independently arrived at notes of the market moves and agreeing the SPs. Sometimes there will be discrepancy and the resultant SP is a compromise. If one has a horse at 5-2 at the last knockings, and the other has it on offer in places at 3-1, they may well compromise at 11-4 if not enough strong layers are going 3-1. (This is how unusual prices, such as 21-20, split between evens and 11-10, or 19-2, between 9-1 and 10-1, are arrived at. For instance, variations in the odds against the 1990 Champion Hurdle winner Kribensis led to his being returned at 95-40, halfway between 9-4 and 5-2. Virtually no one will have laid 95-40 but the SP men felt that as most if not all of the 5-2 had dried up, it wouldn't be fair to return 9-4 – so they split the difference.)

Over the most ordinary race, the fate of tens of thousands of pounds rests upon such fractions; on the Grand National or the Derby, millions. Many disgruntled punters, annoyed at seeing their winner returned 6-4 when it was 13-8 at the last betting shop show from SIS, allege that the final odds are artificially compressed – that SP reporters deliberately compile prices lower than those actually available to money. Returners quite rightly take great exception to such slurs on their integrity – and often (though of course the grumblers don't mention this), the SP returns odds *longer* than the last show.

Vetabet, the independent analysers of all shows and returns, confirm that, over thousands of races, there is no discernible pattern. But punters remember and continually grouse when odds over their winners are shaved, yet accept, as though by divine right, should they lengthen.

As a rule of thumb, if you're backing a horse that is shortening up – say 11-4, 5-2 and 9-4, or 10-1, 8-1 and 15-2 – take the price. It is unlikely to bounce back late and could well contract further. But if it's been easy in the ring, say from 5-4 to 13-8, and you're not put off, hope that it will return 7-4, then don't take the price on offer.

Generally, when off-course money shortens up a horse others lengthen commensurately. That's the acceptable face of the system. What isn't occurs as money comes down so late that there is no time to adjust prices except cut that of the horse involved. There have been occasions when this becomes absolutely diabolical, and I've said so on the box. Firms have a moral responsibility to play fair. When they don't, inevitably and rightly, it fuels justified criticism.

If betting is often perceived by outsiders to be an impenetrably complex affair, the racecourse ring reveals it at its most baffling. But spend a few days prowling around, and you will soon discover how it works. Look and learn. You may well fall prey to so many of the fascinating vagaries and the conspiratorial aura that pervades everywhere. Someone somewhere is plotting and scheming.

It is noisy, hectic, colourful and engrossing.

Standing alone on a stool beside a joint,

RIGHT: Singin' – or is it yawnin'? – in the rain

BELOW A bookmaker literally 'makes a book'

as I've done, is nerve-wracking. Punters are circling sharks ready to grab at any mistake brought about by lack of concentration.

On the racecourse you bet tax-free, and there's nowhere on earth quite like it. I've said it before and I'll say it again: COME RACING!

And be sure, when you come, to take heed of the following. . . .

SP reporters, the *Sporting Life*'s John 'Wormwood' Stubbs (right) and professorial David Smalley (centre) of the Press Association returning prices in the 'huddle'

HEARD IN THE RING

'The splonk is tips with the thumb, exes bar.'

'It's cockle with the fiddlers.'

'Even pony down to me.'

'That ticket, sir, is from the joint over there. They don't like me paying out for them.'

'It's T.H. over there. Have a £50-6. On your bike!'

'Both bets are on the same ticket, madam.'

'If this thing wins I'll go to work.'

'Too late, sir, it's on my finger.'

'Fifty thousand floormen in Britain, and I get landed with you!'

'Who's running for us, then – the starter's hack?'

'How much does the bogey take out?'

'If that idiot on Channel Four again says the bookmakers are committing suicide, I'll kill him!'

'I told you to lay it, not back it!'

'A bank doesn't take bets and we don't cash cheques.'

'You can have half of that.'

'He never tried a light.'

COURSE HINTS

DON'T PANIC!

Many newcomers to racing are put off betting with bookmakers by what they see as the mystique of the betting ring. Here is a bedlam of incomprehensible shouting, waving and occasional bellowing (so much worse if Channel Four's man is there!), certainly no place for the novice.

But don't be daunted. Bookmakers are generally well-mannered (not always!) and patient. They want your custom.

For the uninitiated, you bet with a book-maker simply by approaching his pitch, offering him cash and stating the nature of your bet. So if he has evens Desert Orchid marked on his board and you want to have a fiver on it, say '£5 to win, Desert Orchid' – or, when you feel like doing the sums for him, 'an even fiver Desert Orchid'. (And see below about taking the fractions.) The bookmaker will give you a small numbered ticket (which is your receipt), and the clerk will note down the bet in the field book. Always note the bet on the back of the ticket, to avoid confusion if you can't remember which was struck with which bookmaker. When Desert Orchid wins, return to the same bookmaker, and upon presentation of your ticket you will be paid £10 – £5 winnings and your £5 stake back.

And always, on- and off-course, check winnings instantly. Never eagerly stuff the readies away without first ensuring the payout is correct.

INFORMATION

The best information to get on the racecourse is usually not about winners – everyone thinks they know them – but losers. If you reckon to know that a short-priced favourite is not expected to win, for whatever reason, all sorts of intriguing betting possibilities open up. But always remember, when attempting to glean genuine 'info', the old saying: 'Those who know don't talk, and those who talk don't know'.

FINDING THE CLUES

Going racing properly is hard work, and in order to collate all the clues you'll want to be in several places at once. Already you know about the weight, going, jockey, draw, form, and so on. But only the racecourse provides those essential last-minute clues. You'll need to be by the paddock to assess the condition of each horse. You must watch them going down to the start, study their action – some won't stride out on extremes of going – and look for any signs of untoward sweating or temperament. Also you'll want to be in the betting ring to interpret clues. But remember: because a horse shortens up, that doesn't necessarily mean it is going to win. Rather it demonstrates confidence, a clue in itself. Likewise, because a horse drifts (lengthens in price), that does not ensure defeat, but only confirms bookmakers are willing but can't take enough money for it, and *that* is significant.

THE LAST SHOWS AND THE STARTING PRICES

Statistics compiled by Mike Higgins of Vetabet on races (excluding evening meetings) run between 3 June 1991 and 6 June 1992 show that of winning horses in 6253 races:

Last show SAME as SP 4814 times (76.98%)

Last show SHORTER than SP 723 times (11.56%)

Last show LONGER than SP 716 times (11.46%)

Who is backing a particular horse, why are certain bookies out to 'get' (lay) another can be important. Ask yourself: why is an animal taking a walk in the market? If you reckon the reason is irrational, then step in. Afterwards you can be among those amazed at why the winner was returned at such a big price, having got on late.

A classic occurrence was before the 1991 Group One Sussex Stakes at Glorious Goodwood.

The Luca Cumani-trained Second Set, beaten a head by Marju in Royal Ascot's St James's Palace Stakes, had been quoted as low as 7-4 a few days before the race. But on the Tuesday Cumani's Coalite St Leger candidate Le Corsaire, at 5-2 on, finished a poor last of three in the Gordon Stakes. Jockey Frankie Dettori reported that the horse coughed twice in running and the trainer told the hacks his stable had been hit by the virus.

THE ODDS IN SLANG

Speed and secrecy are essential for the language of the betting ring. The common terms of betting slang are given on pages 59-61, but here are the usual slang expressions for the full range of odds. Some of the derivations are too obscure to discover, some come from tic-tac, some are simply the number spelt backwards (such as 'rouf' – pronounced to rhyme with 'loaf' – for 4).

evens	levels (or one to one or Scotch)
11-10	tips (or bits)
6-5	sais a ching
5-4	wrist (or hand to rouf)
11-8	up the arm
6-4	ear 'ole (or exes to rouf)
13-8	bits on the ear 'ole
7-4	shoulder (or neves to rouf)
15-8	double taps
2-1	bottle
9-4	top of the head (or enin to rouf)
5-2	face (or bottle and a half)
11-4	elef a vier
3-1	carpet (or tres or gimmel)
100-30	Burlington Bertie (or scruffy and dirty)
7-2	carpet and a half
4-1	rouf (or quat)
9-2	on the shoulders (or rouf and a half)
5-1	hand (or ching)
11-2	hand and a half (or ching and a half)
6-1	exes
13-2	exes and a half
7-1	neves
15-2	neves and a half
8-1	T.H.
9-1	enin
10-1	net (or cockle)
11-1	elef
12-1	net and bice
14-1	net and rouf
16-1	net and ex
20-1	score (or apple core or double net)
25-1	pony (or macaroni)
33-1	double carpet

Virtually no press tipster then went for Second Set and the *Racing Post* front page had a nudge-nudge-wink-wink splash headline: SECOND SET VIRUS FEARS FOR SUSSEX SHOWDOWN. After that few punters could bring themselves to back the colt who was duly knocked out in the market from 11-4 to touch 6-1 before late covering office money, which took more than £100,000 out of the ring in big bets alone, cut him back a point.

Second Set, though, hadn't heard the gossip and proceeded to bolt in, holding off 9-4 'jolly' Shadayid by 1½ lengths and amazing his loyal followers with around double their anticipated return. Had he lost badly, of course, the sinking feeling that, as the betting indicated, the creature indeed was sickening with flu would have been inescapable.

As in life so on the fertile breeding ground of innuendo and 'psst' whispers, the racetrack, sussing out reliability or otherwise of gossip and rumour is never easy. When proved right, bombastic know-all 'I told you so' merchants abound. And, as you can imagine, those who got 5-1, and even 11-2 and 6-1 Second Set, were pretty

Mickey 'Hokey' Stuart – 'the fastest hands in the West'

insufferable too.

Fortunately, as you know from long experience, Channel Four's fat windbag has never been guilty of passing on unsubstantiated tittle-tattle from the ring – ever!

TAKE THE FRACTIONS!

Fractions are so important. Never *ever* have a fiver or a tenner on a 6-1, 7-1, 8-1 chance. Rather construct your bet around the 'fractions' which the great majority of racecourse bookmakers will give you. So if your horse is on offer at 6-1, ask for a 'pony'

(£25) to 4, or £50 to 8 or £100 to 16. At 7-1, £50 to 7, £100-14. Or at 8-1, £50 to £6, £100-12. In each case you will be winning a fraction over the advertised odds. A bet of £8 on a 6-1 chance wins £48 instead of £50. (If any bookmaker won't accept 'fracs', find one who will: it won't take a moment.) The more familiar fractions include:

100-6 (16-1) = $16\frac{2}{3}$-1
100-7 (14-1) = $14\frac{2}{7}$-1
100-8 (12-1) = $12\frac{1}{2}$-1
100-9 (11-1) = $11\frac{1}{9}$-1

(continued on page 118)

113

AN 'EXPERT' GUIDE TO TIC-TAC . . .

odds on

evens ('levels')

11-8 ('up the arm')

6-4 ('ear 'ole')

11-10 ('tips')

5-4 ('wrist')

7-4 ('shoulder')

9-4 ('top of the head')

. . . NOW YOU KNOW WHY THIS MAN IS UNEMPLOYA

5-2 ('face')

3-1 ('carpet')

5-1 ('hand')

10-1 ('net')

4-1 ('rouf')

9-2 ('on the shoulders')

33-1 ('double carpet')

50-1

An on-course betting shop – never let me catch you having a punt in one of these!

Never have £3 on a 'double carpet' (33-1) chance – ask for £100 to £3 or even £1000 to £30. So don't hesitate. Stride up to the bookmaker and confidently demand 'a pony to four' about his 6-1 shot.

You can't take the 'fracs' in most betting shops, though now one or two chains are offering the concession.

BETTING AT AN 'AWAY' MEETING

One thing that never ceases to amaze me on racecourses is the sight of punters queueing up at the track's betting shops, run either by the Tote, individual bookmakers, or layers combined under the banner of NARBOL (National Association of Racecourse Betting Offices Ltd). All bets are subject to a 6 per cent deduction, yet a few yards away course bookmakers are going tax free.

Make no mistake. Betting with the 'aways' – as bookies pricing up races at other meetings are called – requires a degree of common sense. Firms have their tic-tacs relaying SIS odds. So if they put 'ear 'ole' (6-4) the 'jolly', you can rest assured it won't in reality be a 'wrist' (5-4) chance!

The only way to make sure you're not 'turned over' is to insist on the starting price. No responsible 'away' layer will demur at such a request. That works for single bets. Yet so many are tamely handed over to racecourse betting shops, where board prices can't be taken and there's that hideous tax. And if you fancy a £1 'away' Yankee, or bigger, you'll soon find a layer, probably on the rails, pleased to accept the business and have you as a customer.

The only time I want to see you near a NARBOL counter is when checking the odds on offer before darting out to get on SP in Tatts, watching the race on SIS, or perusing results.

Don't be so naïve as to give yourself 6 per cent less when you do 'cop' – away.

EACH-WAY TERMS

At last, after a long campaign, the fractions of the full odds which course bookmakers give about placed horses are now advertised in racecards. Mercifully, the monstrous days when a bookmaker need not pay out on the fourth in sixteen-runner plus handicaps, as they do in betting shops, are behind us. So make sure your bookie adheres to these agreed each-way terms:

Non-handicaps:

2-4 runners	win only
5-7	one quarter odds first two
8+	one fifth odds first three

Handicaps:

2-4 runners	win only
5-7	one quarter odds first two
8-11	one fifth odds first three
12-15	one quarter odds first three
16+	one quarter odds first four

All handicaps of five or more runners ought to be a quarter the odds. Do away with the one-fifth 8-11 runners nonsense. Some firms oblige, and even improve on these terms, paying 1-2-3-4 in fifteen-runner handicaps. And, at big meetings, you can usually obtain quarter the odds all handicaps. A few offer that as a regular concession. Shop around! The number of runners relates to those coming under starter's orders: just think how many times layers are let off paying out on the fourth in a sixteen-runner handicap when a late withdrawal reduces the field to fifteen. I'm sick of harping on these infuriating instances on the air, and they do *seem* to occur more often in eight- and sixteen-runner races.

If a bookie tries to 'flimp' (underpay) you, complain at once to the Ring Inspector. He is employed by the Jockey Club for,

among other duties, ensuring fair play between racegoers and layers. Bookmakers, quite rightly, are not compelled to bet each way. But those that do must comply to the accepted off-course terms. And the sooner large signs on every racecourse indicate exactly where the Ring Inspector can be located the better. Why keep so anonymous, lads?

BETTING IN RUNNING

Betting in running – that is, during the race when the bookmaker will adjust the odds as the contest unfolds – is best viewed as an insurance policy. But make sure that you know as much as the bookmaker: he will be watching the race as well, and you'll have to be a pretty expert race-reader to spot something which you can turn to your advantage. If the favourite was 2-1 on at the last show and a bookmaker is offering evens in running, that horse is in deep, deep trouble.

But there is advantage to be had if you back an outsider in running. Say you're on the favourite, and with two furlongs to go he and the 'rag' are clear of their rivals, so that it's roughly evens which is going to win, the bookmaker might offer you 2-1 against the outsider, because if at 'double carpet ' (33-1) the animal might be a 'skinner' (unbacked), so why not get it in the book at 'bottle' (2-1).

STEWARDS' ENQUIRIES

Nothing provokes more controversy than winners being disqualified in the stewards' room. Notorious cases in big races alone, such as Nureyev (1980 Two Thousand Guineas), Royal Gait (1988 Ascot Gold Cup), If Memory Serves (1990 Pigot Diamond Ladies' Stakes), Cahervillahow (1991 Whitbread Gold Cup) and Topanoora (1991 Hardwicke Stakes) still rankle.

(continued on page 123)

119

BETTING ON PHOTO FINISHES

Television freeze-frames of the finish, shown instantly around racecourses, have helped to take much of the fun out of hectic 'insurance' betting while the judge scrutinises the negative and sometimes the print.

But angles, as we are constantly told by commentators hard pressed for anything else to say, can be tricky, especially the sprinting straights up the centre of Kempton and Sandown, and the notorious Windsor and Chester finishes. Unless the television camera is spot on the line anyone can be deceived.

Worst used to be Newbury and Redcar, where the cameras have been sited well short of the line and the horses went away from the viewer.

At Chester's May meeting in 1991 virtually everyone reckoned that Jack Berry's two-year-old Tino Tere (2-1 favourite) had held on to win the Lily Agnes Stakes from Chadleigh House (5-1). On the replay that indeed appeared the outcome, and one punter, absolutely convinced that the favourite had held on, raced round the ring taking any price he could. His bets, including £2000 to win £100 and £1000 to win £50 (both 20-1 on), and £1000 to win £100 (10-1 on), and others, along with hefty wagers made by other punters (including £600 to £1800) were losers when eventually Chadleigh House was declared the winner by – as the print showed – the very tip of her nostril. (How much better it would be to emulate the French and have a new distance – a nose.)

And at Epsom on the eve of the 1991 Oaks, market leaders Stop Press (9-4 favourite) and Adversary (11-4) flashed past the post together in the Sun Life of Canada Handicap. On Channel Four GG (Graham Goode) called Stop Press the winner, and that was the initial reaction. Then one layer asked for 8-1 (you could bet £80 to win £10, or £8000 to win £1000!), followed by 6-1 on, 4-1 on, and suddenly 7-4 on as it was realised that Adversary's last-gasp counterthrust might even have prevailed.

Soon it was evens each of two, take your pick. On the rails Stephen Little laid £5000-£5500 Adversary and another punter had an even £2000 with him. Five 'monkeys' (£500 at 5-1) were taken on a dead heat, which, as the time agonisingly went by, contracted to 2-1.

At the end there was almost as much betting on the photo as the race itself, with replays from various angles being minutely studied. Eventually Stop Press was announced the winner and the official print revealed just how close it had been.

We should all have listened to the original call of eagle-eyed GG!

If a 'rag' at 'double carpet' (33-1) seems to have touched off the favourite, or another well-backed runner, some bookmakers like to 'insure' themselves. So they're often delighted to have 2-1 bet on a beast that only a minute or two before was 'out with the washing'.

For the patient racegoer it's easy money, but beware. If the result is reversed at a subsequent Stewards' Enquiry, or the winner fails to weigh in, then photo-finish bets are settled on the eventual official outcome.

All the same, betting 2-1 on when you've seen the animal indisputably pass the post in front can't be bad. And such 'generosity' happens more often than you think!

(*Above*) Chadleigh House touches off Tino Tere – and (*below*) Stop Press short-heads Adversary

PRINCE MONOLULU

A legend among racecourse tipsters was 'Ras' Prince Monolulu. Forever bellowing his raucous catch-phrase, 'I Gotta Horse, I Gotta Horse', he became one of those unforgettable racecourse personalities whose absence has removed so much flamboyance from the racing scene. In truth, of course, he was no more a Prince than you or I (well, at least I). Born in Abyssinia in the 1880s, he went through life as an inveterate rogue and charlatan, but the racing public loved him.

Married at least four times, Monolulu (real name Peter Mackay) freeloaded around the world, often ending up in jail, but always pretending to hobnob with Royalty and the gentry, owners, trainers and jockeys. In reality, it was a lonely, often sordid existence for a lewd spiv, ever on the lookout for mugs.

Yet people flocked to buy tips from this strange figure in the feathered head-dress. He tried to sell one of his sixpenny specials to the Duke of Windsor, and dismissed Hitler as 'that German monkey'. And his patter never ceased. 'I'm Prince Monolulu

'I Gotta Horse!' – and some fillies

from sunny Honolulu', he'd assure his followers, as he'd launch into one of his famous rhymes:

God made the bees,
The bees made the honey,
The public back the favourites
And the bookies take the money.

His tipping career reached its zenith with the 1920 Derby. 'Have your shirt and a pound on Spion Kop,' he proclaimed, 'and don't forget the Darkie told you.' The colt obliged.

I remember seeing him nearly thirty years ago, shortly before he died. A shabby, hunchbacked, tired old man – the feathers were drooping, the dirty outfit stank. But the myth and the legend that was Monolulu endure, and every Derby Day he's remembered and missed by thousands on Epsom Downs.

Birds will sing,
Bells they ring,
Bees they will make honey.
Punters always study form,
The Bookie takes the money.
Black man for Luck,
White man for Pluck.

For decades Monolulu, a lifelong victim of crude racism, was among the Turf's best-known characters. Yet racegoers from the ethnic minorities remain infinitesimally few in number, despite being keen betting shop punters.

So whatever your colour or background, whether you're an Abyssinian Prince of the Blood or poor and common like me, Come Racing.

I'll look after you!

We go racing and bet on the outcome, not stewards' opinions on anything that should, or ought, or might have occurred.

Some betting shops, especially in Scotland, pay first past the post. And a few independents offer a tremendous concession – settling both first past the post and the eventual winner. But no one pays out on a race declared void, for reasons such as the whole field accidentally taking the wrong course.

Now surely, as in greyhound racing, settling bets, prize money and future penalties should defend on the actual result. Diehards maintain that a jockey, desperate to win at any cost, will force a rival over the rails or deliberately swerve into him close home.

Nonsense. Jockeys have to go on riding, and that behaviour could lead to a warning-off for years, even life, and maybe bring on a criminal prosecution. Penalise jockeys by all means, but not owners, trainers, punters and bookmakers. Put an end to 'interpretation' of what might have happened if . . .

Nothing provokes incidents, and causes horses to swerve, more than the whip. Imagine for one moment that whips had never been invented. Someone then produces one and starts hitting his horse. We would be outraged just as if now electrodes were applied to an animal's private parts.

Racing is a public spectacle and more and more people are sickened at the sight of whips flailing. Without them, except as aids to balance or straightening a horse by tapping it around the shoulder, results would be much the same, with the best horses and jockeys coming out on top. Limiting the use of the whip to ten strokes, as at present, is like giving a man a machine gun with instructions to fire single rounds! It's tinkering with something that's fundamentally indefensible.

MEDIA MESS-UPS

(To spare embarrassing beetroot-like blushes, names have where necessary been changed or omitted.)

Following one big race a leading broadcaster exclaimed over his talkback (the programme's internal communication system): 'Oh my God, we can't have the trainer on – the man's a crook!' Down in the unsaddling enclosure this observation had been picked up by an assiduous assistant who sidled up to his front man and exclaimed: 'We mustn't interview the trainer – Brian says he's a crook!' Unbeknown to the assistant, the trainer concerned was well within earshot, and, incandescent with rage, stalked off spluttering and muttering unprintable retorts not exactly complimentary to Brian. Anyone wondering why no comments were forthcoming on air that day now knows the reason.

*

Before a Derby one trainer kindly allowed Channel Four to film his contender in the yard. After walking the horse up and down interminably to get the best shots, he gave a wide-ranging interview. Then we all went across to his sumptuous abode and were plied with champagne and plenty to eat. Altogether a splendidly convivial evening.

But on the Tuesday morning at Epsom, the eve of Derby Day, a local television company unfortunately decided to solicit my worthless opinion of the prospects. Pointing to the nearby horse we had visited only two days earlier, I blurted out: 'That's one who cannot possibly win. Look at him. He's a rat of a horse – a horrible little thing.'

My inexcusable rudeness was overheard by the trainer's charming wife, who turned witheringly and said: 'That really wasn't very nice, was it? We did try and be hospitable the other day.' Collapse of fatso, stammering meaningless, confused apologies.

A year or two later Channel Four went round to the same yard for another pre-Derby feature and, still ashamed, I wisely was a non-runner this time. That made no difference. Halfway through the filming, the good lady stumbled on the crew and, enraged at their presence, went ballistic, unleashing a torrent of invective before sending the whole lot packing.

One lesson from all this, apart from remembering never to be rude and insensitive: Insult wives, husbands, even children, and you'll probably be forgiven. But never refer in derogatory terms to horses or pets. Such slurs are harboured long after paeans of praise have been forgotten.

*

Just before giving a shriek from the betting ring in a race when Princess Anne had a ride, the panic-stricken voice of executive producer Andrew Franklin came down my earpiece: 'For goodness' sake, John, don't whatever you do say that the bookies want to lay Princess Anne!' The thought had never occurred to me!

Every sympathy for a colleague, when relaying a trainer's comment that his horse 'never leaves an oat' actually said, 'he never leaves a note!'

*

In an amateur riders' event at Newmarket, a few small bets were noted at 'double carpet' (33-1) for the animal ridden by John Oaksey's offspring Sara. 'They're nibbling at your daughter down here, my Noble Lord,' I informed our very own paddock commentating peer – and anyone else who happened to be listening.

*

Try and guess the identity of my Channel Four colleague who observed: 'There, on the favourite, is the unmistakable Pat Eddery' – long pause, gasp – 'or is it Willie Carson?'

*

My apologies to the jockey I accidentally described as having 'pissed a fatness test'. Coming from me, of all people!

Supporters argue that Lester Piggott, for example, wouldn't have won two of his Derbys (Roberto 1972 and The Minstrel 1977) without those rat-a-tat explosive finishes. So what? Beating animals in the name of sport is degrading and unacceptable.

In time it will be outlawed. Why not immediately?

No TAX

The great advantage of betting on race-courses rather than in betting shops is that bets made with a course bookmaker are no longer liable to tax (usually 10 per cent off course). This applies to *any* bet struck with a course layer, not just on that day's racing. So if you fancied lumping a large amount of money on, say, a General Election, go along to the racecourse (though make sure in advance that a course bookmaker will take the bet at the odds you want). Non-Tote bets struck at course offices of Tote Credit are liable to 2 per cent commission (scandalous!), and bets made in the course betting shop to 6 per cent. If known – and that's crucial – you can usually bet in cash with a rails bookmaker, so let's have no more of these stories of punters dumping a bag full of £50,000 in readies onto the betting shop counters – that's strictly for mugs!

(But most course bookies are wary of big wagers on each-of-two events like snooker and tennis. Understandably, many simply don't want to know.)

Tory Chancellor Nigel Lawson's abolition of the 4 per cent on-course betting tax in the 1987 Budget was the finest and most welcome government intervention in racing since betting shops were opened twenty-six years earlier. Thanks, Nigel, old bean.

SHOPPING AROUND

The other great benefit of betting on the racecourse is it gives you the opportunity to choose between different bookies' sets of prices, and shopping around can often reap handsome dividends. It requires, however, alertness, and the ability to nip in quick as soon as you spot the price you want.

Firms have no great love for one another. Competition is keen and for various reasons, either to balance their books or 'get' a particular horse, someone somewhere will be offering over the odds.

A desolate, soggy Silver Ring – if you turned all the sufferers upside down, fifty quid wouldn't roll out of the lot of 'em

Make sure you're around at the right time. And don't be rushed into striking a bet by the floorman shouting up to his guv-'nor, 'Quick, the 9-4 has gone, it's 2-1 on the rails!' That's a come-on. More likely the rails bookmakers are offering 5-2! But if you hear the floorman whispering, 'Quick, no more "top of the head [9-4]", it's "bottle [2-1] with the thumb [good, that price is being taken]",' try then and get on your £90 to £40.

And there's always 'unorthodox' betting – that's without the favourite, to be second to the favourite, winning distances, etc. Bookies are never shy of offering a wide variety of betting opportunities. Get stuck into them if you reckon they've made a 'rick' (error).

And the best of luck to you!

WOE ON THE PITCHES

Every day is Eureka Time for punters, according to Dave Saphir, a leading boards layer.

Echoing a profound pessimism, long nurtured within the world's second oldest profession, Saphir reckons the game has become 'horrendous'. The rest of us, struggling against all sorts of vicissitudes to find the next winner, will retort that he would say that, wouldn't he? But as a failed race-course operator myself it is not so hard to understand the current wave of unease.

Blaming, principally, everyday expenses – an average per joint of £250 – and 'too many books chasing too little money in often contracted rings', Saphir has all but the most cynical reaching for handkerchiefs as the tears of sympathy well up while he vividly describes their plight.

But Saphir, whose opinions invariably

are worth listening to, is not a man prone to reckless exaggeration. And southern rings are still reeling from the default in 1990 of independent rails operator Duggie Goldstein, with accounts reckoned in excess of £600,000 unpaid, and the judgment of Tattersalls Committee not to recognise any claims though, in practice, there is little they can do.

Yet there is nothing new in layers being unable to collect. Virtually since the dawn of time, knockers have been the bane of layers, though rarely from within their own kind. Until gambling debts become recoverable in law, like anything else, that will continue to be so. And the lukewarm attitude of so many towards reform means there remains a lack of any serious impetus for change.

At Goodwood in 1990 Don Morris ('Taffy') cited the example of the opener at Brighton the previous evening when 6-5 favourite Port Vauban beat Zloty (6-4) with Bastin third at 10-1 after opening at 4-1.

The front pair were both available at 6-4 while the 14-1 and 16-1 'rags' had been offered at 'double carpet' (33-1) and a 'pony' (25-1). On these figures they bet to 95.7 per cent and Morris called this another case of 'giving our money away'. There are numerous other similar instances.

Agreed, pouncing at just the right time for the best price isn't easy, though controversial rails layer John Pegley put it starkly: 'Time and again we bet overbroke where it's possible to back every horse and show a profit. There's not enough money going around to fill the books up. Any punter seriously fancying his chances must come racing. No-one can bet off course, taking SPs with 10 per cent tax and make it pay.'

And, along with many others, he pinpointed the source of so many bets circulat-

WEIGHING IN – HORSES AND JOCKEYS

How tolerant British punters can be.

In season after season come instances of jockeys on winners or placed horses failing for one reason or another to weigh in.

Objections by clerks of the scales (often after bets have been settled on and off course) are always upheld, and they would result in riots in less phlegmatic countries.

In America such nonsense cannot happen. On dismounting in front of the stands every rider, unlike usually only the first four over here, has to sit on the scales before being allowed back to the paddock area.

The time is surely not far off when all jockeys weigh in, with none conceivably being able to avoid, or forget, the scales. An end to these infuriating amateurish shambles in weighing rooms is long overdue.

And also overdue is the public announcement of horses' racing weights. Modern progressive trainers regularly weigh their horses. A sharp loss, such as Ibn Bey's forty pounds before flopping in the 1989 Japan Cup, can be an instructive guide to any animal's well-being.

Yet the public aren't given this information, though they are in Tokyo. It would be quite simple to emulate greyhound racing and weigh every animal on arrival at the course. Whether it matters noting fluctuating or constant poundage (I suppose it would all be done in those foreign kilo things) is beside the point.

Punters are entitled to be told.

A Tatts bookmaker, not renowned for generosity or laying 'thick' (big) bets, called out after a close finish: 'I'll take 10-1'.

A workman rushed up asking for £2000 to win £200.

'Nothing', was the reply.

'Well, let me have a "grand" [£1000] on.'

'Nothing.'

'Alright, I'll have a couple of hundred on.'

'No you won't – anyway, you've got no money.'

'I know that', countered the disconsolate workman, 'but I've got to get the fare home from somewhere!'

explains, 'as the odds have been extended before the offices come in and then they shorten up sometimes too late for others to be pushed out.'

'Lord of the Ring' Colin Webster has recently decamped his operation down from Leeds and reckons racecourses in the South, with more activity, offer punters better prospects than northern tracks. But all over the country, he complains, 'it's like trying to sell without customers'.

Outspoken Micky 'Asparagus Kid' Fletcher is contemptuous of his fellows, saying: 'If bookmakers had to pass an exam most would fail. They've no ability. Ninety per cent are born into the game. They inherit the best pitches. It's almost impossible for young blood to come in.' True enough, until the Racecourse Association have the guts, gumption and ingenuity to open up rings by allowing the buying and selling of pitches with adequate safeguards.

On his front row boards pitch Sam Harris acknowledges, as do all bookmakers, how well informed the public are these days. 'Just after the war,' he recalled wistfully, 'the game was so good. So were the figures and the punters didn't understand what was going on. Now Channel Four's Saturday *Morning Line* is just the latest benefit for them. They've got the trade papers, especially the *Racing Post's* Pricewise, *Timeform*, SIS, television, everything.'

John Banks has seen it all and he confessed: 'The game mystifies me. With so many bookmakers turning punter it's become tougher than ever simply to survive.'

And the racecourse is not the place to find criticism of the major firms sending money down. They know that without Ladbrokes – the 'Magic Sign' – and others to a far lesser extent it would be impossible even attempting to make a book. A free market

ing around. 'It's bookmakers turning into backers. There's no doubt it's far harder for us than betting shops. Punters there don't know what they're doing and SPs are always over-round.'

And before irate gamblers, usually losing ones, point to the hundreds of races where the figures top up to a ghastly 130 per cent plus, remember you can always choose when, and when not, to have a slice of the action. Tax-free betting is one of the huge bonuses on British racecourses and the benefits to average punters compensate for high admission charges far, far more than in Tote monopolies, where the take-out can be up to 30 per cent.

Neal Wilkins, the Press Association's chief SP reporter, advises shop *habitués* not to settle for the closing price but opt instead for the show three or four minutes before the off.

'That's when there is greatest value,' he

needs more, not less, off-course money poured into it.

On a wider perspective, one of the top independents, Stephen Little, argues: 'Racecourse bookmaking is one of the most competitive businesses in the world. Nowhere else do you get so many trying to sell the same thing in one place.'

Veteran tic-tac Mickey 'Hokey' Stuart sums it up: 'Punters are so well educated. They even get news from trainers' quarters and meanwhile the books are fighting each other to get clients. But even though the abolition of on-course tax was a great help, the fact is that on the 1990 Derby, I was involved in only fourteen bets compared to 217 when Mill Reef won in 1971.'

Throughout all the catalogue of woe, you'll notice, no one mentioned those halcyon days of twenty years ago when all eight-runner races were a quarter the odds 1-2-3 and 12-1 was 100-8, 14-1 was 100-7, etc. Though, unlike in betting shops, on the course you can still get the 'fracs'.

How extraordinary it all is that bookies, along with farmers, are always moaning, but big and small punters come and go and only a handful of racegoers show a regular profit. Year in, year out, the same tongues still shout the odds from their precious pitches. However, whether you believe the bookies or not – and I suspect few do – one thing everyone is agreed upon. To have any chance of beating them consistently, avail yourself of their 'generosity' over prices and bet tax free. Come Racing!

SCREENS!

Racing around the world enjoys the benefits of huge TV screens situated in front of the stands.

Technology is available, and thanks to sponsorship, Goodwood, Liverpool, Newmarket and York have shown how effective and popular they are.

Crowds gasp with excitement and buzz in animated debate as incidents and photo-finishes are replayed. And they can be taken paddock-side and to the unsaddling enclosure for returning horses and presentations.

Top sporting events in America and elsewhere offer this facility, so do the main athletics meetings. Even cricket at the Oval has at last caught on.

Priority should be to install screens, maybe mobile ones, on major tracks at least, and do away with cumbersome, outdated number boards. To pay for them, there's sponsorship and the extra millions racecourses have collected from SIS since 1987. Or is that totally unexpected bonanza being frittered away?

And while we're on about electronics, when is sectional timing, with all its imperfections, at last going to be mandatory at all courses?

McCririck AT LARGE

A Tale of Shameless Skulduggery

The opening day of the Cheltenham Festival in 1972 is recalled with no small feeling of ignominy – and only publicly now because the central participant has passed on.

In those days, At Large used to scratch a precarious living as an inept floorman, tea-boy, junior partner and arch schemer in minor rings. He had inveigled himself into a firm with a pitch in the centre enclosure, opposite the stands. Transport was a major headache but various pick-ups on the outskirts of London ensured a viable (i.e. trustworthy) car, loaded with guv'nors and workmen.

We set out that morning, like any other, buoyed up with hope. Syd 'The Snot' joined the three of us at White City with a mate of his. Now Syd, flat-nosed ex-pugilist with permanent nasal congestion, belonged to the rough school of pre-war bookies and was one of those unpleasant characters you could do without. Habitual loud abuse used to be heaped on his hapless clerk and floorman. And since he operated next to us, it was a quirk of fate not the least in our favour.

Syd, moreover, between incessant sniffs, could talk. His voice punctuated journeys to the races. Opinions, and occasionally hilarious one-liners, poured forth on every horse on the card, and about crooked plots. A persistent theme dwelt on how he was going to crack it 'this time'.

So we settled down, awaiting the monologue. For once it never came. Pensively settled in the back, Syd seemed morose. Since his pal kept stumm, the rest of us were content to leave them undisturbed. However, when The Snot pushed to the front of the queue in the transport caff and insisted on paying for all our breakfast fry-ups it became clear something odd was afoot. For the remainder of the journey the normally loquacious Syd let the banter pass and, by the time we had set up our joints, the atmosphere between us was more of curiosity than open hostility.

As always, readies were scarce, and if firms like ours reefed up more than a 'monkey' (£500) between us we were already flying.

Syd's intentions never changed: come with little – go home loaded. Invariably, that was the plan, but the fact that he still scuffled around the barren outer regions like the rest of us showed how rarely it had been successfully executed.

In those days the Aldsworth Hurdle, now the Sun Alliance, commenced proceedings. Celtic Cone, unbeaten over hurdles, winner of the previous year's Ascot Stakes and favourite for the Cesarewitch, was the banker, napped all over the place, and regarded as a laydown. But he had been prone to jumping errors, so we set out to give him a right stripping which, for us, meant the full monkey touch.

A Celtic Cone victory would confine the rest of the day to ducking and diving. The price we got him at was all-important. So we stood back amazed as Syd, not normally the most generous of our colleagues, chalked up 'wrist' (5-4) Celtic Cone when the tic-tacs from Tatts were sending first 'tips' (11-10) and then 'levels' (evens) 'with the thumb' (being taken). Pounds, fivers and tenners flooded in as Syd took on all-comers and despite the ever-shortening price he continued trading over the odds.

Then I overheard him confirming he'd laid an even grand (£1000) inside (to Tatts) twice! This was far beyond Syd's, and our, league and still he was smashing away, going 100-8 bar one (8-1 and 10s with us). At such competitive prices we were virtual spectators as punters clamoured around Syd's joint, though having £500-£550 bet on Celtic Cone inside quite late suited us fine.

Near the off, he loudly confirmed £1000-£1100 and several £1000-£80s and £1000-£70s other contenders. Heady stuff, and when Even Dawn, a 40-1 'skinner' beat the 8-11 shot by two lengths, we were ecstatic for ourselves – and not a little envious of The Snot's right tickle.

'How much then?' I whispered to his clerk as the euphoria subsided. 'Took it, took the lot,' he muttered shamefacedly, pointing to a single bet in the Even Dawn column of £5000-£150 laid to the tic-tacs.

Absolutely unbelievable. To stand Celtic Cone for more than four grand, take plenty out of the others, then get a blinding result, yet cop nothing when he could have had the bogey back at 40-1, having laid 'double carpet' (33-1) was stupefying.

So the momentous day went on. Second favourite Royal Relief was worse than odds-on Straight Fort for Syd, though not us, in the Champion Chase; the Tom Jones-trained double, Clever Scot (11-1) and Jomon (8-1), was 'no good' for him and the rucks after 20-1 Charley Winking took the National Hunt Chase were truly horrendous.

The air was alive with expletives (numerous) deleted. Remarks such as 'Should have backed it back' and 'Why wasn't Syd told', 'I told you so' and 'Why won't you ever listen to me?'

Coming to the last contest, having gone 'bar one' (not laid) the Jones pair, we were enjoying the bonanza of our lives with Syd suffering his 'worst day ever'. He had to be the only losing layer on that Black Tuesday for punters, topped up when 16-1 Noble Life caught the future dual winner of the Champion Hurdle, Comedy of Errors, in a desperate finish to the Gloucestershire Hurdle.

'We fell for it. They picked me out like a ripe lemon,' snorted The Snot. His heart-rending misery only enhanced our perverse joy at the prospect of sharing out nearly six grand. In the bar before leaving it was doubles all round for us. It was there that Syd's clerk revealed all.

'Ignore his act,' he whispered, 'the steam tug [mug] is shell-shocked. He can't believe what's hit him. He's confused with all those hundreds of bets we took and only knows he's done four long 'uns [£4000] in readies. Syd decided a quick extraction was better than prolonging the agony over three days. There was no more to come from the steam tug. He was only playing up a fluked betting shop yankee.'

So that's who Syd's quiet pal was. A naïve 'sticker in', doomed to last but one traumatic afternoon as a partner in the heady glamorous world of racecourse bookmaking.

How the bloke ever left the track, with those results, not realising he'd been well and truly stitched up, none of us ever knew. The journey home was tactfully spent in reflective silence.

The next day there was an empty place in the car as The Snot obnoxiously bubbled. He was in top form, richer by nearly £10,000 after phoney 'bets' on long-priced winners had been rubbed out of the book. Why they always came to be the last entries on those horses, the steam tug never got to find out. Syd simply regaled us with how he was going to 'take on the ring' and stand odds-on Bula 'for the bank' in the Champion Hurdle.

The plaintive, nasal whining, and bitter re-criminations on the return have scarred me for life.

But in a strange way justice was, at least partly, done.

7

Coups and Gambles, Stratagems and Schemes

As far as most betting shop punters are concerned there is little doubt that nearly everyone professionally involved in racing is as crooked as a corkscrew. You have only to listen to their cynical post-race analysis to know that.

Speaking through their pockets maybe, but cases like the much publicised one last year involving Harry Bardsley, the gambler and 'race-fixer', who was exposed by the Sun *newspaper, certainly provide fuel for their cynicism. And if those backers made it their business to talk to certain sections of racing folk, they might be forgiven for thinking that many top jockeys are 'on the take', a good proportion of trainers solely concerned with bringing off betting coups, and bookmakers the villainous paymasters behind every evil on the Turf.*

John Karter wrote that in *The Times* in 1985, eloquently expressing the popular view of racing's rectitude – it doesn't exist.

The notion that it must be incorrigibly bent persists. Doping, stopping, foul riding, cleverly planned coups to deceive bookmakers, bizarre methods of preventing horses from winning (such as the absurd 'stun gun' affair) or of making them go faster (with jockeys concealing batteries under their silks, running a wire down to a

contact point held in the hand and administering an electric shock to the horse) – to hear some people talk, you'd think that dishonesty and fraud were rife.

All sports attract cheats. You only have to think of the Olympic fencing scandal, or Ben Johnson's drugs in Seoul to enhance performance, the ghastly Maradona and 'the hand of God', and dozens of other notorious examples, to establish that.

Racing involves a vast amount of money slushing around, and a seemingly endless repertoire of ways to prevent its doing so legitimately. Inevitably there are stroke merchants, but it is certainly cleaner now than ever before. Proven doping was back to haunt racing in 1990, with high-class horses Bravefoot and Norwich victims at Doncaster's St Leger meeting. Culprits should be locked up and the key thrown away, endangering as they do the lives of horses and jockeys. Riders and trainers are hauled in for non-trying, and occasionally handed out severe sentences, but 'stopping' a horse – deliberately preventing it from winning to benefit from the betting market, fool the handicapper or ensure a longer price in a later event – is highly difficult to execute in these days of all-seeing camera patrols.

But racegoers at Kelso on 1 February 1991, and those watching on SIS, were aghast at the outrageous ride given Flowing River, trained by Dick Allan and ridden by Brian Storey, threading his way delicately through the whole field from after the last hurdle, to arrive in front ten yards past the post. The horse would have won easily had he not been prevented from doing so, and that brainstorm cost Storey, and trainer Allan, a three-month suspension.

Other examples are far less easy for the stewards to prove. And proof, good enough to stand up in a court of law, is required before livelihoods can be taken away.

It is glib to maintain that a certain horse 'wasn't off'. Proving it is the problem.

In any case, what punters should fear far more than the horse being deliberately 'stopped' is the one out for the run, who will win if it can but is not expected to. Whether a horse is in a position to run to its best – given the course, the distance, the going, its work at home, and so on – is the very fabric of racecourse gossip, and has a material effect on market moves. If the ordinary punter were privy to all the information about horses not expected to succeed, he would avoid backing many losers – and miss the odd winner at a surprisingly big price too!

That racing in Britain is as straight as it is can largely be attributed to the increased vigilance of the Jockey Club.

Film patrols on the racecourse allow the stewards to watch every detail of a race from various angles to weed out non-triers. Racecourse Security Services is funded by the Levy Board to police the sport, investigating possible shady goings-on and generally encouraging efforts to keep it clean.

RSS employ betting intelligence officers, specialist readers of the market alert to suspicious moves which might indicate something untoward. They discuss with Stewards' Secretaries – professional advisers to the racecourse stewards – fluctuations on every race. If a winner shows form suspiciously better than in recent races and the betting has indicated abnormal support, the evidence will help stewards decide whether that improvement merits further investigation. But the role of betting intelligence officers goes much further. They keep an extensive index of information which might show that a big gambler backs one trainer's horses only when they are ridden by a particular jockey, or that a bookmaker invariably lays a certain trainer's horses heavily when they lose.

Then there is the Horseracing Forensic Laboratory, where dope specimens are analysed. Most (though not all: why not?) winners of races are tested, and other horses can be randomly sampled. Very few tests come up positive (just sixteen in 1989, from over 5000 specimens), and most are attributable to a prohibited substance somehow contaminating the horse's foodstuffs. But when will all drugs be detectable?

Racing is not free of chicanery and never can be. Nefarious goings-on add a dash of spice and intrigue to a mysterious and often secretive activity.

For in essence, betting is a battle of wits. Punters are always trying to put one over on the bookmakers, usually by a perfectly legitimate guarding of vital information about the ability or well-being of a horse, sometimes through a cleverly engineered stratagem, and just occasionally by moving the wrong side of what is permissible within the Rules of Racing and the laws of the land. Though in 1984, when Rachel's Delight, backed from 14-1 to 4-1, won at Wolverhampton, BOLA's reason for advising members to withold payment made them seem ridiculous. They complained about 'information [concerning the horse] which was not available to the general public.' Following howls of derision bookies paid up, and BOLA have never since explained how it is apparently acceptable when bookmakers themselves obtain 'information not available to the general public'.

Big betting coups are not necessarily based on particular cunning or ingenuity, but they often contain a distinct stratagem. This sometimes relates to laying a horse out for one particular event and gearing all its training and preliminary races to that target while steadily backing it in the ante-post market. The horse is unlikely to be even 90 per cent fit in some of those preliminary races and so will conveniently fail to turn in a peak performance: but when the time comes, he will be good enough. The key to such planning is containing information within strict limits, and certainly out of the hearing of the bookies.

That's one reason why ante-post betting, which many claim to lose on overall, continues. Noting who backs what and, often more significantly, when support is lacking, can be an informative guide on the day of the race itself. Money talks – never more so than when owners and trainers reckon they have ten pounds in hand!

It works both ways. Three weeks before the 1991 Derby, I told viewers of the Channel Four coverage from York that Marju, eleventh in the Two Thousand Guineas when 6-4 favourite, was back in the betting for the Epsom Classic, having worked well that morning. This came from Coral, the first firm to oppose Marju in the Guineas betting before he ran as a three-year-old. The day I announced that Coral had brought him back into the Derby betting they had received over thirty calls about the colt (some confirming his well-being at exercise) and had laid several fair-sized bets

at 20-1. Connections of Marju were astounded. Complaining faxes were sent. Some hacks joined in. I was accused of at best 'misleading the public'. The horse hadn't done more than trot. The row and accusations simmered until Marju, at 14-1, finished second behind Generous at Epsom. No one though had the decency to apologise to Coral's PR man Wally Pyrah or even Channel Four's blabbermouth.

With two thirds of horses never winning a race at all, the need to succeed and pay training bills ensures that stopping horses in readiness for a big coup is rare indeed these days.

Not every gamble can be called a coup. Very often public support for a horse simply latches on to the momentum begun within the training stable.

Information has a way of leaking and being embellished, so the edge for insiders is to get on before it becomes public knowledge. A good example of the bandwagon effect of stable intelligence arriving in the public domain is what happened to Nashwan's odds for the 1989 Two Thousand Guineas. A month before the classic this winner of two minor races as a two-year-old, was widely available at 'double carpet' (33-1) for the big race. Then a fortnight before Newmarket he produced a piece of work on Dick Hern's gallops which had West Ilsley staff making comparisons with the mighty Brigadier Gerard, beaten only once in eighteen starts in the early 1970s.

'Suddenly,' recalls Brough Scott, of Channel Four and the *Racing Post*, 'all sorts of quite sane and sensible people around the Hern camp began to mutter behind their hands and shake at the knees.' Before long it was the bookies' knees who were shaking. On the day before the Two Thousand Guineas, Ladbrokes laid the colt to lose £250,000. He started favourite at 3-1,

A BACK-HANDER

I was about twenty-three, a wide-eyed innocent in the jungle of the bookmaking business. I had worked with William Hill, the biggest of the country's odds-makers, before I went into the Army and returned to the firm when the war was over. I was a junior ledger clerk, learning the game from the bottom and, if need be, running the odd errand. On this particular occasion I was to take £2500 in cash – and that was an awful lot of 'readies' in the late forties, worth more than £100,000 today, I suppose – to Mr Fred Harkus at the Dorchester.

Never before had I carried so much money. I was only earning about a fiver a week and as I made the short journey from Hill's offices in Park Lane I was extremely worried about what was in my pocket. Add to this the fact that I was ill at ease in the Dorchester, feeling properly out of place, and you will realise that this was one of those times when I would be very glad to get rid of a large amount of money!

Fred Harkus was a personal friend of William Hill; he was also agent to many top jockeys of his era. In the years immediately after the Second World War it was not uncommon for all the big bookies (Hill, Percy Thompson, Willie Preston and Max Parker) to have one of the top jockeys on their payroll. Most often, a jockey would be riding to trainers' orders; sometimes, however, he would be riding to a bookmaker's orders. His fee for doing so, which they called 'the usual', would be £100 on the winner of the race involved at whatever price it was returned.

This particular jockey had ridden a hot favourite at the Glorious Goodwood meeting. It finished second – not a good result for all those punters out there on the favourite. The big winners were, of course, the bookmakers and on this occasion the jockey. He collected 'the usual' which, as the horse which beat him was 25-1, this time meant a £2500 pay-off. Relieved of my awesome burden, I caught a No. 36 bus home to Peckham!

Ron Pollard, *Odds and Sods*

and after thundering home his price for the Derby went into free fall - before tumbling even faster in the ensuing weeks as it became apparent that none of his Epsom rivals could boast comparable form. He went off 5-4 favourite at Epsom and sauntered home by five lengths from 500-1 Terimon.

At least in the Nashwan case there was a good deal of sense behind the gamble. The same could not be said about Tuppence. Owned by the redoubtable Dorothy Paget (see page 32), Tuppence was an extremely moderate animal whose name is remembered only on account of his being the subject of one of the weirdest gambles of the century, in the 1933 Derby won by Hyperion. On the Monday of Derby week Tuppence was 125-1, then bets cascaded down on him to such an extraordinary extent that he started for the Derby as 10-1 fourth favourite, only four points longer than the market leader Hyperion. Tuppence finished nineteenth of twenty-four runners.

Money came from his indefatigable, gambling-obsessed owner, and small punters, beguiled by his name, were panicked into joining in on the plunge. An odd expensive aberration indeed on an animal not worth much more than tuppence halfpenny.

More outwardly sensible but ultimately unsuccessful was the biggest plunge of them all in the Derby on the non-staying Tudor Minstrel, fourth in 1947 to Pearl Diver (40-1) at 'shoulder on' (7-4 on), having won the Two Thousand Guineas by eight lengths. Backed at 8-1 an hour before winning the Guineas, Tudor Minstrel was stood to lose £175,000 by William Hill alone. Faceless accountants wouldn't stand for such 'betting on opinion' involving these days millions of pounds.

But famous Classic gambles to rank with that on Nashwan include the French-trained 1951 St Leger winner Talma II, cut from 100-6 to 7-1 on the day of the race, and 1952 Derby hero Tulyar, backed on the course from 100-6 to 11-2. ('Don't say I didn't Tulyar', jockey Charlie Smirke had crowed in a telegram to the hacks a few days earlier.)

And the unluckiest Derby plungers? Have no doubt, among them were backers of 2-1 favourite Dancing Brave, almost last at Tattenham Corner before failing by half a length to pull back Shahrastani (11-2) in 1986. Twice subsequently in the King George and the Arc, he proved the Epsom running was wrong.

Some trainers are particularly adept at laying out horses for major handicaps. Vincent O'Brien pulled off a famous gamble in 1944 when training Drybob to dead-heat in the Irish Cambridgeshire and Good Days to win the Irish Cesarewitch. Both were 20-1 shots. For aficionados his succession of 'touches' at the Cheltenham National Hunt meeting, mainly involving non-

handicaps, in the late Forties and early Fifties even outdid subsequent triumphs on the Flat which included six Derby winners.

Barry Hills when travelling head lad to John Oxley won so much on Frankincense (100-8) in the 1968 Lincoln Handicap that he was able to start training in his own right the following year. He is now the master of the well-planned handicap coup: Strike Force in the 1988 Schweppes Golden Mile (8-1 SP, from 33-1 ante-post) and Risen

Moon (the 7-1 'jolly') in the 1990 Cambridgeshire – only the fifth successful favourite since 1915 – are just two of many recent triumphs enhanced by inspired backing at long odds.

That bland phrase 'land a gamble' conceals an exhilarating activity in which careful planning and deft execution can lead to enticing rewards. Those occasions when the battle of wits between punter and bookmaker involves cunning, clever scheming and plotting stick in the mind:

THE 1836 ST LEGER

Lord George Bentinck, the great nineteenth-century Turf reformer and administrator, comparable with Lord Wigg in the twentieth, turned in a nifty piece of work before the 1836 St Leger. His Elis was known to be at Goodwood a few days

A gamble landed. Nashwan (Willie Carson, centre) wins the 1989 General Accident Two Thousand Guineas

before the race, and as horses travelled to race meetings on foot, and Goodwood was at least fifteen days' walk from Doncaster, it was assumed by the bookmakers that Elis could not take part. Accordingly his odds lengthened. But Lord George had the animal loaded into a specially constructed box drawn by post horses and hauled up to Town Moor – where, backed down to 7-2 second favourite, he won by two lengths, landing Bentinck a 'satisfactory' touch.

TRODMORE RACES

On 1 August 1898 the sporting newspaper *The Sportsman* printed a racecard for the jumping meeting at Trodmore, Cornwall. The following day the paper gave the results of the meeting, which were also published in the *Sporting Life* the day after that.

Nothing very remarkable, except for the fact that Trodmore did not exist. It was a fictitious racecourse, the venue for one of the cleverest cons pulled against the bookmaking fraternity. A group of swindlers – their identity was never conclusively proved – persuaded the editor of *The Sportsman* to include the card in his paper, then fed him the 'results' by wire, and they were duly published the next day. The *Life*, offering the Trodmore results twenty-four hours later, had a costly misprint, giving the price of Reaper, the winner of the fourth race, as 5-2, rather than 5-1. This was crucial for the conspirators, for Reaper was the horse which they had backed with several London bookmakers, and soon a rat was smelled.

Most bookmakers refused to pay out, but of all the famous betting frauds, for sheer audacity this is on its own.

'Now we have a result just in from Trodmore. Over to you, JT!'

THE GAY FUTURE AFFAIR

Most coups involving pulling a fast one on the bookmakers are staged at minor fixtures, where they will attract little attention, and in the case of the celebrated Gay Future affair the smallness of the meeting – Cartmel on August Bank Holiday, 1974 – was central to the plan.

This is a complex story, but one so intricate and clever that it gave rise to a book and an ITV epic called *Murphy's Stroke*, brilliantly masterminded by Frank Cvitanovich. Planners of the coup, led by building contractor Tony Murphy, were based in Ireland, and they sent to Scottish trainer Anthony Collins an unnamed horse. Collins entered four runners in races on August Bank Holiday Monday: Opera Cloak (4.15 Southwell), Ankerwyke (4.45 at Plumpton), and Racionzer and Gay Future – the horse recently arrived from Ireland – in the 4.20 (the Ulverston Novices' Hurdle) at Cartmel.

On that hectic Monday morning the conspirators went on a betting-shop crawl in London, staking some £30,000 in doubles (up to £15), Gay Future with Ankerwyke or Gay Future with Opera Cloak. These small doubles are seen as straightforward mug punting, and little notice would have been taken of the accumulation of bets involving one obscure horse, Gay Future. The conspirators were going for a £300,000 payout, but at 12.30 the eagle eyes of the William Hill organization twigged that something was afoot. They stopped taking bets on Gay Future and alerted other firms via the bookies' 'precautionary pyramid' system whereby one office sends the news to several others, who each pass it on to an agreed number of further shops, and so on.

To distract attention from Gay Future, trainer Collins had gone to Plumpton to saddle Ankerwyke – or so it appeared. His wife was dispatched to Cartmel to look after Gay Future and Racionzer, with instructions to back the latter in the ring. Meanwhile the 'real' Gay Future, who had been secretly prepared in Ireland for his date with destiny, had been shipped across the Irish Sea two days before the race and imported as an unnamed gelding. At a rendezvous on the M6 motorway he was swapped for the horse who had been in Collins's charge and taken straight to the racecourse stables at Cartmel.

In the Ulverston Novices' Hurdle Gay Future was ridden by the leading Irish amateur jockey Mr T. A. Jones, rather than the inexperienced amateur who had been down in the morning papers. And, as a final touch of virtuosity, the horse's flanks had soap flakes rubbed into them to give the impression that he was sweating up copiously.

Meanwhile, off-course bookies had swung into action. This was a busy Bank Holiday, and the Extel 'blower' service down which they could have sent money to shorten up prices was not operating at any of the three courses involved – as the plotters well knew. No handy car phones in those days either so representatives of the bookmakers were hastily dispatched to the courses to 'freeze' the market. At Southwell and Plumpton they discovered that the Collins horses had been withdrawn. This meant that all those small doubles had melted down into a huge single bet on Gay Future, but the bookies' man arrived at far-off Cartmel (in Cumbria) too late.

Gay Future won by fifteen lengths at 10-1 (Racionzer was pulled up), and it subsequently transpired that neither Ankerwyke nor Opera Cloak had left their trainer's stable: there had never been any intention to run them in the other two races (and neither of the jockeys down to ride in the morning papers knew anything of their booking!).

BOLA immediately advised affected betting shops to withhold payment, the police were called in, and eventually Collins and Murphy were found guilty of conspiracy to defraud bookmakers.

As *Timeform's Chasers and Hurdlers* annual pointed out, the decision to prosecute was made by the police, not by the bookmakers or the Jockey Club:

The actions of the syndicate in having Gay Future prepared to run for his life on his first outing over hurdles, of running the horse at a meeting at which the 'blower' was not in operation, of backing the horse in the SP offices and betting on other runners in the race on the course – none of these actions was illegal. Backers and bookmakers alike are entitled to use cunning in their enterprise to produce a profit for themselves. The switch of jockey and the rubbing of soap flakes on to the horse's flanks before the parade may have gone beyond the boundary of fair play but no one would regard them as criminal acts.

The voice of sanity, as ever, from *Timeform*. But in court, where it mattered, the law reckoned differently.

Many bookmakers regarded the Gay Future affair as a legitimate coup and settled honourably, but the Big Four (Hills, Mecca, Ladbrokes and Coral) withheld payment, the *Sporting Life* declared bets on the race void, and BOLA advised members to return all stakes.

In an ironic twist to one of the most ingenious betting coups ever, Gay Future was subsequently sold to bookmaker John Banks. But it has taken almost twenty years for the Jockey Club to bring in the overnight declaration of jockeys. They've pushed it through despite fierce reactionary opposition. Punters thank them for that.

THE DAGENHAM COUP

Betting's age of innocence ended with the cunning Dagenham greyhound coup on 30 June 1964.

Three years after betting shops opened punters were still able to opt for SP, or Tote dividends, and chart or track forecasts. The 4.05 race at Dagenham, over 840 yards (long before those appalling metres) attracted 11,756 two-shilling (10p) units in the forecast pool. But 11,487 of them included the two 'double carpet' (33-1) chances, leaving only 269 units involving the other four.

Second favourite Buckwheat beat the third best Handsome Lass, and with only one two-shilling unit for them the dividend was £987.11s.9d! Top whack normally it might have been £3.

A gang had blocked the twenty-eight Tote forecast windows. Regular punters couldn't get on and that eventually scuppered the coup. Amazed punters in shops at the time temporarily rejoiced – as did those in on the plot. The 'rucks' at the stadium proved bad enough but repercussions outside soon ended those halcyon days when bets were settled on tiny track pools.

Bookmaking hardened up and – you could say – came of age after Dagenham. Punters would still try and pull strokes, but defensive mechanisms, from computerisation to the pyramid warning system, were on the way.

Dagenham will go down in history long after Ford cease to build cars there.

THE ROCHESTER COUP

This was the most controversial greyhound racing coup of them all. On 27 May 1978 the small, now defunct track at Rochester in Kent staged an unusual race – two heats over 277 metres and a final later in the evening over 901 metres. The first heat of

what was appropriately named the Long and Short Trip Stakes went to Leysdown Pleasure at 33-1, the second to Leysdown Fun at 4-1. Both dogs were trained privately by Jack Purvis. Leysdown Fun was withdrawn lame from the final and Leysdown Pleasure finished a well-beaten last. The pair had attracted little money at the track in their heats, but then it was discovered that off-course bookmakers – mainly in Basingstoke, Leicester, South London and Peterborough – had liabilities of around £350,000 about the two dogs. BOLA, sensing an illegal coup, advised members to withhold payment – where have we heard that before? – and the official National Greyhound Racing Club launched an investigation.

The police were called in and eventually submitted a report to the Director of Public Prosecutions who decided that no action should be taken. The Big Four bookmakers and some others refused to pay up. Eventually in 1985 Leonard Caplan, QC was appointed arbitrator and decided that the bookmakers were not liable to pay. Caplan's conclusion was that the event involving sprint heats and a long-distance final had been deliberately framed to discourage other good sprinters from taking part, and that the Leysdown dogs had been running in trials over distances which would not reveal their true form. Outstanding stake money was refunded.

The brainy people behind this coup had contacted me at the *Sporting Life* saying that they were going to glue up the locks of the betting shops of some of the offending (as they saw it) bookmakers, and I reported this, making the bookmakers concerned livid. At the time I argued that I was just writing what I had been told, but looking back on the Rochester affair I now wonder whether by reporting the intentions of the perpetrators I was giving them the oxygen of publicity, and should not have done so.

Maybe, though the news of shops having been superglued would have made for equal headlines anyway. But there is no doubt that this was a fair coup. The races had been cunningly framed, and a South London coach operator brought in to sponsor this bizarre event at an obscure track. No criminality was proved, and the few bookmakers who refused to pay shamed their profession.

Imagine holding betting slips worth thousands of pounds, maybe borrowing money on them and dreaming of sun-drenched holidays in Hawaii, and after all the aggro getting nothing. Rochester showed bookmaking at its least acceptable, and now there are strict limits on winnings at evening dog meetings.

RINGERS

To substitute a horse with a 'ringer' (one of similar appearance but very different ability) should be impossible today in any properly regulated racing country, where every runner has a 'passport' giving precise details of its markings. Back in 1844 the Derby was won by a horse called Running Rein, who turned out to be not the three-year-old Running Rein at all, but a mature four-year-old named Maccabeus.

Since the war there have been a few notorious cases of switching one horse for another in very minor events where the perpetrators might expect to get away with the deception.

In 1953 a moderate animal named Francasal won a selling race at Bath at 10-1. He turned out to be a much speedier beast called Santa Amaro, who had been heavily backed off the course (over £5000 was staked on him, a massive sum then), and the phone lines, which would have trans-

mitted some of that money to the course market, were cut. Four of the villains found guilty received jail sentences, the longest being three years.

The finish of the Knighton Auction Plate for two-year-olds at Leicester on 29 March 1982 raised many eyebrows when 10-1 shot Flockton Grey charged in by twenty lengths, an extraordinary margin in an early-season juvenile race. But the horse was not Flockton Grey at all, rather an experienced well-grown three-year-old named Good Hand. After two years of investigation the men behind the deception were found guilty of conspiracy to defraud, and fined heavily. The two innocent parties, Flockton Grey and Good Hand, remained in police custody for five years.

The *Sporting Life* summed up thus:

The truth is that the Flockton Grey affair hardly ranks as something in the pages of a Dick Francis novel. It was rather tatty and tawdry, involving a lot of people. In fact, it is claimed that a sheep pen would have been needed to make a dock if everyone questioned had been charged.

A more macabre fate than police custody was in store for In The Money. Having his first outing for two seasons and completing the course for the first time ever, he won the Hatherleigh Handicap Selling Hurdle at Newton Abbot on 28 August 1978 by twenty lengths at odds of 8-1. He was reportedly found to be so lame on the day after the race that he was put down, but it transpired that this was destroying the evidence in another ringer case. For In The Money had been replaced by Cobblers March, and trainer John Bowles got a £1500 fine and twenty years disqualification.

In all these cases, as in most racing chicanery, bookmakers become victims. Never forget that. Conspirators cannot be

A career nobbled: Pinturischio (Lester Piggott up)

lauded as folk heroes. Punters were defrauded too. Bent races besmirch the game and without integrity it isn't worth the candle anyway. No one realises this more than bookmakers – the few crooked ones, in their ruthless greed, above all jeopardise the public's trust, without which racing would soon become as significant as wrestling.

DOPING

'Doping' – giving a horse an illicit substance to affect its performance in a race – is an emotive term, and covers a multitude of circumstances.

The Jockey Club maintains a list of prohibited substances, any trace of which in horse's urine after the race means disqualification – though for some substances there are very low 'threshold levels', which mark the dividing line between how much is allowed and how much not.

That ensnared the Aga Khan's 1989 Oaks winner Aliysa. The consequences of her disqualification following bitter wrangles which resulted in the King of Kings resigning from the Jockey Club and withdrawing from Britain his ninety horses in training, rumbled on in the High Court. And the Jockey Club's adherence to secret disciplinary hearings, reminiscent of totalitarian regimes the world over, is a dark, intolerable aspect of Turf justice.

Until 1990 no horse had been proved to

have been deliberately doped to lose since Alloway Lad at Epsom in 1969. In 1961 Pinturischio, favourite for the Derby and consistently supported in the ante-post market, was 'got at' two weeks before Epsom, recovered, and then was 'nobbled' again, ruining his racing career for good. (Alcide, favourite for the 1958 Derby, was crippled not with dope but a savage blow in his box which broke a rib.)

The spectre of doping to lose seemed to have disappeared from the racing scene until the 1990 St Leger meeting at Doncaster. The two-year-old colt Bravefoot, unbeaten in his two previous outings, was hot favourite for the Laurent-Perrier Champagne Stakes. Despite attracting a great deal of money in the betting ring – as much as £75,000 in recorded large bets – his odds lengthened from evens to 11-8. For his price to drift so markedly in spite of hefty support was ominous. Witnessing this mysterious market move, I told Channel Four Racing viewers at the time that 'something smelled', and it smelled to high heaven.

Bravefoot's abject performance in the race increased that feeling. Tongue lolling out, he finished a dispirited last behind Bog Trotter at 'T.H.' (8-1).

Within a couple of weeks the pungent truth emerged. Bravefoot, trained by Dick Hern, had been doped, and so had Norwich, 'elef a vier' (11-4) joint favourite for the Kiveton Park Stakes at the same meeting when finishing a disappointing fourth. Norwich was trained by Barry Hills, and another of the stable's runners, Flying Diva, 'rouf' (4-1) in a three-runner juvenile event, was discovered to have been doped when last, beaten nearly ten lengths, at Yarmouth the following week.

Immediate reaction to the Bravefoot case – the most telling of the three, as far as market moves indicated – was that the criminals were bound to be connected with the bookmakers.

If a punter *knew* that Bravefoot would not win, he could bet against him. But he would still not know which of his opponents to back, and might yet end up on a loser. (Betting on all four wouldn't be all that profitable.) But if a bookmaker learned that Bravefoot was 'no good', he could confidently accept as much money as possible at odds which would attract punters, secure in the knowledge that there was not to be any payout.

It is probable that one or two bookmakers were party to Bravefoot's doping, though the fact that the second favourite for the race, Arokat, was backed from 7-2 to 15-8, suggests that the scheme was not necessarily bookmaker-inspired. (And, as it turns out, how good anyway was Arokat? Sent off the 250-1 pacemaker in the Derby nine months later, he trailed in twelfth of thirteen.) What is certain is that the great majority of bookies in that Doncaster betting ring had no inside knowledge, and would have been altering their prices in response to the general market move against Bravefoot, or following their own feelings about the horse's chance.

In time there must be pre-race testing of all horses. Dopers are always trying to keep ahead of the detectors, but scientific advances will surely come up with a relatively cheap, instantaneous test to deter and banish them for ever.

Stories that Dick Hern's Gorytus, the 'wonder' juvenile of 1982, was doped when last of four in Newmarket's Dewhurst Stakes, at 2-1 on, have always seemed to me fanciful and tenuous.

Far more likely, as I repeatedly wrote and broadcast at the time, the over-hyped colt was 'soft' and those who cruelly labelled him 'Gowrongus' were spot-on and helped save less gullible punters' pockets.

Once again, any plot is an attempt to defraud bookmakers. They don't need crooked racing: they can do very nicely without it, thank you. So can the rest of us.

Bookmakers generally provide the honourable part of racing's equation. When there are strokes pulled or wheezes to be dreamt up, it is the connections or punters behind them, rarely bookmakers. The days of the welshing bookie scarpering with the public's money are virtually over, though the 1990 collapse of flamboyant leading southern rails operator Dougie Goldstein, leaving firms and racecourse workmen owed an estimated £600,000, reinforces the necessity of safeguards.

And the 1970s and '80s regularly witnessed high-flying off-course firms who blazoned their attractive odds and offers but then defaulted. Many still remember Rosspoint – 'That's the Point'. Their failure alerted the industry and public to how clever advertising could be used to draw in accounts, and others have followed.

Punters sorely tempted must always ask themselves why one or two new companies alone can afford to offer exceptional prices or tax concessions. It is the same in the City, insurance, and elsewhere. (Witness the collapse involving billions of pounds of the fraudulent Bank of Credit and Commerce International in 1991. They'd offered extra-high interest rates!) Beating the odds, but not being paid, is useless. Don't be conned by promises and attractive packaging.

Competition is ferocious and established businesses, along with genuine newcomers, realise that profit margins do not allow gimmicks like tax-free off-course betting or absurd over-the-odds generosity. Most firms offer concessions. Victor Chandler makes nine per cent deductions. Kinghorns bet tax free on selected races. Mawdesleys go one quarter the odds a place on all handicaps, and Dublin's PM Racing return win single stakes, up to £250, if the horse loses by a short head with the catchy slogan, 'You're not in the red if you're beaten a short head'.

Beware though 'come ons' that your gut feeling tells you are too good to be true. Almost invariably they are!

Already it 'smells' in the ring: Bravefoot cantering to the start at Doncaster

BEGUILED BY A BRUNETTE, WE SUCCUMB TO A STING

'Caterers, caterers!' we chorused out of car windows as gatemen at the entrance to Epsom Downs opted for self-preservation and leapt aside.

Waving, as evidence, a tatty white coat while speeding through was hardly convincing but at least our firm was saved the couple of quid entry to the Hill over each of the four days at the 1971 Derby meeting.

Dishonestly 'blagging in' hardly set us high in any moral league, but racecourse reality that it is overwhelmingly punters, not bookmakers, who pull strokes, was to hit us not once but twice on Oaks Saturday.

All right, we regularly laid under Tatts odds on our pitch in the centre of the course alongside the funfair; though under-exercised consciences were partially salvaged in the knowledge that any punter could ask for starting price, and some did.

But trying to make it pay, with tiny 'tanks', sometimes as little as £100 (equivalent to about £250 these days), put a premium on pure survival. And, thanks to one large slice of good fortune, we were well in front after three days.

In the Derby Mill Reef (100-30 favourite) – never better than 3-1 on our board – wasn't any good, and nor on Thursday had been Tudabula, at 14-1 the outsider of three when flooring Oceanic (6-4) and Leaping Lad (4-6).

Dozens of small bets, from 6-1 to 10-1 Geordie Ramshaw's mount, put him up with the favourite, but stupid reluctance to 'waste money' hedging the 'rag' proved mighty expensive. Still, all was forgiven on Friday, when we had a right result, one of the most memorable of an inglorious, unprofitable racecourse 'career'.

Lester Piggott, whatever price his horse, never helped layers on a major race day so, in normal circumstances, Green God, trained for the late David Robinson by Michael Jarvis, would have been at best a small winner when sent off at 10-1 for the Headley Handicap. But this time he was 'ours'. Runner-up, at 10 lengths, to Mill Reef in the previous year's Gimcrack at York, and back again to six furlongs, we were united in reckoning that if ever there was a race to go 'bar one' – lay all the others but keep a particular beast on your side – this was it.

So we cracked into Dennis McKay's Ballynockan, winner of his previous two contests under Willie Carson and Geoff Lewis. Carrying only 7st 6lb, he went from around 6-4 to even money, while as we laid Green God, popular at 6-1, 7s and 8-1, we backed it back 'inside' (Tatts) at better prices, 'topping up' each time.

Taking on all-comers over Ballynockan and the rest, and still firing into Green God, we ended up with a hopelessly lopsided book. Certainly if Ballynockan had won it would have cleaned us out well beyond Royal Ascot. But with good old Lester doing the business and getting home by half a length from Fireside Chat (8-1), with the 'jolly' only third, we had landed an eight-grand-plus touch.

Jollifications and backslapping all round. And when Green God went on to win the Nunthorpe, before being disqualified in favour of Swing Easy, and Haydock's Vernons Sprint

Cup, to dispute sprint championship honours, it proved what shrewd judges we had been at Epsom on that memorable afternoon.

Flush, and on a high, we approached Oaks day with enthusiasm and almost reckless confidence, though a whispered suggestion that the gateman should be 'dropped' a tenner for earlier misdemeanours found no favour!

In the Classic, Noel Murless's One Thousand Guineas winner Altesse Royale was supported down to 6-4 to enable Geoff Lewis to become the only jockey to have completed the top Epsom treble, after Mill Reef and Lupe in Thursday's Coronation Cup.

Stable-companion Maina (Piggott) was second best at 17-2 with 10-1 bar the pair bringing in Mariel, our each-way 'bar one', and the Queen's Albany. Plenty of fillies were supported and, juggling with the figures, backing back at more generous odds, and not going wild, we didn't end up with a disastrous book, though three-length winner Altesse Royale was stood for a few bob and, agonisingly, Mariel failed by a neck to grab third spot.

Soon, there was a queue in front of the joint replete with happy ice-cream-guzzling punters. Up on the stool I went on taking tickets, tearing them up, and paying out with less than a sincere smile.

After a few minutes a young, well-dressed East Ender handed in his 'brief' and said: 'Two and a half, mate.'

'£2.50?' I queried back.

'Come off it,' he laughed. '250 quid, mate. £100 at 6-4. Always knew it was a cert.'

Turning to our clerk, George, I repeated, '£250, ticket 571.' At that instant, as old George went down to the crowded Altesse Royale column, and the rest, I knew we were in deep trouble. There wasn't a bet anywhere for 571.

Earlier, over 570, I had paid out a tasty brunette in a tight, scarlet mini-skirt who, quite by chance you understand, I happened to remember coming to draw her fiver (£3-2).

Ticket 572 was another £3-2 and a different filly had been backed with 573 but no sign of 571. This was going to be tricky and the punter hardly seemed the kind of bloke meekly to settle for any ring inspector's adjudicated 'split' (£125), let alone anything less.

Anyway, we had as much chance as an outsize lobster, picked out of a posh restaurant tank and about to be plunged into a steaming pot. After a brief acrimonious confab, the grudging consensus was to swallow it – no, not the lobster! – and cough up the half-monkey (£250), with as much aplomb as we could muster.

Without the previous day's eight 'big 'uns' this would not have even been contemplated but, with the crowd showing signs of getting restive, I took the ticket, ripped it up into little shreds, and handed over the 'readies'.

We had been well and truly done, and we knew it. George should have realised bets were not in sequence at the time. That's why sensible layers tape-record every transaction just in case of dispute or of two tickets being issued at the same time. (Roll on the day when the present antiquated number system gives way to computerised betting with the date, race, horse, stake, price and time clearly down on the slip!)

Shortly after that trauma, as we continued blaming each other, another punter handed up his ticket and, when I asked how much he wanted, he mumbled something unintelligible.

'592,' I called to George.

'£50,' he replied and off the fellow went with five £10 notes.

He was barely gone when George spluttered: 'Hey, that £50 geezer should only have copped a fiver. He had a couple of quid on, not a score. We've been kippered again!'

Sending out search parties, as we'd done in two similar instances elsewhere before, was hopeless in that widespread throng and, anyway, it could have been worse. Moreover, there was work to do.

The punters had got away with two diabolical strokes within five minutes. Imagine the screams if layers behaved like that!

Yes, mistakes can happen but there isn't a racecourse regular, at least that I know of, who would ever deliberately pull a 'fast one' on his customers. Yet, time and time again, smart alec punters try it on, acting the aggrieved innocent when challenged. If those much-maligned bookies had the same lack of scruples, we would have had a Tote monopoly decades ago.

And a final memory of Oaks day 1971? Trudging back to the car, humping some of our gear, and suddenly spotting the £250 wise guy in a flash open sportscar sitting alongside this gorgeous bird, her brown hair flowing in the breeze.

You've guessed it. The same one who must have been given two tickets when having her £3-2.

As the chap went by he took his hand off her ample thigh, grinned towards us and contemptuously put two fingers up before roaring off.

Don't ever lecture me about shady bookies.

8 'Totegate' – or the Carlisle Cock-up

After being voted up the 1978 Specialist Writer of the Year in the British Press Awards, Big Mac was named the 1979 Campaigning Journalist of the Year for exposing the practice of Tote Credit sending winning off-course bets into the course Tote pool after the race had been run. This article, originally published in the Sporting Life on 5 February 1980, summarises the story.

Totegate – the exposure of the Tote's system of putting bets into the pool after the results of races were known – began routinely enough when their PRO Geoff Webster called an emaciated dividend at Carlisle on Wednesday 4 July 'inexplicable'.

Shine On (11-1) coupled with Tina's Gold (20-1) had paid just 45p to 10p for the dual forecast in an 18-runner handicap. Whatever else the explanation might be it could not be 'inexplicable': there had to be a reason, albeit an innocent one.

The Border Handicap was the last race on the card and, quite by chance, I happened to have an interest in that run-of-the-mill contest. On the previous Monday, trainer Albert Davison had made a late switch of jockeys for his two horses in a Windsor seller while Patrick Haslam did the same at Yarmouth 24 hours later. Professionally ridden, instead of by apprentices as stated in the morning papers, both had won to the obvious disadvantage of off-course punters and I wrote a piece pointing this out in Wednesday's *Life*.

Then Jeff Ballard, responsible in our New Fetter Lane office for collating the results as they come off the Extel teleprinter during the afternoon, noticed that a similar switch had occurred in the fateful Border Handicap. Denys Smith's apprentice Robert Sidebottom was now riding Shine On and number one jockey Lindsay Charnock had switched to Wharton Manor.

As it turned out, this was a genuine error, which connections vainly attempted to rectify. It meant Shine On shouldered 9lb overweight yet the mare still won. Soon afterwards came news that Charnock had failed to weigh in on the fourth-placed Wharton Manor and had been disqualified and placed last. With each-way punters paid four places, it meant we already had a story on two counts.

The Tote dividends came up – and that 45p forecast put the lid on it.

I was quickly on the phone to Tote House, where a spokesman refused to divulge the size of the pool, the number of units invested on the winning combination or even whether they had been staked on the course or sent down from London. Meanwhile the Press Association quoted Webster as saying: 'I have been in contact with the course and there doesn't seem to have been anything particularly abnormal about the pool. It was one of those inexplicable turn-ups.'

But no Tote dividend is totally inexplicable; somebody must be able to account for it. Was there simply a lucky punter at Carlisle whose fluke wager had swamped the pool? Or had a large off-course bet been sent down? If so by whom, on whose behalf, and when?

I set about finding out. No success that night.

Next day I tried Webster again. No help. 'It's not our policy,' he said, 'to explain dividends or how they're made up.'

'Strange,' I answered, 'reasons have been forthcoming in the past.'

'They aren't now,' was the instant retort.

It was time for the personal approach. With genial Webster, an ex-*Life* man, it had worked before.

'Geoff, old chap, off the record, let me know what happened. I'm sure there's a perfectly innocent explanation – just save me bothering about this any more.'

'John,' came the reply, 'you know I can't. Leave it alone – it isn't worth your while – just forget it!'

But I couldn't. That 45p danced before my eyes. The more I thought about it the stronger became the near-obsession to solve the mystery.

Friday – Day Three of probing – was spent sniffing for clues at Sandown. No joy. But on Saturday came a break of sorts. Bird of Prey (33-1) beat Another Dove (9-1) at Haydock and the dual forecast, for 10p, was £107.31. The disparity between that dividend and the one at Carlisle was so huge for similar results that it didn't make sense. Had something in the system changed?

All the time I was expecting some other paper to run the inside story of the Carlisle affair. Surely I wasn't the only hack on the trail – however little scent there was.

Then, out of the blue, at 4.50 p.m. on Monday 9 July, came the decisive breakthrough: a phone call to the *Life* office and from the man's opening words – 'You want

to know what happened to that dividend at Carlisle last week?' – we were on our way.

Who made that call I still don't know. But the voice was youngish and this in essence is what he told me:

The Tote sent £50 down for the winning combination after the race – that's why it returned 45p. There was about £200 in the pool before this bet was put in and two winning tickets.

It all started with a 50p forecast. The transmission room manager and his assistant were off that day and somehow the instructions got mixed up.

It's been going on for years, usually in dual forecasts. A few bets are sent down after the race and almost always the winning combination is amongst them. Mainly it's for £5 units.

I'm sickened by what's going on. Something's got to be done.

The caller sounded nervous. He wouldn't say who he was. I asked him to ring back in half-an-hour. He never did, but never mind. So this was it – after-time betting! The dream of punters down the ages. The obvious, but unbelievable explanation. Yet elated as I was, one unidentified voice on the phone was not enough. Where was the corroboration?

The one piece of evidence which slotted in was that the Tote Credit manager, Jeff Wells, had been off on the crucial Wednesday. That I already knew from my call to the Tote immediately following the race. 'Shy Throat', on the solitary piece of his evidence which could be checked out at that moment, was accurate.

Not only did it encourage belief in his reliability; almost certainly, it placed him in or close to the Tote's transmission room on that day. Was he directly involved? Had it even been he who sent down the £50 bet by mistake? Had he been saddled with the can when the recriminations were flying?

Sometimes, in the heat of an inquiry, the obvious person to give a lead is ignored. In looking for the far-fetched, the long shot to turn up, likelier sources are stupidly overlooked. And my fundamental error in this respect delayed publication for four days.

On Tuesday I tried Webster again, telling him of the new information. The un-Geoff-like reply was curt, even threatening: 'I'd strongly advise you to leave this alone. I've nothing further to say on the matter.' With the phone banged unceremoniously down on the hook the last chance of amicable assistance from within Tote House was gone. It was back to basics – checking, phoning, asking, pleading – but still no progress.

Then came another 'ton' dual forecast – £104.72 over Luck of the Draw (11-2) and Elisheba (25-1), in the opener at Newmarket. A second whopper in four racing days was stretching coincidence too far. Clearly dividends weren't now being doctored.

The next break came on Wednesday evening when one of our SP men, Mick Bass, came up to the office after working at Newmarket. I asked him almost casually whether he knew anyone on the Tote. 'John Broadway's your best bet,' said Bass. 'He used to work for them.'

Of course – our own SP man! Why hadn't I thought of him? And how fortunate the *Life* had only recently taken him on the staff following his seven years with the *Sporting Chronicle*.

When I rang Broadway that Wednesday evening his opening words told me we'd cracked it. 'You're calling about that Carlisle dividend, aren't you?' he asked unprompted. 'I know Bill Baxter, the Tote's racecourse manager that day at Carlisle; he's an old friend of mine.'

What a slice of luck – and just at the right time, too!

Broadway went on: 'I've talked to him about this and do you know he had already calculated the dividend from the £200 pool. There were two on-course winners, one with a £1 ticket and another 50p. It came to over £10 before he was told there was a £50 winning bet on the combination from London. He couldn't believe it and was very annoyed. And when one of the punters complained to him about it there was absolutely nothing he could do.'

And Broadway also confirmed that after-time betting was a regular occurrence though, since Carlisle, an edict had gone out ordering course controllers to ring Tote House for instructions, not the other way round.

So Carlisle wasn't just a one-off blunder and, even more important, the figures given to me by 'Shy Throat' and to Broadway by Baxter – £200 pool, £50 invested by London, two winners – matched. But until the Tote hierarchy had been given a chance of explaining, there was still nothing we could print. Repeated calls, and messages left, had failed to contact them.

During the next day I must have telephoned Tote House over a dozen times. Eventually bluff became the only weapon left. Wyatt's secretary was informed that the *Life* was running the story even if we failed to hear from him. Whether that did the trick is uncertain but shortly after 5.00 p.m. the familiar high-pitched tones of the millionaire former Labour MP for Bosworth, speaking from Hull, were on the line.

With the editor listening in on an extension – no chances now of Wyatt being 'misquoted' – the conversation began innocently enough with Wyatt saying:

'Hello, old boy, it's about that Carlisle

dividend, isn't it? Well, to be perfectly honest, it was a monumental cock-up – as simple as that.'

Almost jocularly he continued: 'All of us make mistakes – even you do at the *Life* – and we did here. There was a stupid mix-up but I'll tell you what we'll do. If the punters come forward we'll pay them the full dividend. Now could we be fairer than that?'.

On the surface it was a convincing performance from a man skilled at extricating himself from tight corners – the frank admission of error and now restitution. But when the questions started the facade of joviality was swiftly dropped.

'But, Mr Wyatt, was £50 put into a £200 pool after the race?'

[Long pause] ' . . . Naturally we have to collate all the bets laid in our 230 shops, and those on credit. This takes time. Indeed bets can be put into the pool up to five minutes after the result is known.'

'What bets are sent down?'

[Longer pause] ' . . . Only bets actually struck by punters are ever sent down. The delay is inevitable, considering our widespread operations.'

'How can you justify anyone, anywhere being able to place bets after time?'

[Even longer pause] ' . . . As we take pool bets right up to the off it is part of procedure to send our hedging commissions down after time. There is no conceivable way it could be done before the off. Nothing, other than bona-fide bets from punters, are ever transmitted to the course. I give you my word on that.'

'But how can you, Mr Wyatt? How do you personally know what is happening at any given time in the transmission room?'

The longest pause of all. Then the boisterous tones of Bill Balshaw (had Wyatt been asking Balshaw for the answers to my questions?) boomed down the line: 'Now look here, John, you're making very serious accusations and you'd better be very careful indeed. There are courts which deal with this kind of situation. It is mischievous and malicious to insinuate this was anything more than coincidence.'

'Bill, are bets placed in racecourse pools by Tote Bookmakers after-time? One former employee has assured me they do.'

'Untrue. It doesn't happen and there is no question of impropriety by Tote Credit or Tote Bookmakers employees. We've offered to pay those involved in the wrong dividend at Carlisle. What more do you want?'

There was nothing further to say. Here was the great admission by Wyatt and Balshaw. Both were tough fighters, one in the political and the other in the bookmaking jungles. Balshaw had clawed his way out of the Glasgow betting arena to rise to head of the multi-million pound Hills Organisation.

For both of them the motto 'Hit back, and hit back hard again,' had served them well. But these were not the correct tactics now.

'That's it,' said Ossie Fletcher the moment Balshaw rang off. 'Wyatt's admitted after-time betting – and he has actually defended it! That's the lead for the paper tonight.'

On Friday 13 July – unlucky as it proved for the Tote! – under the strapline 'Woodrow Wyatt calls it "the Carlisle cock-up"' and headline 'HOW AFTER-TIME BETS GET INTO THE TOTE POOL', we splashed the story accompanied by an editorial – the first of four that were to be penned as the scandal developed. Calling the after-time bets situation 'a desperately unhealthy state of affairs', and saying the excuse of administrative convenience 'simply isn't on', the editor ended:

On a previous occasion and in a totally un-connected context, I accused the Tote Board before the Select Committee of the House of Commons on Nationalised Industries of an irresponsible disregard for the interests of its clients and dereliction of its duty to the public in general.

I do so again.

Once the starting stalls open, no further bets should be admitted into Tote pools. From whatever source, for whatever reason.

On Friday morning BBC Radio 4 inter-viewer Brian Widlake recorded interviews with Wyatt and myself separately on the lunchtime 'World At One' programme. I simply reiterated the facts as I knew them and then returned to the office and sat with the editor listening to Wyatt's response. It contained a searing attack on the *Sporting Life*, which was echoed in a statement the Tote chairman issued to the Press. This said:

The loss-making Sporting Life, *which could not survive without bookmakers' advertise-ments, devotes much of its space to violent attacks on imaginary defects in Tote proce-dures, but is very gentle in its criticisms of the real defects of the procedures of the big book-makers.*

John McCririck and the editor in Friday's Sporting Life *pretend to be shocked that Tote Headquarters transmits to the pools on-course bets which have been struck before the start of the race after the off.*

As bets in our 230 betting shops and our Tote Credit offices all over the country are allowed up till the off it would clearly be im-possible to collate bets all over the country and transmit them to the pools on course before the off. Ever since the Tote began, bets taken before the off have been transmitted to the pools as soon as they have been collated. As we do not have telepathic but telephonic communication

there is inevitably a delay of a few minutes while the bets are transmitted after the off. The alternative would be to close all betting at Tote odds off the course five to ten minutes before the off. This would doubtless please the Sport-ing Life *as it would give their friends the book-makers a considerable competitive advantage since betting at SP would still continue up to the off.*

This mistake in transmission which caused the lopsided dual forecast dividend at Carlisle on 4 July arose from human error from which the Tote is not always entirely free. The same mistake would have been liable to occur even if the transmission of the bets concerned had taken place ten minutes before the off.

The Tote has offered to pay any punters who can prove they had the correct dual forecast on that occasion what they would have received if the mistakes had not been made.

Under the heading 'Bunkum and balder-dash, Mr Wyatt', the editor retorted:

Let us now dissect Mr Wyatt's blustering and condescending attempts at self-justification.

His snide opening gambit is to suggest we are in the pockets of our bookmaker-advertis-ers – blissfully overlooking the fact that he is one. And if he thinks we are never critical of the others, well, where's he been throughout the unending saga of the Rochester coup?

Next he talks of 'imaginary' defects in Tote procedures. They are clearly imaginary to him. But they're not to those of us who've pro-gressed beyond the kindergarten stage in bet-ting education.

At the Sporting Life *we don't pretend to be shocked. We are shocked. Shocked not only at what has gone on, but even more at Wyatt's attempts to justify it. Shocked at the conflict be-tween what he says now and what his PRO said last year.*

He makes great play of the fact that bets are

Woodrow Wyatt – 'Hello, old boy, it's about the Carlisle dividend, isn't it? Well, to be perfectly honest, it was a monumental cock-up – as simple as that'

allowed up to the off in the Tote's 230 betting shops and their credit offices and speaks as though all bets have to be collated and all sent down to the course.

This is unadulterated balderdash. Every bet placed at an off-course Tote office is placed not with the pool, but with one or other of their bookmaking subsidiaries. That's what we've repeatedly been told. None of the bets has to go to the course at all.

The Tote accept them just as any other bookmaker would do. If any other bookmaker wants subsequently to get any of his Tote-odds commitments into the pool, he must do something about it before the race. Tote Bookmakers and Tote Credit Ltd should do likewise – not wait till they're in a position to know which bets will cost them and which, if retained, will swell their profits. Why should Tote Bookmakers or Tote Credit Ltd have this improper advantage?

Similarly, it is bunkum to talk about all Tote-odds betting having to cease five to ten minutes before the off. Let Tote Bookmakers and Tote Credit Ltd stick the late bets as other bookmakers do. The question of 'competitive advantage' to other bookmakers does not arise.

The final nail in the coffin of Wyatt's credibility in this matter is his claim that on 4 July a £50 dual forecast on Shine On and Tina's Gold could as easily have been sent to the course in error ten minutes before the off as after.

Anyone who believes that will believe anything.

And would the two lone backers of the forecast on the course have stood any chance of getting their rightful dividends had the Sporting Life *stayed silent?*

All that was published in Saturday's *Life* but on the Friday morning, enter Bruce George, MP. I had known the Labour member for Walsall South for ten years – he first won the marginal seat in 1974 – and had recounted his advocacy of greyhound racing

having its own levy. There is no love lost between the former Labour MP Wyatt and current Labour members. To them he is a turncoat and George felt no compunction about attacking him now the 'after time' scandal was breaking.

On reading Friday's *Life* he told me: 'This is a truly remarkable story of yours. I find it amazing that the chairman should condone betting after the results of races are known.' So on the Saturday, as well as Wyatt's statement and the editor's riposte, we ran the splash headline: 'RESIGN! THE TOTE BOSS MUST GO CALL BY MP.'

Once again, fortune and teamwork played a major part in strengthening our case. At lunchtime on Friday a Mr Goldring telephoned and claimed Geoff Webster had denied in the *Life* a year previously that after-time betting ever took place. In the confusion of a hectic day that information – dozens of other calls were flowing in at the same time – was relegated but, fortunately, deputy editor Graham Taylor kept reminding everyone about it and his words eventually fell on fertile ground when mentioned to assistant editor Colin Simpson.

He recalled Webster's letter, traced it and triumphantly produced it at the editor's conference. By now it was 6 p.m. – too late to change the composition of the front page – but this new evidence was both startling and damning. We reproduced a 'tear-out' of just one paragraph:

'Tote Credit and the Tote's on-course cash division are two separate operations and the suggestion that they could or would collude to put money into the pool "after time" has no foundation in fact and is an unwarranted slur on those concerned.'

Above it we ran the headline, 'This is what they said a year ago' and below it ' – but it isn't what they're saying today.' Teamwork had combined to smash through the Tote's defences. They stood condemned out of the very pen of their own PRO. Things were going well.

Saturday's *Daily Mail* was the first of the other papers to realise the significance of the story and, in a two-paragraph item headed 'Now tell all, Mr Tote,' they wrote:

'The practice of inserting bets into Tote pools after the off is fraught with danger for punters and the machine. ... Tote boss Woodrow Wyatt must devise a fairer system. Better still, publish full details of pools and let all see what's happening.'

On Sunday Bill Maclelland, in the *News of the World*, summarised the facts in a dozen paragraphs and the *Observer*'s Robin Lustig, decently crediting the *Life*, gave it four paragraphs. But their racing correspondent Richard Baerlein, under the telling headline 'Tote caught in time lapse', tore into Wyatt and refuted the chairman's claim that the after-time system had been used by the Tote for years.

That morning was spent contacting former Tote executives such as ex-chairman Sir Alexander Sim, ex-secretary Captain 'Buster' Graham, ex-director-general Dudley Bartlett and former Board member Lord Wigg. All denied selected bets were sent down late when they were in charge.

Wyatt had also claimed there was 'one trusted Tote Board official who has been doing the job for thirty years and who makes the decision as to how much money is sent down to the pool from monies collected before the race.' In Monday's *Life*, alongside Mr Goldring's full letter and Webster's reply, I wrote:

'Public confidence in the operation of the Tote is being undermined by these latest revelations and calls are likely to be made to the Home Secretary to arrange for a senior firm of accountants to investigate every after-time bet placed in the past three years.'

That morning the *Daily Mirror* and *Sun* entered the fray. In three paragraphs, under 'Call for bets probe', the *Mirror* updated the situation and James Lewthwaite in the *Sun* reported Wyatt's defence.

Journalists need long memories and this was crucial in the case of Mrs X, a long-serving racecourse employee of the Tote. She had helped us several years earlier over another story, the editor recalled, and she produced some startling allegations. Her inside evidence, having proved accurate once, added to other leads coming in, made it safe, we felt, to run her story on Tuesday which claimed that Tote on-course managers had been under instructions to telephone the London credit office when there were only one or two winners of the dual forecast pool at the course.

Usually, she recounted, they were told to add at least ten units (£1), and often more, on to the successful combination. And she went on: 'This manipulation of the forecasts looks so bad on us and we're all relieved the whole business is at last being brought out into the open. Take it from me. Very few of the late bets put in the pool are losers. Hardly any of the late "reads" from London contain solely losing bets.'

Finally she told of how one exasperated controller, infuriated at being made to add winning units into the pool after the result, scrawled across the sheet in red pencil: 'This dividend was altered after receiving a reading from London after the race.'

Her statement was dynamite and accompanying it went an Editorial Opinion headed: 'Why Wyatt Must Go.' It began:

It will be a major scandal if Woodrow Wyatt survives as chairman of the Horserace Totalisator Board.

Out of his own mouth, he had demonstrated that in this role he is either an incompetent ass or an opportunist with little regard for the truth.

Bruce George was keeping up the pressure at Westminster and lobbying for support among his colleagues – including Front Bench spokesmen. The Home Secretary's reply to his inquiry was eagerly awaited though both of us felt pessimistic as to the outcome.

A letter from Tote chief executive Geoffrey Rae-Smith in Tuesday's *Life* purported to show how after-time wagering had been common practice down the years – documentary evidence was given backing up the claim – but that no bets had been struck after the off.

In the *Daily Express* Bill Balshaw came out swinging in an interview with Peter O'Sullevan. Headed 'Tote in a tizz – Backers can't get on after time, says Balshaw', O'Sullevan began: 'Suggestions that Tote bets may be placed in the pool after results are known so as to influence dividends were strenuously denied by Bill Balshaw yesterday.' He quoted the former Hills chairman as saying: 'It was simply a clerical error, whereby a clerk transmitted £50 instead of ten different £5 units – and should have been corrected earlier.' As for the after-time allegations, Balshaw said: 'It does not mean a backer can get on after time.'

What a red herring! No one had ever suggested they did. O'Sullevan, unusually for him, had allowed himself to be sidetracked from the main issue of Tote Bookmakers getting on when they knew the result.

But the Balshaw line had been swathed through by Mrs X's simultaneous attack and his arguments were to prove the last serious defence of the indefensible from Tote House.

That Tuesday began for me with a call from Tom Clarke, sports editor of the *Daily*

Mail, asking me to do a Racemail feature on the scandal. Agreeably flattered, I promised to bring it round on my way back from the Commons, where Bruce George hoped to question Mrs Thatcher during Prime Minister's Questions. Also, the Home Secretary's decision about an inquiry was expected.

Almost miraculously, George managed to 'catch the Speaker's eye' and, to growls of approval from the packed benches, he asked:

Will the Prime Minister meet with the chairman of the Tote to discuss allegations that bets were placed by a subsidiary of the Tote after the results of races were known? Is there a secret laundering system for these bets and how many punters have been swindled out of their rightful winnings? And will she order an immediate inquiry into this matter of grave public concern?

Mrs Thatcher replied: 'I am not very expert at betting' – she paused and smiled as laughter echoed round both sides of the chamber – 'and I pass the buck to my Right Honourable friend the Home Secretary, who might know more about it.'

But the dogged Walsall South MP had alerted Parliament and the Press to the seriousness of the scandal and, by managing to raise the matter at the most publicised Commons set-piece of the week, the Tote's last fleeting hopes of containing the crisis had ebbed away.

It was a 'Phew, what a scorcher!' afternoon and, sitting on the terrace of the Commons as a cooling breeze wafted up from the Thames sipping iced Coke while waiting for Mr Whitelaw's statement Bruce George was already discussing his next moves. They would be needed, for, in two paragraphs, the Home Secretary attempted to wash his hands of the affair. The statement read:

The activities of the Horserace Totalisator Board were exhaustively examined by the Select Committee on Nationalised Industries in July 1977.

On the information available to me I see no need for an amendment of the Act. I am informed that only bets received before the 'off' from whatever source can be included in the pools.

Though that left the door ajar it signalled the arrival of a relief column to the besieged Tote and, with just twelve days left to hold out before the sanctuary afforded by Parliament's summer recess, it appeared as though Wyatt, battered but unrepentant, would make it. But, as George said: 'The Prime Minister may not know about betting but even she knows it wasn't possible to back the Tories after the Election!'

Tricycling down Whitehall to Northcliffe House with the Racemail article, I wondered how we could 'top' the peak of PM's Question Time. Somehow momentum had to be maintained and the stonewalling of the Home Office overcome.

But coming over the tapes inside newspaper offices at that very moment was the sensational news that the Tote had climbed down. After-time betting was to cease. In a Press statement they said:

In view of the attacks made by the Sporting Life *on its Chairman, Mr Woodrow Wyatt, the Horserace Totalisator Board at its meeting today affirmed its total confidence in Mr Wyatt.*

The board reviewed the procedures for transmission of off-course bets to the racecourse pool. It is entirely satisfied that there is no impropriety in these procedures. The transmission after the result of bets struck before the off has been the practice of the Board since 1962.

The Board recognises, however, that such procedures, although perfectly proper, are open to malicious misrepresentation. To ensure that misrepresentation of this kind can no longer occur, the Board decided that, starting from today, all off-course bets which it is desired to include in the Win, Place, Dual Forecast, Daily Double and Daily Treble pools will be transmitted to the relevant racecourse pool before the off.

The Board regrets any inconvenience which this requirement may cause to bookmakers holding the Tote Authority and wishing to lay off into the pools.

Off-course bets for the Jackpot, Placepot and any other special pools will as hitherto be transmitted in full to the relevant racecourse pool.

This of course was exactly what the *Life* had been campaigning for since the Carlisle cock-up story broke.

Also, the Tote rushed out figures ahead of time to show how profits had soared 42 per cent to £2,324,029 for the financial year ending 31 March 1979. ('No wonder,' one wag observed, 'if they're able to bet when races are over. I'd be in front doing that!')

But the skimpy fig leaf of financial success – didn't President Nixon talk about China and world peace while being engulfed by Watergate? – proved inadequate protection as the carrions of the Press descended on the Wednesday.

The Tote received their worst press ever. My Racemail piece, covering almost a full page, was headed: 'How the "Nanny" became a black sheep' and, separately, the *Mail* talked of the Tote's 'astonishing climb-down'. Bob Rodney, in the *Daily Mirror*, wrote that the Tote 'had stopped their race to self-destruction' and that the 'Hate-the-Tote' fortnight had been self-inflicted. He added that the paper's Punters Club members were 'amazed by the revelations'.

The *Guardian*, reporting the Tote had been 'under heavy fire recently' confined the previous day's drama to a paragraph but Ken Lawrence, sports editor of the *Daily Express*, in a strong editorial headed 'Milking the Nanny', asked, 'Has someone been milking the "nanny goat"?' before saying: 'Already the *Sporting Life* and bookmakers have cried "foul". If it requires an inquiry there should be one. Whatever is going on certainly won't be to the advantage of the punter. It never is!'

And on page three of the *Express* Peter Hardy, in a twenty-paragraph story, quoted Bruce George as saying he was not opposed to the Tote but 'as a socialist I would love to see it running to everyone's satisfaction'. The increased profits smokescreen was buried in the final paragraph.

Throughout it had proved virtually impossible to ascertain the forces at work within Tote House itself. But now, fortuitously, help was at hand and a high-level source revealed a 'searching in-depth inquiry' had been initiated after the Board had demanded all the facts and figures. The source revealed how the Board had met for their routine monthly meeting on Tuesday and how, up till then, the defence had been marshalled by a triumvirate consisting of Wyatt, Balshaw and Rae-Smith.

Until the meeting, so I was told, most Board members were unaware of any after-time betting and insisted the practice stopped at once. (Board members were Woodrow Wyatt, Dame Elizabeth Ackroyd, Sir Alexander Glen, Frank Chapple, Tony Stratton-Smith, Nigel Broackes, the Duke of Devonshire and Rae-Smith.) And separate lawyers, called in by the Board and also Wyatt himself, were studying all that had been written to date.

Significantly, on the Wednesday the editor received by hand from Wyatt's solicitors a letter informing him that Wyatt was taking 'urgent advice' on the content of our stories. The letter added: 'We think it right that you should take this fact into account when determining your own future course of action.' The intention was clearly to scare us off but we don't scare that easily.

That Wednesday evening I went to Kempton and, coincidentally, a coachload of MPs, invited by the Commons All-Party Racing Committee, was there. This was to prove unfortunate for the Tote to say the least. As the position stood they had survived the shock of the revelations, the ill-advised practice of late betting had ceased, and there the affair could have rested. Extra pressure, inside and outside of Westminster, was needed fast and the men to give it within the Palace walls were the committee chairman and vice-chairman, Sir Timothy Kitson and Bob Mellish.

Sir Timothy, the Tory member for Richmond in Yorkshire, and I had worked together on other racing matters and when he popped up to the Press box at Kempton I wasted no time bringing him up to date with Totegate. Later I talked to him and Bob Mellish (Lab. Bermondsey) and emphasised the need for an inquiry. Mellish, of course, was particularly concerned about the nationalised aspect of the Tote and Sir Timothy promised to see his old friend Mr Whitelaw personally.

As I reported in the *Life* next day, Sir Timothy said: 'I can't see any other way out for the Tote. This whole matter has to be cleared up to the public satisfaction.' Mellish said: 'Something has to be done. These allegations are so serious, only a full inquiry will clear the air.' The all-important momentum was not being lost.

This hardening of the Racing Committee's position, and news of the 'searching internal inquiry' was given in Thursday's *Life*. And that morning Peter O'Sullevan, in the *Daily Express*, led his column with: 'Woodrow to act – He is seeking legal advice'.

Wyatt spoke of meeting the formidable libel lawyer Lord Goodman – we all knew what that could mean! – and the chairman showed he at least, from the bunker of Tote House, remained defiant. 'It would be sheer madness,' he said, of the dichotomy of aims inherent in the Tote and Tote Bookmakers, 'to conduct internecine warfare, even if granted the opportunity, and I would draw your attention to Tote profits and the consequent sums made available to racing.'

So it had sunk to this! Totegate, in relation to the supposed good of racing, was a minor misdemeanour. It was as though Wyatt was pleading for past indiscretions to be forgiven in view of the goodies to come. The defences had indeed been shorn away.

But that attitude was strong in many quarters. One leading trainer told me: 'All this Tote uproar, John – maybe there's something in it, but don't forget Wyatt has pulled them round. Now they pump money into racing – that's what matters in the end.'

Does it? Leaving aside the fact that the profits increase in ratio to the number of betting shops purchased, is the pursuit of money to override all ethics?

But any complacent thoughts that the Tote Board were shell-shocked into inaction were dismissed that Thursday afternoon when Wyatt complained that my morning report of Tuesday's Board meeting was 'wrong'.

In a formally issued statement he said the decision that off-course bets for inclusion in pools would now be transmitted to the respective courses prior to the race concerned was taken *before* the board met, not

at the meeting as my report suggested. A distinction with hardly a difference! It gave editor Ossie Fletcher the lead-in for this piece in Friday's *Life*:

The Horserace Totalisator Board are clutching at straws in attempts to discredit the Sporting Life *following its revelations about after-time betting.*

Yesterday they went to the extraordinary length of issuing a formal four-paragraph Press statement saying the report on yesterday's front page 'purporting to describe the proceedings' at Tuesday's Board meeting was 'wrong'.

While we have no wish to waste space on semantic trivialities, we are bound to point out that the reason we said the decision was taken at the meeting was that that is what the Board themselves said in their written statement immediately afterwards.

Ouch!

Phone calls offering information, stories, the querying of countless past Tote dividends and some plain mischievous were pouring into the *Life* office and, by sifting these and checking known statements, I was able to reveal that a ferocious internal struggle for the control of the Tote – with the traditionalists on one side and advocates of profit through betting shops ranged on the other – was decided in the autumn of 1976.

But the Tote still had one unfailing ally even at this stage. Ian de Wesselow, *Raceform*'s boss, strove to shore up the Tote's shattered credibility by attacking the *Life* in his roundabout article in the weekly racing paper *The Racehorse*. He lashed out at Bruce George, talked of 'confusion' and produced the hoary discredited alibi of 'long lists of bets, probably beginning before the off and continuing until after the race has been run'.

'It is not suggested Tote subsidiaries are passing winning bets to the pool while retaining losing bets,' he wrote.

Wasn't it? Where had de Wesselow been hibernating for the previous fortnight?

The Friday produced the final artillery assault which was to shatter the Tote's efforts to resist the setting up of an official inquiry – the Savage revelations. Dennis Savage, 53, had worked for the Tote for thirty-two years until February 1979, by which time he was in a senior management position. But, more important, he was still branch secretary of ACTSS, the white collar section of the TGWU, having previously been chairman for six years. He knew Wyatt, Balshaw and Rae-Smith personally through union negotiating meetings and his evidence was damning.

Over lunch Savage told me of the late 'reads' sent down from London which almost invariably contained winning bets. And he revealed how sheets containing those 'reads' existed and could be used to prove by analysis the percentage of winners laid off.

It was as though the White House tapes had suddenly been discovered. As Savage explained:

Each gives the amount staked on the winner, placed horses and forecasts from the various racecourse rings, on-course credit – and the extra inclusion from London.

And, from personal experience ever since the selective system of transmitting bets was introduced in 1976, I know most of them were phoned through after the race. Before then the practice was to send virtually all off-course bets into the pool. Nearly always this was completed before the race was over and those too late for inclusion became 'broken money' in London and were 'stood' by the Tote.

These racecourse control reads – they are kept for about three years – contain all the necessary evidence.

The problem was to convince the diffident Savage of the need to come out publicly and reveal all. This he reluctantly agreed to in Saturday's *Life*. This proved the crucial shove needed. Bruce George realised at once the implications of the Savage exposures. 'That's it,' he said, 'there must be an inquiry now!'

On Sunday John Oaksey, in the *Sunday Telegraph*, was in full cry:

Independent inquiry vital for the Tote's image' headlined a piece which began: 'There can no longer be much doubt about the need for a completely independent inquiry into the operations of the Tote.*

. . . to my mind it had already become inevitable as early as last Tuesday when the Sporting Life's *tireless investigator John McCririck quoted 'a long-serving female racecourse employee of the Tote'.*

. . . even my sparse knowledge of betting machinery tells me that, if true, the allegation reveals a straightforward criminal offence.

On Monday I quoted Sir Timothy Kitson: 'There has to be an inquiry. A *prima facie* case has demonstrably been made out.'

Bruce George kept nagging at the Home Secretary with another demand for an inquiry on Tuesday and he stated his determination to have a Commons debate on the issue before the recess at the weekend. And he told me of 'fantastic stories' passed on to him by individuals and concluded: 'This is a statutory body we are talking about – public money is involved – and attempts at covering it all up must end, and be seen to have ended.'

A reader, A. H. Coeshalls, wrote an amusing letter to the paper at this time: 'I would like to be the first bookmaker to support Mr Woodrow Wyatt. In turn, I assume he will give me a hedging account that allows me the same facilities as Tote Bookmakers Ltd!'

Then, on Wednesday 25 July – just twelve days after the scandal broke – the Home Office somersaulted on the issue and issued the following statement:

The chairman of the Horserace Totalisator Board has discussed with the Home Secretary recent allegations in the Press about the transmission of Tote bets.

Mr Wyatt has informed the Home Secretary that he is calling in the police to investigate whether criminal offences have been committed.

He has also asked the Home Secretary to hold an independent inquiry into the Tote's procedures for the inclusion in their on-course pool of bets made off the course.

Representations to this effect have also been made by the Parliamentary All-Party Racing Committee.

The Home Secretary has agreed to their request and will announce, as soon as possible, the person who will carry out the inquiry.

The inquiry will be without prejudice to any police investigations that may prove necessary and any criminal proceedings that may ensue.

Its findings will be published.

Under the banner headline 'TOTE: WHITE-LAW CALLS INQUIRY – WYATT CALLS IN POLICE', Graham Taylor made over for the second time virtually all the front page to the culmination of the campaign, quoting Sir Timothy Kitson: 'It's great news and a fine piece of work by your paper. It is very important this came to light.'

And Bruce George: 'It shows how the Press and MPs together can produce action. At least punters can now place bets with the

Tote knowing already that nothing will be done to tamper with the pools after-time.'

The rest you know.

*

'The rest' was the independent inquiry headed by Francis Aglionby QC. It found the Tote guilty of sending bets to the course after the result had been known. But the report exonerated Woodrow Wyatt and members of the Tote Board. Blame was placed on 'misplaced enthusiasm' of Tote employees lower down the ladder. The Life's *headline read, 'THE TOTE GUILTY, BUT MINNOWS TAKE THE RAP'. The Great Survivor was awarded a life peerage as Lord Wyatt of Weeford in 1987, and in 1990 his tenure at the Tote was again extended, this time by two years.*

DAZED AND CONFUSED IN THE GOLD CUP CAULDRON

Never can a Cheltenham Festival winner have cantered back past the stands to such stunned disbelief as 100-1 Norton's Coin after the 1990 Tote Gold Cup.

'Who won it?' and 'Number 7 – what's that?' and even 'Who's in the black colours?' were among the incredulous queries as punters and workmen bemusedly stared at their racecards.

On the floor of Tatts, alongside joints and by the rails, it was impossible for all but a privileged few on stools to see the action save for occasional glimpses of jockeys' caps or horses' rear sides.

United in relying on racecourse commentator Raleigh 'Bwana' Gilbert's call, often drowned out as eventual third Desert Orchid's progress was observed to loud accompanying cheers, we were mainly oblivious to the reality of the drama climaxing barely a few hundred yards away.

From the last fence the only name coherently coming through was Toby Tobias, though I did reckon at the time that bookies unashamedly punching the air in delight were stretching joyful celebrations a bit far, as the 8-1 chance had been persistently supported second favourite almost up to the off.

One stocky Scottish punter was leaping up and down shrieking: 'I canna see it – oh, there's the winning post!' While next to him a demented fiend urged: 'Come on Toby, Toby's got it, go on my son, Toby, Toby . . . oh no, what's the thing that's done him? I don't believe it – Norton's bloody Coin! Just my luck – I didn't do Toby each way, that's the finish for me.'

Compared with the mass hysteria in 1989, when hats blackened the sky as Dessie battled past Yahoo and the noise was deafening before emotional punters hugged strangers in sheer exuberance, the applause this time for the Welsh unknown, except from some bookies, could scarcely be heard.

Instinctively jockey Graham McCourt acknowledged muted clapping from Tatts on his way back but in fact it came from sympathetic Dessie loyalists, while one punter joked: 'I don't know what that Norton's Coin had for breakfast, but I could certainly do with some of it myself!'

Down in racing's heartbeat, the betting ring, there was no sentimental talk of the 'magic of steeplechasing' or lofty ideals of triumph for the little man over established stables and stars.

Instead irrational anger, which does the game no credit but is so frequently evident in betting shops and racecourse, was expressed by one embittered ignoramus loudly proclaiming: 'Richard Pitman was the worst jockey I've ever known in my life until today. Now his son takes the biscuit. How could he let that no-hoper go past him? Ben de Haan would have won on it.'

Coming from someone whose view of the race, like thousands of others including my own, could only have been at best spasmodic and fleeting, such an outburst was valueless and told all who listened more about the complainant's peanut brain than anything else. Nevertheless it crudely expressed the sheer frustration of backing the correct horse to turn over 11-10 on Dessie and still not having a draw.

Another fellow in danger of failing to collect was a genial but upset Welshman who claimed to have a £20 bet on Norton's Coin to win, or be second to Dessie, at 66-1.

Apparently a boards bookmaker had refused to pay, though on what grounds wasn't clear. 'Where's the Ring Inspector – where can I find him?' he implored, getting more and more agitated.

Good question. Amid the teeming throng his chances seemed about as promising as finding a successful backer. It is about time the Racecourse Association, with so much SIS cash sloshing around, instructed their members to put up large signs, prominently displayed, as to where anyone aggrieved can immediately seek out the independent arbiter before festering, irrational resentment takes over.

On a big race day I defy stewards to locate the Ring Inspector straight away at any of our courses. In various minor capacities I've been floating around the periphery of many of them for a few years now and frequent requests, such

as the Welshman's, have invariably been met with unsure finger-pointing in some vague direction or another.

Inspectors themselves should insist that their locations are well signposted though, more important, all bookies ought to use tape recorders. And, looking to the future, computerised betting slips such as they have in Australia – not numbered tickets which can always be subject to dispute – are a must.

For hard-pressed clerks on the busiest jumps day of the year, that welcome blank column under Norton's Coin, an absolute 'skinner' for so many layers, took the pressure off for a few minutes. With virtually nobody to pay out, early prices on the following Ritz Club National Hunt Chase were being chalked up even before the winner had been unsaddled.

There was, however, one other cause of delay, a particularly nauseous spectacle – bookmakers dipping into their 'hods' gathering great wads of cash and counting out each note with a smug self-satisfaction as if to say: 'It's our turn, lads, you've done it all this time, and it won't be coming back.'

In the centre enclosure, opposite the stands, an ambulance, lights flashing, was inching its way through the throng near the winning post. An insensitive workman, summing up the mood, turned to his guv'nor and whispered: 'Quick – put up some prices. They're starting to carry them out over there!'

For most, though, financial and not medical resuscitation was all that was required.

9 *Losers*

The ebullient Terry Ramsden. No one more enlivened the game during the Eighties, but in that ruthless betting jungle lions are so often tamed!

Take heed of what happened to Terry Ramsden, once Britain's 57th richest man, whose Glen International crashed in 1988 with £140 million losses. An ebullient, daredevil character to interview on TV, Ramsden in the mid-1980s owned 100 racehorses and is said to have lost £77 million gambling! The rags-to-riches financial tycoon is described by Ladbrokes' Ron Pollard in *Odds and Sods* as 'the biggest loser of the latter-day gamblers . . . a wild, wild gambler'. Pollard elucidates:

Sometimes he would have a £1000 Yankee, which would cost £11,000, but there were times when he would have a £5000 one, which meant a lay-out of £55,000. Over a period of years, betting in this way, on both horses and dogs, was to lose him an estimated £100 million to bookmakers at large. I was very sorry indeed when, in 1988, he owed Ladbrokes so much money that I was forced to take the action that ended with him being 'warned off'. I tried to protect and help him to the very last, organising a deal and preparing a letter for him to sign agreeing to pay us a certain amount each month. Time and again I warned him of the consequences of not paying if he did sign the agreement and time and again Terry assured me that it would not be a difficulty for him. Yet we did not receive a single payment and we were left with no other option. . . .

The tragedy of Terry Ramsden was that he was a clever man – too clever, you would have thought, to get himself into such a mess.

But a mess is just what too many punters can find themselves in, and we must not forget the dark underside of the world of betting – so fascinating and absorbing one minute, yet tragic and bleak the next.

A fight broke out in a Yorkshire bingo hall over one lady taking the regular table of a pensioner, who died from her injuries in the ensuing brawl. Child gamblers become addicted to playing fruit machines, even stealing money from home to fuel their obsession. A distraught Berkshire father reported his 15-year-old son to the police for stealing £800 from him to play fruit machines.

Thieving to finance compulsive gambling was brought to a more sophisticated level by crooked accountant Nicholas Young, who between 1985 and 1990 placed £10.9 million in bets on horses - averaging £5000 daily. His prey, some seventy of them, were taken in by his firm's respectably opulent West End offices and readily believed promises of two to three per cent interest *per month* on their investment – 'almost as much as the credit card companies are charging you', he'd say.

For a while these rates were paid as others were lured in, but inevitably the 'snowball' pyramid collapsed and Young was jailed for four years (not excessive, you might think). Of course investors were both greedy and gullible, but how they've suffered for it – some becoming destitute overnight.

A prison visitor described Young, public-school educated and a son of the Queen's chaplain, as having 'under his carapace of bland cheerfulness an enormous hostility. To take his victims' money and throw it away on the gee-gees is just about the most effectively murderous thing he could have done. He was killing them. When we discussed his case and the position of his victims, he spoke about himself as if it was another person, as if somebody else had done all this.'

Self-delusion entraps many chronic gamblers. Their crimes, from fraud to stealing from their friends and relatives, are the downside of gambling which is always there. Compulsion takes many forms. Few are sadder or more distressing than excesses brought on by a compelling urge to bet beyond your means.

One postscript to the sorry Young saga, and many others: those unscrupulous bookies who accept such enormous bets without asking any questions have consciences too – or have they? Never forget those who share our fascination with the world of betting and gambling but let it build into a compulsion. They may go to Gamblers Anonymous (081-741 4181) to help beat such a destructive addiction, or resort to their own devices. These include a sincere promise to some Divine Being never to have another bet ever again 'if this one wins'; and a pledge after another losing day, 'that's it – no more betting – that's the last penny bookmakers will ever get from me'. Such vows, made under stress, are rarely adhered to!

The appalling drawback of so many human activities which can bring such pleasure, relaxation and fun when pursued in moderation – betting, drinking, eating and sex – is that they can be over-indulged, with unexpected and disastrous results.

Don't let betting bring you even near such a calamitous situation. Never forget that most fundamental law for any punter, large or small : always – *always* – bet within your means. Once you allow that overriding rule to slip, be it ever so slightly, betting is no longer fun.

We can't, and mustn't be blind to gambling's dark, occasionally tragic consequences. People lose – like the Saudi Arabian Sheikh Eynani, who played two roulette wheels simultaneously on the French Riviera in 1990 and lost £8.8 million in just four weeks, beating his own world record for the greatest losses (£8 million, set in 1985). During one particularly tricky four-night period in the 1990 bout with the wheel he lost £6.5 million.

For him that wasn't 'tragic'. For someone else having a 'case' (last) tenner on a horse, it could be.

People cheat, as we've seen in the section on coups, and there are many cheating on a far more professional level – like gamblers at a Coventry casino who indulged in 'top hatting', whereby a pair of players stand at a roulette table, one betting on the winning number just as the ball drops and the other distracting the croupier at the key moment. In the days before strict controls, the essential balance of wheels could be tampered with.

Gambling, with cash slushing around, undeniably has its seamy side. But the Chief Constable who approved of betting shops because if his boys wanted to nab a few minor crooks, they simply had to go to the betting shop and round them up, was out of date. He might just as well have suggested a pub or restaurant. Villains are all around us – even on racecourses!

How Arkle's Defeat Upset the World's Worst Loser

There was precious little seasonal goodwill flowing around Kempton's Silver Ring on 27 December 1966.

After the most dramatic King George VI Chase of them all, when 10-1 chance Dormant came again to floor the peerless Arkle (2-9), we lowly denizens from afar were neither short of opinions nor slow to express them. After all, how incredible it was that Arkle, the greatest equine athlete any of us had ever seen, had lost only his fourth steeplechase in twenty-six after being well clear at the last.

And the most embarrassingly vocal complainant was my mate 'Nifty' Eddie. He liked to think his nickname reflected unconcealed admiration for his sharpness and fleetness of foot as he ducked and dived in life and on the racecourse, much like the far more illustrious 'Dodger' McCartney today. In fact, in our gang, we slyly used to add, though he never quite cottoned on, that 'Hey, Shifty' sounded much the same in the wind as 'Hey, Nifty'.

Anyway, hyperactive, ever-bustling 'Shifty', a sprinter of some distinction apparently in his younger days, was a 35-year-old, lean, fit, Scot. Tall, gangling, with a shock of reddish hair, he was forever twitching and could never be still for an instant. But in life, like the rest of us, he was very much minor league – a failed Arfur Daley really.

How his wife, a sweet uncomplaining little thing called Sue, put up with this zany mixed-up character defied any human explanation, though perhaps his prolonged absences from the nest must have helped. On the few occasions I met her, Sue was always optimistic about some upcoming 'deal' and loyally maintained that he genuinely cared for her. In our company evidence of that was a little thin, and the only constant in his existence used to be his unavailability on Sundays.

Not reckoned to be a devout churchgoer, Shifty worked the outdoor markets every Sabbath. Though how this exertion kept him financially solvent, let alone Sue as well, remained a mystery none of us attempted to solve.

Yet he was never a downer and he brought an infectious enthusiasm to his racing selections, much the same as he must have shown as a stallholder barking his wares whatever they happened to be and wherever they came from.

Now, as you know, there are two kinds of punters – one who cannot believe his beast has somehow overcome the numerous vicissitudes and won; and the other unable to accept, in a sporting manner, the harsh evidence of bare results. Shifty was King of the after-race moaners. If his choice wasn't placed it must have fallen, been left or disqualified by biased stewards. Fate, villainy, the trainer or the jockey – and often a long-winded invention involving all four – had to be to blame.

So when his big-race 'business' was scampering around for the 3-1 or even better Arkle to beat Dormant, leaving out Woodland Venture ('A boy among men here'), and the other quartet, he was leaping up and down with joy after the 6-1 second favourite capsized at the second last while still upsides Arkle. No remorse for the gallant animal or that brave, swashbuckling cavalier Terry Biddlecombe, from Shifty.

Thumping me on the back as Arkle went past us approaching the last a good five lengths clear of Dormant, with the rest nowhere, including the soon-to-become-immortal 100-1 Grand National winner Foinavon, he was bellowing his approval. Run on a Tuesday, it was clear all Sunday's takings were on the line.

Now there is a problem sizing up close finishes from most Silver Rings – Ascot's is the worst – in that it is impossible to tell from the receding backsides of the protagonists exactly what's going on.

With the course commentary drowned out by the noise of the huge crowd all we could see was that Dormant (receiving 21lb) was making a race of it up the run-in, though 'obviously' that was because 'himself', as Arkle's Irish legions called him, was simply easing down.

Eventually though, when the premature celebrations collapsed as the dreadful outcome sank in that Dormant had sneaked back up to win by a length, Shifty was beside himself in voluble fury. Jockey Pat Taaffe 'didn't try, did he? – you saw for yourself, he went to sleep – what are the stewards doing? – this will kill the game – I'll never have another bet, that's it – look at those [expletives deleted] bookies' etc., etc.

All total nonsense. Apart from the fact that in the Silver Ring Dormant would have been a far worse result than the unbackable favourite, save for those cunning enough to offer 6-1 and 7-1 while laying off at 10-1 inside, from what I'd seen that old-style horseman Pat Taaffe had been vigorous and alert.

But nothing could placate the enraged-to-the-point-of-apoplexy Shifty. Always a rotten loser, this seemed to unloose the last screw that held him together and for the rest of the day he was the boring epitome of nature's biggest complaining pain.

Worst of all, as so often, those closest to events knew least. It was only on reading the next day's papers that, for us, the awful truth emerged. Arkle had suffered a broken pedal bone in his off-fore and, as it eventually turned out, would never race again.

Had we been informed of that down in the Silver Ring perhaps Shifty, and others somewhat less irate, would have been mollified. Though knowing the world's worst loser that is unlikely. He would probably have retorted, 'They would make up something like that, wouldn't they?' To Shifty, nothing could beat 'Ankle', as he always called him, except some kind of ramp.

Incidentally, if you ever have the nerve to wind up The Noble Lord, be similarly irreverent about his hero – though make sure you don't hang around afterwards!

Anyway, Shifty went his own way shortly after that. Some in our gang suggested that perhaps he had become a guest of Her Majesty or, more exotically, finally cracked it and was living the high life in Rio or Acapulco. Whatever the intervening years brought, it would be spiffing to meet up again.

'Nifty' old chap, or even sweet Sue, luv, please come to Kempton on Boxing Day. If you search you are liable to find me – dashing, debonair, handsome as ever – lurking around the rails still trying pathetically to earn a crust to keep going.

Things at this end have been hard since we last met and if I appear to be wandering about talking absolute nonsense to myself, please be understanding.

Take pity. It has come to this.

By the way don't fret, as you used to, you old reprobate, over your round. Apart from the odd glass of bubbly, I'm on diet Cokes these days. You'll be able to judge for yourself how effectively they're working!

10 *Around the World of Betting*

A part of my soul expired with Alexandra Park.

I've told the Booby that when I die, there's to be no period of national mourning. No state funeral, or 69-gun salute. The nation, in its grief, mustn't come to a standstill. I know very well there's a space allotted for me in Westminster Abbey. A stonemason is already sculpting my monument.

But I'll have none of this. The Booby understands that I'm to be cremated, and the ashes scattered where the furlong pole used to stand at Alexandra Park. I've taken her to show exactly where it's to be done, so there'll be no excuse if she lets me down. She wouldn't dare fail her boy anyway.

Part of me died when Ally Pally shut in 1970. Nothing could match the atmosphere of that tiny course near the foot of Muswell Hill, at the time of its demise the only racecourse within the boundaries of Greater London.

But it was on its uppers by the end of the Swinging Sixties, and because its fixture list was dominated by evening meetings, which were no use to the Levy (betting shops being closed in the evenings), the Levy Board declined to fund the course. Badly managed, closure became inevitable.

In some ways the villain of the piece was former Labour MP George Wigg, chairman of the Levy Board from 1967 to 1972. He could have saved Ally Pally but didn't. Though conspiratorial, vindictive and cunning – his machinations were labelled 'Wiggery Pokery' – the ex-Paymaster General and troubleshooter for Harold Wilson was a man you took on at your peril, for he did his homework thoroughly. A controversial figure, George did much to save Epsom and Liverpool when both were threatened. For that, and for knocking some sense into the racing establishment, he deserves gratitude. But his sound business sense overrode any sentimental affection in which Alexandra Park was held, and he let it go.

Ally Pally had only three distances. Races over one mile 160 yards and one mile five furlongs started in front of the stands before the runners went off to negotiate the famous 'frying pan', the circular part of the course – once round for the shorter distance, twice for the longer. Five-furlong affairs started on a chute obscured from the stands by a wall of trees: what used to go on in the early stages of those sprints – before stalls and all-seeing film patrols – is too horrendous to contemplate.

But I, along with thousands of other Londoners who flocked to the evening meetings there, loved the place. And we 'adopted' horses who acted so well on that peculiar circuit: Induna, Cider Apple, Cantab, Marly Knowe and plenty more.

I miss Ally Pally desperately. But on a fine summer evening visit Windsor, which must be the worst viewing track in the world, and see the crowds cramming the stands revelling in the chance to go racing after their day's toil.

'The Frying Pan' – Alexandra Park in all its glory. And there I am, lurking in the Silver Ring

If Windsor can be made to pay, why not Alexandra Park? My greatest ambition in life is for somebody to come along with £20 million to revive Alex. The stands have long gone but the outline of the course is still there (you can see the five-furlong chute on the left from the train going north from King's Cross). No doubt we'd need to build a supermarket and sports centre to help the scheme along, but that's fine. Surely the local council would be enthusiastic to encourage jobs and business.

My dream is to see racing again at Ally Pally before I die, so if anyone reading this has a spare £20 million or so, please get in touch.

Meanwhile I'm reduced to traipsing around some of the lesser arenas of the world of betting. Gambling in some form or other takes place across the globe, but the facilities differ significantly from country to country.

Of the major racing nations, only Ireland has the same set-up as Britain, with bookmakers on- and off-course, plus tote facilities.

France has the best racing in Continental Europe, and – appropriately – the highest turnover. All betting is on the Pari Mutuel, a pool system like the Tote, and the national bets on selected days are the high-flying Quinté (first five from 18 runners) and long-established Tiercé (first three in correct order) and Quatre Plus (first four). Tickets are sold not only on racecourses but in corner shops and bars.

These pools account for more than 60 per cent of Pari-Mutuel investments; 28 per cent is forecasts and just 11 per cent win and place!

But don't bank on the accuracy of pre-race Pari-Mutuel shows. At the off for the 1991 Group One Prix Jacques le Marois at Deauville, Hector Protector, coupled with

One for the patriots – but British punters proved reluctant to put 'readies' alongside their emotions, and Linford Christie's breathtaking victory in the 100 metres at the Barcelona Olympics in August 1992 was a 'result' for the books. A 50-1 chance with Hills early in the year, Christie lined up for the final top-priced at 3-1, behind odds-on American Leroy Burrell. But chauvinists were bemoaning their impartiality when the lad from good old Shepherd's Bush powered to victory by six hundredths of a second – the sprinting equivalent of hacking up.

The Greatest Show on Earth produced record-breaking betting turnover, with prices available on all major sports and many of the more obscure.

As usual, greatest interest was in the track events, where Britain's other gold medallist was Essex Girl herself, the dishy Sally 'Top' Gunnell in the 400 metres hurdles, backed from 2-1 to evens ('By far the best-backed winner of the Games', reported Ladbrokes). But latecomers to the patriotic bandwagon were stung by defeats of warm favourite Colin Jackson in the 100 metres hurdles, Steve Backley (javelin) and Liz McColgan (10,000 metres).

Some time before the '92 Games, Liverpool electrician Alex Robb placed £200 to win £100,000 (500-1) about his son Curtis winning the Blue Riband 1500 metres gold at Atlanta in 1996. Did his boy peak too early when reaching the 800 metres final at Barcelona? He finished a staying on sixth, and that 500-1 voucher looks well worth keeping safe behind the mantelpiece clock . . .

Yet the greatest Barcelona memory for British fans has to be team captain Linford Christie's 100 metres. 'Had it been a horse race,' reported Matthew Engel in *The Guardian*, 'you would have emptied your wallet on Christie the moment you saw him in the paddock, all biceps and pecs, physically dominating the field.' Just like me among the Channel Four Racing team!

Atlanta here I come . . .

pacemaker Mousquetaire, was priced at 2.3 francs (over 5-4). Yet the declared dividend returned 1.8 francs (5-4 on). *Incroyable!*

The biggest day of the French racing year, and the afternoon which gets most attention from punters on the other side of the Channel, is the first Sunday in October – Longchamp for the Ciga Prix de l'Arc de Triomphe.

Over 30,000 people make their way through the Bois de Boulogne for the Arc, one of the great days of world racing. A vast amount of francs are wagered there, although for the ordinary punter having a bet involves standing in a queue for ages as it inches towards the window (forget any paddock inspection if you want to get on!). In 1991 Longchamp punters that Sunday put the equivalent of £1,749,676 into the Pari-Mutuel pools, £49.90 per head. Compare this with the £21.27 per head wagered on average on our Tote on each day of Royal Ascot that year, or the £17.15 at the Goodwood July meeting – but remember British racegoers have the welcome alternative attraction of course bookmakers, who take at least 85 per cent of business.

Advocates of a Tote monopoly in Britain bang on about how much better the facilities are in countries which do not allow bookmakers, how much better the prize money is, and so on. They conveniently forget that British punters have the precious privilege of *choice*. They also forget – or perhaps they've never subjected themselves to it – the frightful experience of trying to get a bet on during a big day like the Arc. Plenty of punters who've crossed the Channel for the most glamorous day in European racing have been reduced to gibbering wrecks by the necesssity to queue for half an hour to get your bet on and then queue for another half hour to get paid out once *votre cheval* has obliged. Computerisation will fundamentally ease the travail – one day. But you still won't be able to take a price.

Such grumbles apart, Arc day is a magnificent occasion, with the cream of European society – well, I'm there, though not the Booby – producing a stylish parade of fashion and wealth. Situated close to the heart of Paris, Longchamp is France's equivalent of Ally Pally, geographically at least. Perhaps that's why I feel so at home there!

A recurrent issue for British punters betting on the big French races such as the Arc is whether to wager at British bookmakers' odds, or take the Pari-Mutuel return. The advice used to be that if you wanted to back a British challenger, opt for the course Pari-Mutuel return; if you preferred a home-trained runner, plump for bookie's odds. The reasoning was that the weight of on-course money for the locals would compress their odds, and native ignorance of the form of our brave challengers ensure that their returns were outsized. Our clever

bookie chappies would have a different perspective on the race from the hordes of onion-sellers at Longchamp.

This rule of thumb no longer applies, as the odds of some of our recent Arc day challengers testify. Even the most chauvinist Frenchman knew that Dayjur would win the 1990 Prix de l'Abbaye (and after Whippet had unceremoniously dumped John Reid at the start, there was no French runner in the race anyway). There was no chance that lack of appreciation of Dayjur's form would ease his odds, and he duly bolted in at 10-1 on, the smallest price which the Pari-Mutuel will return for a win bet (and for a place bet it can simply return stake money – *mon Dieu!*, though it's happened here too).

Nowadays around a quarter of the crowd on Arc day are British, so that any bias of the on-course market towards home runners is effectively removed. And, of course, it is not unknown for representatives of our astute bookmakers to join the cross-channel expedition, with in-flight bags full of readies to lump into the course pools. And let none of them dare do any private business at the course. Parisian cells can be cold and forbidding!

At French meetings where the influx of British visitors is less, you can often do well by backing the challengers at on-course odds. Sanglamore, who in 1990 became the second British-trained winner of the Prix du Jockey-Club (French Derby) at Chantilly, after Old Vic (9-2) in 1989, paid 9½-1, having been generally 6-1 with the big British firms the day before.

Chantilly for the Prix du Jockey-Club – run on the Sunday before the real thing at Epsom – is a far cry from Longchamp on Arc day. While other Derby Days – at Epsom or Churchill Downs (the Run for the Roses) – are wonderfully popular events, the courses teeming with people hell-bent on enjoying themselves, Chantilly evokes an era of Flat racing from the distant past. A crowd of under 20,000 occupy the stately stands of this most classical of world race-courses, with the Grandes Ecuries, the magnificent chateau stable block at the far end of the track, providing an unparalleled backdrop. (The Grandes Ecuries was built by the Comte du Condé, who was convinced that he would be reincarnated as a horse, unlike another nutcase who knows he will again be a floorman at Alexandra Park.)

Chantilly's atmosphere is reminiscent of a quiet mid-week meeting at Salisbury. The action is unhurried, the ambiance genteel and quietly sociable: racegoers are there as much for the garden fete atmosphere as the sport. About midday, two hours before the first race, early-comers sit down to an *al fresco* lunch of lobster and champagne, then saunter off to make a bet with an impersonal Pari-Mutuel machine. All is decorum.

Much like elegant, stylish, incredibly expensive Deauville – the August seaside haunt of those who have it and those that haven't but pretend they have. Chic and chicanery sum up Deauville's charm.

In contrast, America's great Triple Crown days, highlighted by the Kentucky Derby on the first Saturday in May, generate tremendous excitement and hoopla. Seeing the triumph of Winning Colors in 1988 matches any sporting experience I've been privileged to enjoy. Also magnificent is the championship Breeders' Cup series, first run in 1984. The venue moves from year to year, different tracks imparting their own atmosphere. Fortunately I've managed to inveigle myself into every one. Each has been special, and if there's a racing trip abroad you must try and save up for, it has

to be the Breeders' Cup. (Incidentally, for any overseas racing, contact Ian Fry at Horse Racing Abroad (Golden Key Building, 15 Market Street, Sandwich, Kent CT13 9DA; phone 0304 612424): his expertise and individual attention ensure any trip to the races, sometimes combined in an exotic package tour, turns out 'brill'.)

Breeders' Cups generate fabulous betting. The unforgettable 1990 staging at Belmont Park, New York – Dayjur jumping the shadow of the stand when about to win the Sprint on dirt, the tragedy of Go For Wand, Lester and Royal Academy – attracted a crowd of over 51,000. At Churchill Downs in November 1991 more than 66,000 produced an on-course 'handle' equivalent to £5,627,118.

Those privileged to be there that day saw one of the most staggering performances of all time when Arazi won the Breeders' Cup Juvenile, weaving his way snipe-like through the field. But the dream shattered abruptly on the same track six months later in the Kentucky Derby. More money was bet on Arazi (10-9 on) than on any other horse in the 118 runnings of the 'Run for the Roses'.

That familiar Hollywood-scripted speed was there down the far side – but not where it mattered, and the 'wonder horse of the century' faded into eighth place behind Lil E Tee (168-10).

In the USA there are no bookmakers as we know them. Odds-makers in Las Vegas and other cities in Nevada will quote prices about certain events, and some states have Off-Track Betting (OTB's), like our betting shops (though generally far more primitive in conditions) but providing betting only to the on-track pool dividends. New York was the first city to open OTB's in 1971, and now has over 100, with around 250 in the whole of New York State. Some American

BETTING ON OVERSEAS RACES

Bookmakers, unless they pump huge sums into the local Pari Mutuels, have no control regarding dividends on overseas racing.

Tolomeo's 1983 Arlington Million triumph – when trained at Newmarket by Luca Cumani and ridden by Pat Eddery – at 38.2-1 wasn't popular with the layers. He was priced as low as 6-1 in Britain! Disputes arose as disgruntled punters claimed the bonanza odds.

But it was far worse in 1988 when Ladbrokes tried to settle at their 12-1 over French-trained Mill Native, returned at 40.6-1, in the Million held at Woodbine, Toronto, and televised live on Channel Four. The furious reaction was predictable.

Claude Duval, 'The Punters' Pal' in the *Sun*, opened an Actionline which blasted the whole mess asunder and demolished the at times contradictory Ladbrokes defence. The firm's much vaunted 'Bill of Rights' was in danger of being discredited until public pressure and some ridicule, including from Channel Four Racing, forced an about-turn.

Clients were paid at 40.6-1, and the 'Magic Sign' showed itself big enough to hold hands up and admit they were wrong.

Now all overseas bets are settled, tax free, on the country's returned dividends. Only if you specify that you want to take a price will that general ruling be void.

Fifty-four-year-old grandad Lester Piggott and Royal Academy (14-5 favourite) collar the blinkered Itsallgreektome in the 1990 Breeders' Cup Mile at Belmont Park

states do not allow betting at all, though slowly that's changing.

The question raised about whether to bet on British horses running in France at home

prices or on-course returns also applies in the USA. With European riders increasingly frequent in the big American races, and consequently punters' interest in those events rapidly growing, betting from the UK will become more common.

But again, the presence of a thousand or more British racegoers at a top event like the Breeders' Cup and the regularity with which our bookies can put money into the course pool are altering the situation. Royal Academy returned odds of 14-5 favourite when winning the Breeders' Cup Mile at Belmont Park. The morning of the race he was easily available at 11-2 and 5-1 from the big British firms. On the other hand, Ibn Bey, best-priced 20-1 for the Classic, paid $30.60 a place and $13.60 for the show (to a $2 stake).

The answer is that there is no answer.

Use your judgement depending on the nature of the event and the horse. When Dancing Brave ran in the 1986 Breeders' Cup Turf, America appreciated that the Arc winner was outstandingly the best horse in Europe, and he ended up at 2-1 on, but still flopped in the heat of Santa Anita. However, when Tolomeo went to Chicago in 1983 for the Arlington Million, none of the natives knew much about him – though a visiting British pundit known locally as 'Brow' Scott assured the nation on NBC TV that Tolomeo would win. He did so, and paid odds of 38.2-1. It took the locals a few years of 'Brow's' tips to realise that even he could fluke it occasionally!

And if you troll over to Vegas their sports books offer Breeders' Cup prices from early spring – and they don't 'reckon' our beasts!

In Nevada, where casinos in 1991 won over $5 billion, betting tax at a quarter of one per cent is not passed on to the punter. So it's hardly surprising that Las Vegas is the gambling capital of the world. For twenty-four hours a day, 365 days a year, the place throbs to a cornucopia of roulette, craps, blackjack, poker, baccarat – and 85,000 fruit machines. These are everywhere – even at McCarran Airport to hook you on arrival and offer a final fix as you leave. There's only one way to guarantee a profit from fruit machines, and that's not legal, though whizzkids, by picking and choosing machines, manage to win so long as their eyesight holds out! Part of the humbler end of the gambling spectrum, these machines have proved extremely profitable: in Nevada the average player loses 78 per cent of the bank he or she starts out with – but one lucky Jackpot winner at the Mirage in 1990 won $5 million!

Fruit machines are simple gambling. Blackjack (the card game similar to pontoon where the object is to be dealt a hand

> **AIR!**
> Perhaps the excitements available in Nevada put too much of a strain on those whose minds are ever active but whose bodies are not.
> When the contents of a leading brothel, the Mustang Ranch, were auctioned in 1989, among the items found inside were fifty oxygen canisters!

of 21 or near to it, though not more) is not. It's based on chance but the outcome is not purely random, and any player able to keep track of the changing composition of the deck can assess when the odds of winning are favourable, and stake accordingly.

'Counters', sharp operators often with hidden mathematical devices, are not welcome in casinos anywhere. In August 1985 one Philip Preston Anderson was playing blackjack at the Westward Ho casino in Las Vegas when he was arrested by security guards for exhibiting 'suspicious body movements'. It turned out that he was wearing 'computer shoes': he had a tiny card-counting computer strapped to his calf under his trousers and controlled by switches which he could work with his feet. By tapping his toes Anderson was able to tell the computer which cards from the blackjack deck had been dealt. The computer then calculated the remaining cards with the dealer and sent back messages which advised him of the best way of playing his hand – by means of a wire that delivered coded electric shocks to the rear strap of his athletic support. I've heard about gambling giving you a buzz, but this is something else!

In blackjack, as in poker, you've got to know when to hold 'em and when to fold 'em. But whatever the plan, as locals are quick to point out: 'If you bet slow you've got to go – if you bet fast you won't last.'

The money bet at the Breeders' Cup would seem small change on the racetracks of Japan. For the 1991 Japan Cup at Fuchu, Tokyo, a crowd of 143,532 (described by the Japan Racing Association as a 'disappointing' turn-out – would Epsom say the same about such a figure on Derby Day?) wagered £100 million *on the Japan Cup alone*, and about half of that was in dual forecasts, Japan's most popular bet. But with ex-Clive Brittain horse Golden Pheasant, now trained by Charlie 'Bald Eagle' Whittingham in America, coming in at 172-10 from Arc runner-up Magic Night (5-1), there was a distinct nip in the air around the winner's enclosure.

The average amount put into Japan's tote system every day is around £40 million, much of it through the medium of 200,000 telephone accounts. Despite the attractions of a lively betting interest in other sports (notably powerboat racing), the Japan Racing Association sees over 2000 billion yen a year – mind-boggling enough for you to work out yen by yen – going through off-track betting centres. Forget any comparison with our homely betting shops. These fever-ish centres, located mainly around Tokyo and Osaka, are marvels of high-tech punting – to the extent that you can bet with a computerised machine, which says 'thank you' after taking your money.

MISSING PERSON

When I slipped into Vegas for a fortnight in 1986 I instructed the Booby not to ring me unless in an emergency. So a restful holiday was spent in Caesars Palace without a phone call from home.

But there had been a mix-up. The increasingly distraught Booby had been continually trying to contact her beloved boy, but the hotel reception kept reiterating that I had checked out after one night's stay.

Was I dead, kidnapped, or had I finally left her as promised for a pneumatic teenager?

Eventually, after the British Consul in San Francisco and colleagues in Britain had been alerted, two friends flew over to Vegas, and checked with Caesars before going straight to the morgue looking for a 'fat Englishman'.

Several shrouds were ghoulishly peered under, but no luck.

So it was off to the local police station. After studying a photo, a bemused sergeant queried: 'Aw shucks, you don't really want to find him, do you?'

Most helpful. Eventually the computer error was discovered, and a tearful Booby, reunited with her boy, lived blissfully ever after.

But thoughts of multi-million dollar lawsuits against Caesars for gross negligence and causing untold heartbreak were short-lived. In the witness box what answer would I have had to the obvious question: 'If you loved and missed your wife so much, why didn't you bother to call her during that fortnight?'

Perry Mason couldn't have got out of that!

Tokyo has the distinction of housing the biggest betting shop in the world, the JRA centre at Korakuen. This has thirteen floors to accommodate the betting-obsessed – somewhat different from Jack Swift's old shop in Dover Street (page 66)!

Gambling mania extends throughout the Far East (and stays with those who emigrate, as any Soho betting shop bears witness). In Hong Kong horse racing is the only legal gambling (apart from the state lottery), and crowds pack those massive stands at the territory's two racetracks: Happy Valley and Sha Tin (built on reclaimed land and opened in 1978). Atten-

Fast bucks!

dances average more than 40,000 a day, and the amount staked annually on-course and in Hong Kong's off-track shops is around £2000 million. A third of a million inhabitants have telephone betting accounts – though only on deposit, not on credit.

Some profits, up to £50 million, go to charity, and it has been said that gambling forms such an important element of Hong Kong's economy that income tax would have to be raised two per cent if racing were to cease. What will happen when China takes over the colony in 1997 is one thing no one is prepared to accept bets on!

In Australia punters are a little less single-minded, but they certainly enjoy themselves and have even been known to throw sheep dung at losing jockeys! A crowd of around 100,000 attends the Melbourne Cup at Flemington on the first Tuesday in November, putting around £3 into the course Tote. But racegoers have the choice of Tote or bookmakers, so the atmosphere is not unlike that in Britain.

There are, though, interesting differences between bookmakers in Australia and Britain – apart from there being none off-course Down Under. Australian layers are obliged to price up every horse in a race at all times. Also, according to their position in the ring they must guarantee to lay a horse to a stated amount. Compulsion goes against all my political instincts but a case can be made that a similar system would benefit British tracks. Nevertheless I am loath to make anyone do anything with their own money. Perhaps, after all, it's best left here to normal market forces.

There are no legal bookmakers off-course in Australia. Anyone yearning for the Aussie method shows utter contempt towards ordinary horse players by forcing them to bet on the machine. Choice. That's why Britain's unique system is best for the people who matter most – all punters.

Down Under the Totalisator Agency Board (TAB), founded at the instigation of Sir Chester Manifold, owner of that gallant front-runner Crisp, the 1973 Grand National runner-up to Red Rum, have a monopoly. Would anyone in Britain, except for greedy racehorse owners and their tame acolytes, want a similar restriction?

India – where many of our Flat jockeys ride during the winter if the lure of all-weather days at Southwell or Lingfield can be overcome – is the same as Australia: on-course tote (each owned by the regional racing club), bookmakers on course but not – legally, anyway – off.

But there's no place like home, and our own biggest betting race, and the world's most famous single horse race, is the Grand National. A global audience of hundreds of millions are said to watch the Aintree spectacular, and in Britain more than £55 million is staked on the race (sensibly run on a Saturday). If you have only one bet a year, it's odds-on to be in the National.

In the late 1970s, after the course had been sold, first, to the eternal shame on his name, by the fabulously rich, heirless Earl of Sefton, then for £3¼ million by Mrs Mirabel Topham to property developer Bill Davies, it became odds against the race surviving over the historic Liverpool fences. No more Becher's, Valentine's or the Chair. When Davies was unable to develop part of the site in the way he had been led to believe he sought to sell the course again, and the spectre of closure loomed. Ladbrokes ran Liverpool on a seven-year lease until 1982, when a public appeal was launched. The negotiations with Davies over the sale of the course to the Jockey Club were headed by Lord Vestey, who had an unlikely sidekick in his dealings, as Brian Vine in the *Daily Mail* described:

It was going to be up to Sam Vestey to beard Bill Davies in his lair, and as Mr Davies was hardly about to bend the knee to the scions of the Jockey Club, there was something of a sociological stand-off. The breakthrough came when Vestey got the feeling that the odds would be more in their favour if he used a pure people's man, punters' friend John McCririck, the Channel Four odds pundit, to cosy up to Davies. And to explain that the Jockey Club hierarchy were not all decadent squires or Ivan the Terribles who ate peasants for breakfast.

It's what your right arm's for!

'McCririck and I both travelled up together on the train to Liverpool. He wore his Old Harrovian tie and I wore my Old Etonian tie. But I think the whole idea of this show of propriety was lost on Mr Davies. However, John was able to break the ice and present me as an honest

BETTING LIKE THERE'S NO TOMORROW

On 7 June 1992, the final day of the season at Hong Kong's Sha Tin racecourse, punters yet again smashed turnover records. They wagered £85.2 million on the nine races, including £14.3 million on the last race – some Getting Out Stakes!

A few days earlier Hong Kong racegoers had crammed into the colony's other track Happy Valley and after six races watched a simulcast of the Derby, plonking £2.5 million on the outcome. But they didn't much fancy the chances of Dr Devious, who started 25-1 on the Hong Kong tote, as opposed to 8-1 second favourite at Epsom!

tuating negotiations, speculated wildly and incessantly. Being on the inside of a major national drama turned out to be most revealing.

Outrageous stories were printed and it was no use gently telling the hack responsible how far off beam he in fact was.

I am more proud of the small role I managed to play in helping to save the Grand National than anything else in an undistinguished career reeking of mediocrity – especially when I call to mind the short-sighted 'to hell with Bill Davies, let him stew' attitude so frequently heard at the time.

Aintree and all it stands for had to be far more important than any petty vendettas, and those who in the course's darkest days advocated ditching it and staging the Grand

Only by knowing the irascible Davies, and earning his trust, was the link-up maintained through tortuous on-off months as the rest of the hacks, unaware of the fluc-

ABOVE Ah so! Japan Cup day – not Wolverhampton on a wet November Monday

LEFT Is this why they call it Flat racing? Not much chance of an early night's kip for residents overlooking Hong Kong's Happy Valley

National at nearby Haydock or Doncaster, Newcastle, Newmarket – yes, there was a proposal to construct a steeplechase course on the Heath – ought to be ashamed. And I'm not one to remind others of their folly – being riddled with absurdity myself – but Julian Wilson's proposal that the world's premier chase should be run at the Larkhill point-to-point course will haunt him for ever.

And I've kept the generous letter from Senior Steward Lord Manton, written after the saga was over and Aintree had become the property of Racecourse Holdings Trust run by the Jockey Club, in which he kindly acknowledged help received. And Sam Vestey hasn't forgotten the favour done all those years ago: he regularly invites the Booby to his prime box throughout the Cheltenham Festival!

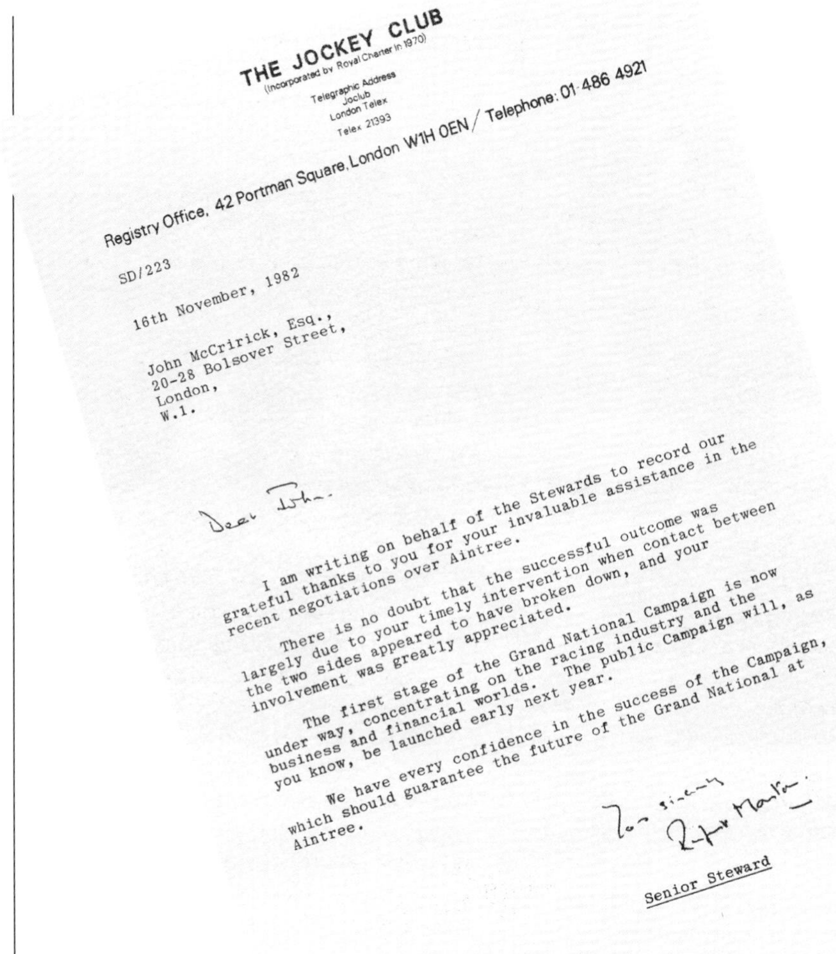

THE JOCKEY CLUB
(Incorporated by Royal Charter in 1970)

Telegraphic Address
Joclub
London Telex
Telex 21393

Registry Office, 42 Portman Square, London W1H OEN / Telephone: 01 486 4921

SD/223

16th November, 1982

John McCririck, Esq.,
20-28 Bolsover Street,
London,
W.1.

Dear John,

I am writing on behalf of the Stewards to record our grateful thanks to you for your invaluable assistance in the recent negotiations over Aintree.

There is no doubt that the successful outcome was largely due to your timely intervention when contact between the two sides appeared to have broken down, and your involvement was greatly appreciated.

The first stage of the Grand National Campaign is now under way, concentrating on the racing industry and the business and financial worlds. The public Campaign will, as you know, be launched early next year.

We have every confidence in the success of the Campaign, which should guarantee the future of the Grand National at Aintree.

Yours sincerely,
R J M Martin

Senior Steward

Sam – the key player – joins Ladbrokes, stewards Lord Manton and Johnny Macdonald-Buchanan, Nicky Henderson's father Johnnie and current sponsors Seagram, with their Old Harrovian supremo Ivan Straker, on Aintree's roll of honour.

Gentlemen: Let no one forget that you were there when racing needed you. Saving Aintree has been the Jockey Club's finest achievement. That alone justifies its existence. Generations to come will forever be in your debt.

VEGAS: ALL STEAM, NO SUBSTANCE

Getting on steamers at the morning line is even harder in Las Vegas than over here. And if you're thinking of nipping over to Nevada and plunging on big-priced European Breeders' Cup prospects, then beware.

Anyone reckoning that the gambling mecca of the world is a punters' paradise, where sports books readily accept bets of all kinds and sizes without flinching, is in for a shock. The hard reality is that our much maligned bookies seem accommodating philanthropists compared with their panic-stricken Vegas counterparts.

Studious Andrew Beyer, of the Washington Post, keeps his own form figures, and is one of the few American hacks to understand the game. Recently, he took time off from the Turf to investigate the downside of Vegas. His report, in the Los Angeles Times, makes devastating reading for those reckoning that our layers are the pits.

Take ante-post betting. In February 1989, I couldn't believe that Easy Goer, the champion juvenile despite his Breeders' Cup defeat, was being offered at only 2-1 for the Kentucky Derby three months away. It was diabolical. Imagine in mid-winter the Derby favourite being priced up at 'bottle'!

But Beyer tells of a punter wanting $200 (£140) on 60-1 Sunday Silence, who hadn't even won a stakes race. At the Frontier Hotel, he was offered half the bet, and the rest at 30-1. Wise for the hotel, as it turned out, following the triumph of Sunday Silence, but that didn't mollify Beyer.

'What makes this conservatism so absurd,' he writes, 'is the odds are stacked so heavily in the race book's favour. Even the "steamers" who inspire such fear from the race books are usually losers.'

Explaining the phenomenon, not unknown over here, Beyer goes on:

'Although few people have ever wound up in the poorhouse by booking horse bets, the race books do run a risk of losing on any given race if they are overloaded with wagers on the same horse.

'This can easily happen because tips on supposed hot horses, called "steam" in the local parlance, circulate every day, and everybody wants to jump on the same bandwagon.'

Stardust race book manager, Al Sinatra (good old Al) acknowledges that 'in this town most people don't know how to read racing form. All they're looking for is the steam'.

Apparently computer screens flash the words 'GET APPROVAL' as soon as a bet is requested for the steamer. The seller yells out 'KEY' and a supervisor has to type in a code to let the wager go through.

Apart from steamers, Al Sinatra admits that 'the most dangerous thing to fear are the exotics [forecast pools]: exactas, quinellas and parlay'.

Beyer relates this exchange he had at the Sands Hotel (300-1 limits on exactas and quinellas) when asking for a $30 (£20) exacta (forecast 1st and 2nd) combining the two favourites at Philadelphia Park.

'The ticket seller called for a supervisor who told me gravely that this was too big a bet. I pointed to the odds displayed on the television screen. "This is a 7-2 shot over a 6-5 shot," I said. "If I win, my profit would be $400 (£260) tops." The supervisor replied that I could have a $2 (£1.50) each way. Thanks a lot.'

Beyer accepts that was an extreme case but maintains it typifies the prevailing spirit. Instead of encouraging all the betting action they can get they are paralysed by fear of losing. When he tried to talk to the race book manager at one of the big hotels, Beyer says he had to get approval from various levels of the company's hierarchy just to ask a few innocuous questions.

'The race book manager has a boss, who has a boss, who has a boss, and all of them are looking at the bottom line of the race book each day. They don't want to see any minus signs.'

For instance, Bob Gregorka, the Sands Hotel sports book manager, candidly confesses: 'If we were to lose $50,000 to $60,000 (around £35,000) a day I wouldn't keep my job and I've got two kids to feed.' It tears at your heartstrings, doesn't it?

Gregorka agrees that 'when you turn down bets you're going to run out a certain amount of customers but in the long run you're better off doing it. The slot machines make more in a week than race books make in a year. We're like a loss leader, here because you don't want your customers to leave the hotel'.

Beyer sums up the restrictions as 'enough to make would-be serious bettors leave out of exasperation'.

'The race books are marvellously entertaining, an equine three-ring circus, but a serious horseplayer can find as much action on an average afternoon at Laurel as he can in America's gambling capital.'

Certainly with live televised racing, trotting and greyhounds non-stop, including Sundays, for twelve hours from 10 a.m., opportunities are unlimited. At 12.30, I've actually seen five live races running simultaneously, late events on the East Coast and starting up in California. All this, tax-free (deductions, of course, at source from the pool), unless winnings come to more than $10,000 (£7500). Then the dreaded IRS (Internal Revenue Service) get in on the act.

So that trip to Vegas, which Alex Bird for instance did before Dancing Brave went under in the 1986 Breeders' Cup Turf at Santa Anita, needs to be meticulously planned. Better still, ask Beyer's view of the day's business.

Pestered by a group of Brits in Ballys Hotel, I resorted to Andrew, the US answer to Timeform and Channel Four's 'Jimbo' Jim McGrath, in the Press box at Gulfstream Park, Florida. He pointed me towards an animal called Favorable Dawn in the seventh. Three were preferred to it in the betting but the beast held off all challengers to win at 5.8-1!

Whether Favorable Dawn became the day's steamer I don't know, but seemingly some visitors paid for their holiday in one hit and ended up reckoning that, in Nevada at least, At Large had cracked the system. Declining persuasive offers to mark their cards again, and wallowing with feigned modesty in Andrew Beyer's reflected glory, was the safest way to prevent any disillusionment.

So don't yearn for Vegas. There you wouldn't even sniff an obtainable morning line.

Winners

Let's end our prowl round the world of betting with a few big winners, who might serve as inspiration, or at least encouragement, to punters everywhere:

● Brad Daugherty landed a prize of $1 million by taking the 1991 World Poker Championship in Las Vegas – with a pair of jacks. The thirty-nine-year-old gambler from Sparks, Nevada, said: 'I don't give up until I'm broke. Now it will be a little harder for me to go broke.'

● Mike Wittkowski won the Illinois State Lottery in 1984 and netted $40 million for an outlay of $35.

● The inhabitants of Alcoron, near Madrid, shared £54.6 million, the first prize in the Spanish lottery known as El Gordo – the Fat One (no, not named after me) – in December 1990. In Malaga the hairdressers' association scooped £2.9 million. 'It's just as well we didn't get the first prize,' said spokesman Narciso Pinero: 'There wouldn't have been a hairdresser left working in Spain.'

● Australian tycoon Kerry Packer raked in £7 million over a month playing blackjack in London clubs.

● Legendary Irish punter J.P. McManus, feared by all bookies, enjoyed one of his biggest touches with £25,000 on 8-1 winner Trapper John at Cheltenham in 1990.

● Noel Furlong set the 1991 Cheltenham National Hunt Festival alight with the very first race of the meeting when his horse Destriero won the Trafalgar House Supreme Novices' Hurdle. Newspaper reports had it that the Irish carpet tycoon had taken as much as £3 million out of the Cheltenham ring and from other bookmakers, but the true figure was much lower – probably a little less than a million (as if that isn't enough!). Furlong had made a deal with the Customs and Excise over a VAT claim before being allowed into the country, which must have dented winnings. He doubled Destriero with The Iliad in the Champion Hurdle, and if that horse had come in Furlong's bundle would have been up to £10 million. But The Iliad blundered away his chance, and the Dublin-based gambler had to be content with winnings on Destriero alone. Not bad, though, especially when you remember that the same horse had been the subject of one of the biggest ever successful ante-post plunges in Irish racing, when backed from 'double carpet' (33-1) to 7-1 for the 1991 Ladbroke Hurdle at Leopardstown. The sponsors admitted laying £330,000 to £10,000 each way when the weights were published, and that was just the start!

- George Rhodes of Aldershot collected £86,056.42 (after tax) for a 5 pence ITV Seven accumulator from William Hill in September 1984.
- Don Stewart, owner of a greyhound named Monday's News, backed his dog for the 1946 Greyhound Derby before the opening heats with bookmaker Hector Macdonald, who laid him £1000 to an old sixpence (2½ pence) or, some say, a Havana cigar. When Monday's News won the final by seven lengths, Stewart's winning odds were 40,000-1.
- Margaret Regan, a seventy-eight-year-old widow, was robbed of £75 while out shopping in April 1991. The following week she was at London's Dorchester Hotel being presented with a Littlewoods cheque for £1,646,108.20. She and her daughter Colleen Gooderham had staked 45 pence on the winning coupon.
- In June 1992 a man from Bournemouth who wished to remain anonymous (though some of the tabloids blew the gaff) hit the jackpot with a pools payout from Littlewoods of £2,246,113.20 for an outlay of 54 pence.
- Richard Mussell of Havant, a supervisor for a cleaning firm, won £567,066.26 on Cheltenham Gold Cup day 1992 for a stake of £8.14. In a variety of doubles and trebles he combined winners Duke of Monmouth (33-1), Tipping Tim (20-1), Cool Ground (25-1), Dusty Miller (9-1) and Repeat The Dose (14-1). He cleaned up all right!
- And how about jammy bookies? At Royal Ascot 1992 a punter asked leading layer Victor Chandler for a £100 treble in the final three races on the opening day. Chandler's clerk, aiming for a quick getaway and not wanting to settle after the last race, directed the punter elsewhere. The trio obliged, to the tune of £130,000!
- You, with your next bet – may it come in at 'double carpet'!

Index